From Sambo
to *SUPERSPADE*

The Black Experience
in Motion Pictures

Books by Daniel J. Leab

A Union of Individuals: The Formation
of the American Newspaper Guild

From Sambo to Superspade: The Black
Experience in Motion Pictures

From Sambo
to *SUPERSPADE*

The Black Experience
in Motion Pictures

BY DANIEL J. LEAB

Houghton Mifflin Company Boston · 1975

A portion of this book has appeared in another form in
Political Science Quarterly, March 1973. Copyright
© 1973, by The Academy of Political Science.

Library of Congress Cataloging in Publication Data
Leab, Daniel J
From Sambo to Superspade.
Bibliography: p.
1. Negroes in moving-pictures. I. Title.
PN1995.9.N4L4   791.43'0909'352   75-11948
ISBN 0-395-19402-4

Printed in the United States of America

A   10   9   8   7   6   5   4   3   2   1

For My Parents

ACKNOWLEDGMENTS

IN CHRONICLING the development of the black movie image I benefited greatly from the encouragement and advice of Jay Leyda. Other patient friends read and commented on various chapters; for this, thanks go to James Boylan and Linda K. Kerber as well as to Lisa Pontecorvo, who drew my attention to various items I otherwise would have missed. Conversations with my Columbia University colleagues Nathan Huggins, Hollis Lynch, and Elliott Skinner were helpful and enlightening. I was also aided in my quest for film material by James Card of Eastman House, Sam Kula, formerly archivist of the American Film Institute and now curator of the National Film Archive of Canada, Patrick Sheehan of the Library of Congress, and Bebe Bergstern of Historical Films.

My search for stills was enormously eased by the help I received from the curators of the stills collection of the British Film Institute. And the staff of the Theater Collection of the New York Public Library were generous to the extreme in their help and thoughtfulness, as were librarians at Columbia University, the University of California at Los Angeles, the Schomburg branch of the New York Public Library, the Museum of Modern Art, and the National Film Archive.

Columbia College students Garry Gail, Sol Grossman, David Ritchie, and Peter Tuttle guided me in my use of the black press. Nancy Estes was able to type from my handwriting, a praiseworthy feat often accomplished under difficult conditions.

A special note of thanks is due Doris Safie, my former secretary, who typed, xeroxed, collated, and otherwise prevented me from being buried in tens of pounds of accumulated material.

Unfortunately the manuscript for this book was finished before I could benefit from the publication of Donald Bogle's *Toms, Coons, Mulattoes, Mammies & Bucks,* but thanks to some enterprising Columbia students he and I had the chance recently to comment on each other's point of view.

A grant from the Columbia University Council for Research in the Social Sciences made possible some important research.

Lois Wallace did her usual superb job of finding this book a home while it was still just an idea.

I am very much indebted to Robert Cowley for his ruthless use of the editorial blue pencil. The manuscript has benefited immeasurably from his efforts and those of his ever-willing assistant, Barbara Brier.

Finally, to my wife, Katharine Kyes Leab, I owe a debt that cannot be fully described or adequately repaid.

To all who aided me I give sincere thanks. They have saved me from making errors of various kinds. For whatever errors of fact or interpretation may remain I alone am responsible.

CONTENTS

From Sambo
to *SUPERSPADE*

The Black Experience
in Motion Pictures

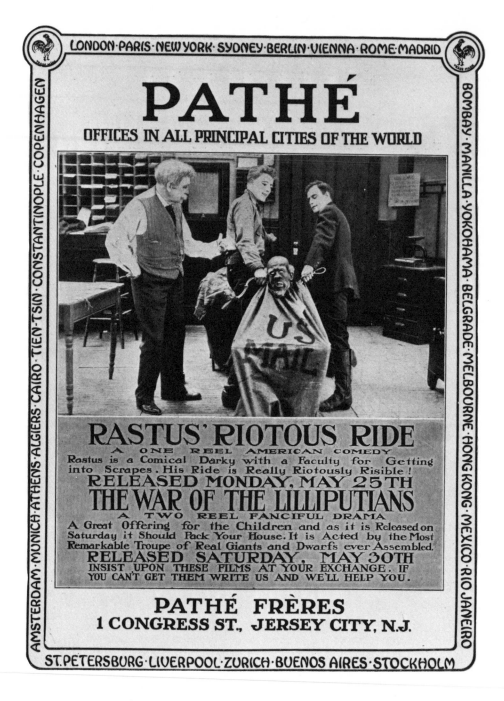

Sambo, 1910: In this ad for a one-reel comedy, from
the *Moving Picture World,* the black was the inevitable victim.

INTRODUCTION: THE LACK OF HUMANITY

UNTIL RECENTLY the movie image of the black has been a "Sambo" image. Sambo, to quote the historian Stanley Elkins, "was docile but irresponsible, loyal but lazy, humble but chronically given to lying and stealing." Just about everything traditionally held to be of some value in the United States was absent from this stereotype. The movies presented blacks as subhuman, simpleminded, superstitious, and submissive. They exhibited qualities of foolish exaggeration and an apparently hereditary clumsiness and ignorance as well as an addictive craving for fried chicken and watermelon. Their relationship with whites was depicted as one of complete, and frequently childlike, dependence.[1]

Take, for example, the central character in the 1910 Lubin comedy *Rastus in Zululand*. Rastus is described as "an odd-jobs man, that is he did odd jobs when he has to, but when there are a few small coins in his pocket he prefers to sleep." The film begins with Rastus searching for a place to sleep. He finds one in the sunlight. This rather odd choice is explained by the plot synopsis: "a darky needs warmth." The sleeping Rastus dreams that he has gone to sea and has been shipwrecked in Zululand. Captured by cannibals, he has been placed in the community cooking pot. The entreaties of the chief's daughter save Rastus from being part of the stew, but she is so obese and ugly that he chooses to return to the pot. He awakens just as the water has begun to boil and "is much relieved to find himself within walking distance of a place where nerve tonic is sold."[2]

Rastus in Zululand accurately reflects the racial prejudices and beliefs of pre–World War I America. In ascribing a certain *joie de vivre* to Rastus, it actually treated the black less viciously than many contemporary movies treated other ethnic groups. Over the years, however, there could be no better evidence of the gradual assimilation of these other groups into American society than their depiction in the movies. The black remained an outsider — as the industry was never reluctant to note. So ingrained had the Sambo stereotype become that in 1935 an "all-colored" film made for black audiences by a black filmmaker contained a scene in which each time an employer dictating a want ad uses the word "Negro," his assistant (played broadly for laughs) writes "nigger."

The British filmmaker Lindsay Anderson has said that "everyone who has seen more than half a dozen films with his eyes open knows that if the cinema does not create the significant social movements of our time, it intimately reflects them." There have been strong divisions of opinion about whether movies influence an audience or whether they mirror its ideas, but there can be no argument about the part that movies have played in shaping the American Dream. Almost from the beginning, the American film industry left the black out of that dream, either by ignoring him or by presenting him as an object incapable of enjoying it because of a nature that was not quite human.[3]

As early as 1914, this treatment of the Negro caused the respected black journalist Lester Walton to denounce the movies. Walton condemned them for ridiculing blacks and "constantly representing the race at its worst." Noting the success of such other ethnic groups as the Jews in moderating the unfavorable caricature drawn of them by motion pictures, Walton argued that the industry had a duty "to emancipate the white American from his peculiar ideas" about the black and not to further propagate "incorrect notions of the colored American . . . hurtful to both races."[4]

Walton's comments would be echoed again and again. Among the more unusual and poignant outbursts against the Sambo image was published early in 1940 by Andy Razaf, a noted black lyricist and contributor to Negro musical shows like *Shuffle Along:*

I always leave a picture show disgusted — Holy Smokes!
Don't they know colored people are just like other folks?
Why do they always think that all we know is sin and strife,
Tho' we have many of our race in every walk of life?

Are Hollywood producers mindful of their harmful acts,
Or are they just plain ignorant and do not know the facts?
They show us all as comics, gangsters, and slowpokes,
Don't they know colored people are just like other folks?

In 1944, Dr. Lawrence Reddick, the black curator of the Schomburg Collection of Negro Literature of the New York Public Library, surveyed one hundred American films from the beginning of the silent period to the 1940s: he judged three quarters of them to be "anti-Negro." He found that despite "the Negro people's oft expressed overwhelming desire" to be treated on screen like everybody else, there had been only a limited range of black characterizations in the movies. There was a "ceiling" above which blacks portrayed in films rarely if ever rose, and Reddick angrily pointed out that "this ceiling on screen is lower than the ceiling for the Negro in American life itself."[5]

Today the American movie industry no longer imposes such a ceiling; the Sambo image has virtually disappeared. This change can obviously be attributed in part to the shifting legal posture of American society and its social attitude toward blacks. But the movie industry has also come to appreciate and to depend more and more on the money spent at the box office by black moviegoers. The traditional film audience has shrunk drastically in recent years and has undergone great transformations in the process. Blacks now form a substantial part of that audience, a change heightened by shifting demographic patterns. As whites have rushed to the suburbs (which have newer but smaller movie theaters), blacks have inherited the urban centers and the older, larger, downtown movie houses.

Even though black has become box office, the Negro is not often presented on screen "just like other folks." The old Sambo caricature has simply been replaced by a new one, dubbed "Superspade" by a number of film critics as well as by one ambitious producer who has registered the title for a movie. Superspade is an uneasy but fascinating amalgam of Aristotle, D'Artagnan, Dick Tracy, Hercules, Robin Hood, and at times a militant yet forgiving Christ. Initially the term was used to label Sidney Poitier, the first black movie superstar; now the Superspade description has come to be applied to the whole range of black movie heroes. Typical is the main character of the 1971 MGM movie *Shaft*. Indestructible, flippant, romantic, and triumphant in Hollywood's best private-eye tradition, John Shaft is Sam Spade as Superspade.

The black on screen is no longer an object of condescension or ridicule. Sambo rarely if ever won, could do nothing right, and could at best hope to survive; Superspade can do no wrong and almost always comes out on top. But this transformation notwithstanding, Superspade is just another caricature. Despite some progress on the part of the movies in depicting blacks

Superspade, 1971: Richard Roundtree guns down a white Mafia hood in *Shaft*. (From the MGM release "Shaft" © 1971 Metro-Goldwyn-Mayer Inc.)

naturally and despite a tendency of the industry to utilize them in the *mise en scène* and to publicize black actors and actresses as "people not props," as yet relatively few movies treat blacks as they treat other characters. And even more rare is a film like the 1965 independent production *Nothing But a Man,* whose main characters are black, but whose theme is universal, dealing as it does with the emotional adjustment of a young laborer to steady employment and the acceptance of family responsibilities.

If box-office returns are to be believed, the new stereotype of Superspade is obviously (and understandably) more pleasing to the black community than was the earlier one. Yet whether Sambo or Superspade, the black image on screen has always lacked the dimension of humanity. With all too few exceptions this human dimension has been lacking in the movie treatment of the black ever since the 1890s, when the first motion pictures were produced.

Little Eva is dead, and Uncle Tom prays for her soul in the 1913 *Uncle Tom's Cabin*. The white Tom, wig askew and in uncertain blackface, is Harry Pollard. (National Film Archive)

1

THE GAMUT
FROM A TO B

THE PERIOD between the mid-1890s and 1915, when the movies became one of the most important forms of mass entertainment in the United States, was a period in which racial libels abounded. At the turn of the century, the mayor of San Francisco could declare, with self-righteous assurance, that Japanese "are not the stuff of which American citizens can be made." Jews were described as unethical, ill-mannered, and vulgar Shylocks: in 1907, the journalist Burton Hendrick could warn that New York was being turned into "a city of Asiatics" by the "Great Jewish Invasion." Describing new productions, movie companies felt free to refer to "the dago with his fruit stand" and "a group of greasers playing dice outside the saloon."[1]

The prevailing attitude probably victimized blacks more than any other group. It was, as historian C. Vann Woodward has pointed out, an era in which "the extremists of Southern racism probably reached a wider audience, both within their own region and in the nation, than ever before." Newspapers and magazines used the words "negro," "nigger," "darky," "colored," and "coon" indiscriminately. A staff member of the film industry journal *Moving Picture World,* who claimed to be without prejudice, vowed that "never again will I go to a theatre, knowing that fellow citizens of African descent form part of the audience [because] . . . so many of the colored people are like children and insist on laughing at the pictures, no matter how tragic they may be." As late as World War I the Cincinnati *Enquirer* carried a headline "Yah Suh! Black Boys Are Happy" above a story on Negro troops in France. The literature of the day viciously lampooned the black, glorified the plantation tradition, rationalized lynchings, and explained away inequitable treatment of blacks. Their depiction in early American movies, however, was probably influenced most profoundly by the treatment of the black on stage and in the minstrel shows and vaudeville. The minstrel shows — whose performers appeared with faces blackened by sooty burnt-cork makeup — followed an elaborate ritual in their burlesque of Negro life in the Old South. Already well-established before the Civil War, they succeeded in fixing the black man in the American consciousness as a ludicrous figure supposedly born, as one show business history puts it, "hoofing on the levee to the strumming of banjos." He was prone to frenzied dancing, shiftlessness, garish dress, gin tippling, dice shooting, torturing the language, and, inevitably, was addicted to watermelon and chicken, usually stolen. So fixed was this tradition that in the latter part of the nineteenth century when professional black companies began to present minstrel shows, the performers found it necessary to adopt almost completely the minstrelsy ritual, even to the use of burnt-cork makeup. The result was what the black critic and poet James Weldon Johnson called "a caricature of a caricature."[2]

During the 1890s black performers began to break with the minstrel show formula, and they had some success in all-Negro musicals and in vaudeville. The cakewalk, described by Langston Hughes as "the first dance of Negro origin to sweep this country," made its mark at this time. But black performers, even the most talented, could not escape the fantastic artificiality of the caricature in which they had been imprisoned. The light-skinned Bert Williams, for instance, was an extraordinarily gifted man whose speech was impeccable; on stage, however, the erect, distinguished-looking Williams appeared as a slouching, dialect-speaking, inept shuffler wearing a burnt-cork mask he hated. Williams and George Walker, his partner of many years, were billed as "The Two Real Coons." Around the turn of the century, the "coon" concept of the black found different kinds of expression on stage. The sentimental "darky melody" gave way to the raucous and bawdy "coon song." These were often performed by whites in blackface, and had titles like "You May Be a Hawaiian on Old Broadway but You're Just Another Nigger to Me." The so-called "coon shows" such as *The Coon and the Chink, Jes' Lak*

In the early days of film, black roles
were usually taken by whites, like
Lillian Leighton. She is seen here, in
character and out.

White Folks, Bandanna Land, and *Dat Famous Chicken Debate* ("Resolved that Stealing Chickens Ain't No Crime") further fixed a warped image of the black in the public mind.[3]

In the contemporary theater blacks did not fare much better. Attempts at photographic reality dominated the stage — of one 1897 production it has been said that "the Chinese quarter of San Francisco was reproduced almost to its smells" — but blacks were invariably portrayed by white actors in blackface. And at a time when many of the more popular stage vehicles were Civil War melodramas, plays about the ante-bellum South, and versions of *Uncle Tom's Cabin,* the "real" stage black was either the comic stooge or a faithful retainer. The stooge differed little from the caricature presented in the minstrel shows and vaudeville. The retainer presented a different image, but one that also failed to suggest that the black is a human being with individual traits. Loyal, uncomplaining drudges, the retainers were — in the words of one study—"the plantation uncle, the broad-bosomed mammy, . . . kindly tyrants of kitchen and garden, hard working, good natured, quaintly humorous, obsequious, affectionate, and faithful." For them, emancipation made no difference. They continued to serve.[4]

Two other stage stereotypes less frequently encountered were "the brute" and the "tragic mulatto." Probably the best known example of the "brute" can be found in the dramatization of Thomas Dixon's novel *The Clansman,* which later served as the basis for the film *The Birth of a Nation.* Interestingly enough, the black-as-threat was not limited to menacing males. Just after the turn of the century the young and then well-known Northern playwright, Eugene Walter, described the characters in his drama *The Easiest Way.* "Particular attention," he wrote, ". . . should be called to the character of the negress Annie, who . . . must not in any way represent the . . . traditional 'mammy.' She is cunning, crafty, heartless, sullen . . . The actress who plays this part must keep in mind its innate and brutal selfishness." The stage mulatto served to reinforce popular notions about white superiority. The merest drop of Negro blood was a taint from which there was no redemption: by the same token, a character's white blood was responsible for any positive features he or she might have. A mulatto in these "mixed blood" plays avoided a tragic end only if, just before the curtain rang down, it became clear that he or she was really all white.[5]

The movies readily picked up, and improved on, the same caricatures, which soon reached more people than ever. By 1908 the gross revenues of the industry exceeded those of the theater and vaudeville combined: more than four million people a day, it was estimated, went to "the flickers." Moreover, American movies were rapidly finding an audience abroad as well: by 1910 about 75 percent of the movies showing in London suburbs were American productions and in the years before the outbreak of World War I American films were widely shown in Germany. Yet the Kinetoscope, a peep-show device that allowed one person at a time to see pictures move, had not been invented until the beginning of the 1890s. By the end of that decade crude projectors and screens had been perfected, and commercial public showing of movies had begun. The usual fare included comedies of some sort and travelogues, news reports, documentaries, and sports films — many of them faked — each two to three minutes in length, strung together to make a show. After the turn of the century, the industry began to produce motion pictures that told some kind of story, although often a rudimentary one. It took time for the plots to evolve into something more than a peg on which to hang a slapstick sequence or a horseback-chase. But the more technical and artistic the attempted innovations, the more detailed and complicated plots became; by 1915, the story film of feature length was well-established. These changes in the American film industry, however, made little difference in the treatment of black characters.

The screen black in this period was usually portrayed by a white in blackface as wooly headed, thick lipped, and very dark skinned. Occasionally actual blacks are found in subordinate roles or as part of the *mise en scène* in the films with large casts. At least one social scientist has contended that "the white man in blackface serves the psychological function of reducing audience anxieties that might occur if real Negroes were used, especially in scenes of overt and covert sexual nature or when the Negro gets the upper hand over the white man." But it is more likely that white actors were used because the filmmakers of the time, a crude and pragmatic lot on the whole, accepted the prevailing beliefs about the limited abilities of the black and proceeded accordingly. Certainly their treatment of blacks indicates that

Edith Storey is the Egyptian princess surrounded
by her black retainers in *The Dust of Egypt*.

they shared popular prejudices. The Gene Gauntier Feature
Players, filming in Jacksonville, Florida, boasted in their publicity
for the 1913 film *Mystery of the Pine Tree Camp* that for one
scene the company had borrowed a "real" black convict from the
authorities, given him a "start of fifteen minutes over the dogs," let
the bloodhounds loose, and had him treed in short order. Not to
be outdone, another film unit in Jacksonville, the Lubin Company, reported on the "fun" its directors had enjoyed at the
expense of their "cullud fellow citizens" in trying to hire a black
driver for a supposed grave-robbing expedition.[6]

Toward the end of 1912, partly for economic reasons and partly
as a commercial gimmick designed to attract a larger black
audience, more companies began to use black players. But this
occasional use of black actors and actresses did not present any
real opportunity for such star performers as Bert Williams. He
remained a victim of a cruel racism that allowed him to be
proclaimed the hit of the Chicago company of the *Follies of 1910*
even though none of the daily newspapers in that city would
carry his picture. In 1916, Williams did make a number of short
films of his most successful stage turns, but these movies found
little market except in movie houses patronized by blacks. All the
distributors approached gave the same apologetic response: they

would like to use the film, but "the southern territory would resent and would not exhibit the pictures of a Negro star." This, apparently, was not the response made to the companies that featured their black performers in vicious comedies about what was imagined to be black life.[7]

John and Mattie Edwards as well as some other blacks appeared in a series of such films for the Lubin Company, which advertised in the black press for "characteristic stories . . . for the Negro stock company of the comedy section of the Lubin Company. All ideas will be paid for . . ." The Historical Feature Film Company of Chicago, utilizing the talents of what it called "the well-known negro comedians Bert Murphy, Frank Montgomery, and Florence McClain," made a number of movies such as *Money Talks in Darktown.* (An outraged critic for a black newspaper attacked these Chicago-made films, describing them as "what is commonly called crap" and urging exhibitors not to show movies "humiliating to the race.") The production company filming *Uncle Tom's Cabin* in 1914 claimed greater authenticity than any of the earlier movie versions, perhaps because a seventy-two-year-old black actor, Sam Lucas, described by the New York *Age* as the "dean of the colored theatrical profession," played the title role. Lucas received good notices in a trade journal, but the attitude of the reviewer toward the other black actors in the movie is summed up by his praise for the director on his handling of the film: the result, wrote the reviewer, was "all the more notable by reason of the fact that . . . Daly was using many colored players . . ." And in notices of other films in which blacks appeared in more than mere background roles, there was often a tone of incredulity: ". . . well acted, considering that the cast is made up of genuine colored people . . ."[8]

Whether or not they were portrayed by blacks, black characters appeared only in certain kinds of films among the hundreds produced between the mid-1890s and 1915. Still, stereotyped images of the movie black developed rapidly. The earliest motion pictures usually showed blacks dancing. The 1894 Edison peep-show catalogue, for example, lists *The Pickaninnies Doing a Dance;* two other items — one in which blacks do a buck-and-wing, the other, a cakewalk — are described as "the best negro subjects yet taken" and "amusing and entertaining." This "dancing fool" caricature of the black even found expression in the first filming of *Uncle Tom's Cabin* in 1903: one scene begins with a long cakewalk sequence that has absolutely nothing to do with the action preceding or following. True, it was not long before the mere showing of blacks dancing became passé, although the movies accepted, as in the 1907 Essanay production *The Dancing Nig*, what a note on this film refers to as "a well-known fact among Negroes . . . that a darky finds it impossible to keep his feet still whenever he hears the sound of music."[9]

The supposition that "they got rhythm" notwithstanding, the comic stooge and the faithful retainer were probably the most common images of the black in the early days of film. Images often overlapped, of course — the faithful retainer was a dancing fool as well, or was used for the purposes of comic relief. They drew heavily on the stereotypes presented in the theater, minstrel shows, and vaudeville — but with an important difference. The movies added a larger-than-life dimension to these stereotypes; films, short and without sound, depended on an exaggeration even greater than that practiced in the contemporary theater to make clear what was happening on screen. Thus, an actor would not just show, say, humility: he would be a suppliant beyond the wildest dreams of Uriah Heep.

This style of playing only heightened the ludicrous aspects of the black as comic stooge in what commentators liked to call "coon subjects." The 1904 Biograph movie *A Nigger in the Wood-pile* is a crude early example. Wood is being stolen from the farmer's shed, and he places a stick of dynamite among the kindling: then, to quote the plot synopsis, "in the next scene, a colored deacon, one of the shining lights in the African church, is seen making away with the wood; the loaded stick, is, of course, put into the fire, and there is a terrific explosion . . ." which blows off the roof and enables the farmer to identify the culprit.[10]

Chicken-snatching, too, was a common plot device: a 1910 advertisement for *C-H-I-C-K-E-N Spells Chicken*, an Essanay production, began "Ah love mah wattah melon but Oh, You-OO Chicken." The black man, usually dubbed Rastus in the title or in advertising blurbs, generally was shown in these movies to be childlike, foolishly pretentious, shiftless (except where gambling or chickens were concerned), clumsy, and vulgar.[11]

With the increased production of story films, the servile black retainer became a screen regular. One of the most popular subjects was what a Kalem Company publicity release described as "the comfortable, unpretentious, slaveholding aristocracy of rural Dixie." *His Trust* and *His Trust Fulfilled,* 1911 motion pictures by D. W. Griffith that form a two-part story, recount how "the old trusted body servant," as the *Biograph Bulletin* calls him, stays with the family during the Civil War, saves their little daughter and his late master's sword when Union soldiers fire the house, and after the war and the death of the mother sacrifices his meager savings to educate the girl and make it possible for her to marry well. At the conclusion of the second film, "old George at a distance views the festivities with tears of joy streaming down his black but honest cheeks, and after [the newlyweds] . . . depart for their new home, he goes back to his cabin, takes down his master's saber, and fondles it, happy in the realization that he too has fulfilled his trust." Old, alone, without funds, the only reward he receives is a handshake from the white lawyer through whom he had secretly paid for the girl's education and who earlier had ignored the black's proffered hand.[12]

These and other films by Griffith present his particular view of the South before, during, and after the Civil War, but they are no different in theme from what the rest of the industry was turning out. For most black characters, emancipation seems meaningless. The "mammy" is usually a blindly constant surrogate mother, neglectful of herself and her own family when it comes to "missy" and the rest of "massa's family." She and her male counterpart are gladly willing to accept blame that is not theirs to cover up for the master's children, to sell themselves into slavery to pay the master's gambling debts, and to sacrifice their lives to help "massa's" fight for the Confederacy or "missy's" romance.

If the black character is employed at all, he is a menial. From time to time a newsreel would show, say, Cuba-bound black troops disembarking during the Spanish-American War, but on the whole films of this type that include blacks show them as laborers and deal with such topics as banana harvesting in the West Indies, tobacco planting in Kentucky, and cotton growing in the South. The filmmakers' attitude toward such "actualities" is epitomized by this statement from a publicity release from a 1913 Lubin documentary on coffee plantations in Jamaica: "The natives work very rapidly and wear little beyond the perpetual smile which is noticeable in the negro race." In story films, blacks typically are cooks, agricultural laborers, scrubwomen, or servants of one kind or another. Jungle adventure movies showed either ignorant, often vicious savages or servile black gun bearers and "Number One boys." Although an increasing number of blacks found work in factories in the years before World War I, and although filmmakers made a substantial number of movies dealing with the prevailing labor unrest, rarely are blacks shown — except, perhaps, as servants of the managerial upper class. Even the depiction of blacks as servants or agricultural laborers is often a sort of shorthand device to indicate the regional setting.[13]

The movie black often was presented in ways that tended to give the character humiliating or demeaning aspects. The 1914 Vitagraph film *A Florida Enchantment* is a complex comedy about sex changes caused by the swallowing of unusual seeds. The main character, Miss Travis, has suddenly become a man. She/he makes a black maid swallow some "so that she may be valeted by a person of the proper sex." The Dutch protagonist of the 1908 Biograph comedy *King of the Cannibal Islands* is captured by the natives and (in the production company's words) "it looked like Stew à la Hollandaise for Heinie . . . when the Queen does the Pocahantas bit, and throwing herself on the prostrate form of Heinie declares they shall strike him only through her . . . They desist . . . as the Queen is so thick

While the black servant cowers, the white hero glowers, in *The Terrors of the Jungle* (1913).

through that the longest spear would hardly reach the victim . . . she is that obese she looks like a crowd. Heinie takes his fiddle and discourses sweet music, which places him in such high esteem with the tribe . . . that he becomes the husband of the Queen and King of the Islands." In *The Thirteen Club,* a 1905 Biograph production, a Negro waiter is efficiently setting the table for the club members' dinner when he suddenly notices a death's head centerpiece; instantly he gets the shakes and the bugeyes.[14]

That the movie industry, like white America generally, gave little thought to the dignity of the black is further revealed in films whose basis for comedy was confusion among the races, the humor, derisive and vicious, invariably at the expense of the Negro. The 1909 Edison comedy *Drawing the Color Line* based its slapstick action on the main character having his face blackened with burnt cork while drunk: to friends, barbers, tradesmen, servants, and family, he becomes just an anonymous black man. The *Moving Picture World* reviewer rather thoughtfully declared that this "picture shows very graphically how merely putting a little black on a man's face changes status" but added that the "subject is one that never fails to arouse much merriment." A trade magazine reviewer of one such film said in 1913 that "there have been more jokes perpetrated on the colored race than on any other" and added almost in surprise and obviously in ignorance of statements by such outraged members of the black community as W. E. B. DuBois and Kelly Miller, "yet our darker brethren never complain." The writer then went on to extol as "the cutest little thing" the Pathe comedy *Mixed Colors.* Its humor was based on the aftermath of mischievous boys painting a black baby white and a white baby black and placing each in the other's carriage.[15]

But if a mixup between the races was considered cute and a subject for comedy, a mixture of blood was the occasion for tragedy. In film as on the stage, the mulatto found, in the words of one commentator, that only death provided "a logical escape from a world in which to be partly colored is considered an even worse disgrace than to be a full-blooded Negro." Perhaps no movie emphasized this more starkly than *In Humanity's Cause,* a 1911 production. A melodrama set in Civil War times, the film has as its main character a Confederate officer who is saved from death on the battlefield by a blood transfusion from a black man. After a title reading "Blood Will Tell," the Southerner is shown as a changed man, in the words of the *Moving Picture Word* reviewer, "a brute who disgusts even his long suffering sweetheart." Having found out about the transfusion, he hunts down the black blood donor, finds him at the edge of a high cliff, and grapples with him: they fall to death locked in each other's arms. This film is the epitome of the whole good-white, evil-black equation with a bit of the *Doppelgänger* theme thrown in.[16]

Then there is *The Nigger,* a 1915 Fox film based on Edward Sheldon's powerful but contrived popular play of the same name. It tells how a newly elected, antiblack Southern governor discovers that he has black blood and feels compelled to give up his office and to renounce the white patrician woman he loves (even though she apparently is willing to overlook his heritage). This grim film, which has the matinee idol William Farnum in the title role, is noteworthy for the vigorous reaction it engendered in the black community. The brouhaha over *The Birth of a Nation,* which was released shortly afterward, has obscured the strenuous but relatively ineffective campaign waged against *The Nigger,* a campaign that succeeded only in having Fox retitle the film *The New Governor* in some areas and in having bits of the more inflammatory scenes cut for showing in a few communities. The arguments put forth by the black community for halting the showing of the film were either ignored or twisted. A report about black protests in Wichita, for example, played up the fact that "one Negro minister wasn't sure but that it would have been all right for Georgia, the white girl, to marry Phil."[17]

Departures from the stereotype met resistance. In a letter to *Motion Picture World,* a New Orleans reader named William Walker complained about the attitude of the black actors in a 1911 Civil War story called *The Soldiers Ring.* Asserting that the actor who portrayed a servant displayed "a stiff unwillingness in placing chairs for the Confederate generals," Walker pointed out that "the Virginia darky knew his place." The same trade journal described another 1911 Civil War melodrama, Champion's *A Southern Girl's Heroism,* warning Southern exhibitors that their audiences "won't like the scenes where the Union officer, accepted lover of the Confederate officer's daughter, kisses Topsie [her slave] nor will they like Topsie's taking the Union officer's left arm

Jack Johnson beats Jim Jeffries for the heavyweight championship in 1910. The victory of a black man over a white led Congress to ban films of live fights. (Culver Pictures)

and marching off with him and the Southern heroine on his right arm in the closing scene." The universal belief that such scenes would alienate a significant portion of their audience obviously restrained film companies from making changes in the stock depiction of the black.[18]

It was sometimes the same in real life. In 1910, when the black heavyweight champion, Jack Johnson, beat the former white titleholder, Jim Jeffries, a Federal law was passed that barred from interstate commerce "any film or other pictorial representation of any prize fight" intended for showing to the public. To be sure, prizefighting had aroused the ire of many church and community groups. Promoters had difficulty finding sites: the Johnson-Jeffries match had to be staged in Reno, Nevada. Moreover, a large number of these groups, reflecting a Puritanical spirit that still flourished in the United States, had expressed considerable antipathy to the movies and had vigorously campaigned for censorship. And yet, it was only after a black fighter had soundly beaten a white one that Congress acted. Many argued at the time that exhibition of such films might lead to racial conflict, an opinion that was not limited to the United States: shortly after the Johnson-Jeffries fight the London County Council passed a resolution stating that in its opinion "public exhibition . . . of pictures representing the recent prize fight in the United States . . . is undesirable."[19]

Significantly, few films of this period, not even comedies, portray black violence against white people or their property. As one scholar has pointed out, this may have been "due to the fear of whites that to portray the Negro so . . . was to affect a possibility of its realization." And whenever there is conflict on screen between black and white, the end result is almost always the same: the white wins. It makes no difference whether the film is a melodrama such as the 1914 Selig production *The Loyalty of Jumbo*, in which a number of hostile African natives are held off by a hardfighting white mother while her little daughter's pet elephant goes for help, or a comedy such as the 1915 Vitagraph movie *Some White Hope*, in which Negro boxer Sam Bangford (obviously patterned on the noted and then active black pugilist Sam Langford) is accidentally kayoed by Kid Limburger of Hoshkosh.[20]

The American movie industry's view of the black prior to *The Birth of a Nation* is what one scholar called an "unformed image." This judgment has some merit, given the different stereotypes that became established, even given the fact that they often overlapped. But it also is abundantly clear that, to echo a famous stage criticism, the range of these stereotypes runs the gamut from A to B. Between the 1890s and 1915 the movie black — whether played by a white or not, and whether presented as an uneasy menace, a dancing machine, a comic stooge, a faithful retainer, a cheerful flunky, a tainted unfortunate, or an ignorant savage — was presented as a composite of qualities that were the opposite of the values treasured by white American society. There was no upward social mobility for blacks in these films, just as there was no way out of the stereotype for black actors.[21]

Certainly this demeaning, ludicrous image of the black on screen did little to alleviate the scabrous relations between the races that so often ran to blood during those years. Though significant numbers of middle-class people had begun to attend the movies, for much of this period motion pictures were the major form of entertainment for the poor, especially for the mil-

The black savage was a stock movie character. But try as he might, as in *Voodoo Vengeance*, he never harmed a white.

lions from abroad and from American rural areas, who were pouring into the cities. As cheap as a glass of beer, available to those who could not understand English or who had little education, the movies, in one scholar's words, "provided the worker with a refuge from the perplexities of his outside world . . . an avenue of escape from a cruelly oppressive slum environment." Indeed, the first nickelodeon was opened in 1905 by an enterprising showman in a Pittsburgh industrial district. By 1910 the national motion picture gross receipts for the year totalled over $90 million, and across the country an estimated twenty-six million people went to the movies every week. The movies — posing neither language nor price barrier — became a school of popular American mores and values. True enough, both the immigrant and the rural hick were endlessly caricatured; but even before World War I most of these caricatures were giving way to more fully developed characterizations — or at least to less outrageous portrayals. The single exception was the black.[22]

As far as blacks were concerned, the patterns set in these early motion pictures would remain unbroken not for years but for decades. The movie industry, as the black author John Oliver Killens has charged, may well have become "the most anti-Negro influence in this nation." Killens has also called the first real film masterpiece, D. W. Griffith's *The Birth of a Nation,* "Hollywood's first big gun in its war against the black American." The castings for that gun were forged in the movies made between the mid-1890s and 1915.[23]

2

THE BIRTH
OF A NATION

ON A QUIET DAY in April 1915, Mayor James Curley of Boston convened a hearing. The subject was D. W. Griffith's new film, *The Birth of a Nation,* and whether or not it should be banned in the city — there had already been threats to dynamite the theater where the film was to be shown. About three hundred people crowded into the hearing room, most of them (as one reporter put it) "interested in the uplift of the colored race." Support for those speaking against the film became so vociferous that a number of times Curley had to ask policemen to restore order.[1]

But it soon became apparent that the hearing was little more than a sham concocted by Curley in the hope of retaining support among black voters. When a white New York social worker who was also an officer of the NAACP objected to the grotesque expressions on the faces of the black women in the film, the mayor told her that "the expressions . . . on the faces . . . of characters . . . in Shakespearean productions could be considered likewise." To Moorfield Storey, the white Bostonian who headed the Boston NAACP branch, Curley said that the objections to *The Birth of a Nation* as racist propaganda would be no more valid than protests against Shakespeare's *Henry VIII* for maligning the Roman Catholic church.[2]

The defenders of the film were often forced to raise their voices so they could be heard over the hisses and shouts of the protestors. Griffith himself was loudly booed when he declared that "if protests of this kind" succeeded it would mean "that the Indian could protest moving pictures, for in most Western pic-

A sporty D. W. Griffith posed for this portrait during the period when he made *The Birth of a Nation*. (Museum of Modern Art)

tures they are depicted killing white men." He then read letters from prominent educators who endorsed *The Birth of a Nation*. A few days earlier, he had offered to pay $10,000 to charity if Storey could "find a single incident in the play that was not historic." After the conclusion of the hearing, Storey demanded of Griffith whether "it was historic that a lieutenant had held a white woman in a room . . . and demanded a forced marriage!" Griffith replied with an invitation to "come and see the play." The director held out his hand to the NAACP official. Storey drew back icily, saying "No, sir."[3]

Storey's aversion to Griffith and his film no longer seems remarkable — for no movie has played quite such an unfortunate role in the history of the black in America. A melodrama of the Civil War and Reconstruction glorifying the Ku Klux Klan, *The Birth of a Nation* includes just about all the stereotypes of the black that had been developing in the movies since the mid-1890s. But it is also one of the few movies produced by the industry until recent years that treats the black as something more than a powerless cipher. Although *The Birth of a Nation* has its share of what a subtitle calls "faithful souls," the movie stresses the concept of the black as a brute and menace. The black is presented as a person lusting for white women, grasping for white property, and unwilling to accept a preordained station at the bottom of the social order. *The Birth of a Nation* argued that the Negro was a serious danger to established society unless checked, as in the film, by a white force such as the Ku Klux Klan.

This view of the black was all the more pernicious because of the extraordinary impact of this film as a work of art. *The Birth of a Nation* is almost universally recognized as a milestone in the development of world cinema. As obviously unbigoted a critic as James Agee stated decades after the film was released that "among moving pictures it is alone . . . as the one great epic, tragic film." It powerfully influenced all aspects of the film medium. Griffith used existing cinematic techniques such as the closeup, cross-cutting, the tracking shot, the fadeout, and effect lighting in new and exciting ways that inspired his contemporaries and future filmmakers as well. Although nearly three hours long at a time when a feature rarely ran over sixty minutes, *The Birth of a Nation* was engrossing entertainment; and it clearly demonstrated the tremendous potential of the motion picture when filming was done with vigor, boldness, imagination, and skill.[4]

Several aspects of David Wark Griffith's background found expression in this film. Born in Kentucky in 1875 and raised in various parts of that state, he was the son of "Roaring Jake" Griffith, a Confederate veteran who died when D.W. was still a small boy. The younger Griffith was a high-school dropout who, before turning permanently to the theater in his early twenties, worked at a variety of jobs including elevator boy, bookstore clerk, salesman, and casual laborer. The lean, rangy, hawk-nosed Griffith achieved some success as a journeyman actor touring with stock companies. Always ambitious, he aspired to be a playwright and even managed to have one of his efforts, a turgid melodrama about the California hop fields, produced in Washington and Baltimore. His first experience with the movies, in 1908, was as an actor portraying the hero in Edwin S. Porter's *Rescued from an Eagle's Nest.* In this Edison company film he played a character who fights an eagle with his bare hands and saves a child from the giant bird. Later that year Griffith was hired by the Biograph Company. He reluctantly accepted assignments to direct films, for he knew almost nothing about directing and he feared that failure would prejudice his chances as a writer or actor. Those fears proved baseless: by the time he left Biograph late in 1913 he had directed over four hundred films (mostly one- or two-reelers) and had helped to transform the medium. That he sometimes had to produce two films a week during this period gives an indication of his capacity for work. During 1914 Griffith shot four feature-length films before embarking on *The Birth of a Nation.*

Griffith's movie, filmed in and around Los Angeles during the summer and early fall of 1914, is based on a poisonously racist 1905 novel, *The Clansman,* and on an equally vicious play based on it that was produced the next year. The overblown theater version incorporated some episodes from an earlier novel called *The Leopard's Spots,* and subtitled "A Romance of the White Man's Burden, 1865–1900." The author of all these works was Thomas Dixon, Jr., who was characterized by a contemporary magazine as "preacher, lecturer, novelist, and Southern country gentleman long known for the earnestness, we might say fanaticism with which he deals with . . . the Negro problem." The novel *The Clansman* opens at the end of the Civil War and continues through Reconstruction. The play — whose theme was described at the time as "Hit the nigger!" — limited itself to part of the Reconstruction period. Griffith, alive to the dramatic aspects of the Civil War, began his movie with the eve of the conflict.[5]

The plot of *The Birth of a Nation,* which was called *The Clansman* when it was initially released on the West Coast, revolved around the relationships of two families — the Camerons of South Carolina and the Stonemans of Pennsylvania. The movie opens with a prologue, which includes a scene showing blacks being sold into slavery at auction. The title introducing it indicates one of Griffith's main theses: "The bringing of the African to America planted the first seeds of disunion." Indeed, the film argues over and over again that the black presence in the United States serves as a barrier to the firm establishment of a unified country. The story proper begins with the visit of Phil and Ted Stoneman to the Cameron home in Piedmont, South Carolina, the fictional locale for much of the movie. The Stoneman boys are boarding-school chums of Wade and Luke Cameron. Phil falls in love with their sister, Margaret; Ben, the oldest Cameron son, is smitten with a picture of Elsie Stoneman. The Cameron slaves are shown, happy and contented, in their quarters. Despite a long work day stretching from dawn to dark, they dance gaily for the Camerons and their guests.

The impending war puts an end to the visit, and the movie shifts to Washington, D. C. There the Stoneman boys' father, Austin Stoneman, closely patterned on the antislavery Republican congressional leader Thaddeus Stevens, is an important political figure ("Master of Congress") as well as an unthinking advocate of black rights. He also has a mulatto housekeeper-mistress, described in a title as the "weakness that is to blight a nation."

Griffith presents a grim picture of the Civil War and its im-

Thomas Dixon, author of *The Clansman.* (University of North Carolina Library)

mediate aftermath. Ted Stoneman is killed in battle, as are the younger Cameron boys. Black guerrillas attack Piedmont. The South suffers from "ruin, devastation, rapine, and pillage." In some of the most exciting yet graphic battle scenes ever filmed, Ben Cameron — "the little Colonel" — leads a series of deperate charges against the Union forces besieging Petersburg. Ben is wounded, captured by Union troops commanded by Phil Stoneman, and committed to a Washington, D. C., hospital — where Elsie Stoneman is a nurse. (Coincidences never seemed to bother Griffith.) Ben's strong feelings for Elsie are soon reciprocated. Distressed to learn that he has been condemned to death, she helps his mother to gain an interview with President Lincoln ("the Great Heart") and obtain a pardon. As the war draws to a close, the question of Federal policy toward the Confederate states becomes a vital issue. Austin Stoneman is the leader of those who would force the South to grant the black equal rights. And he and the president are shown clashing angrily over how Reconstruction should be undertaken. The first half of the film ends with the assassination of Lincoln (witnessed by Phil and Elsie Stoneman) and the Cameron family symbolically speaking for the whole South in a gloomy title: "What is to happen to us now?"

The answer to that question is the second half of the movie, which depicts what is described in a title as "the agony which the South endured so that a Nation might be born." Griffith's rendering of that agony includes the representation of such disparate actions as blacks pushing whites off the sidewalk, grabbing their possessions, preaching marriage between the races, attempting rape of a white teenager, and flogging and killing blacks who remain loyal to the whites. A prime mover in all this activity is Austin Stoneman's mulatto protégé, Silas Lynch. An ailing Stoneman sends Lynch to the South in order, as a title puts it, "to aid the carpetbaggers in organizing and wielding the power of the Negro vote." Soon thereafter Stoneman determines to go south himself; at the behest of Phil and Elsie, he settles with them in Piedmont. Meanwhile, Lynch and his agents have stirred up the black population. He is elected lieutenant governor. Blacks become local officials, county sheriffs, and judges. Following a title that reads "The Negro party in control of the State House of Representatives, 101 blacks against 23 whites, session of 1871,"

Griffith presents the black legislators lasciviously debating a bill legalizing intermarriage. They are shown taking off their shoes, eating joints of meat, and guzzling whiskey in the course of the debate.

Meanwhile, in Piedmont, blacks harass whites. Ben, described as being "in agony of soul over the degradation and ruin of his people," wanders disconsolately along a river bank. He sees two white children hide under a long white sheet, which they use to terrify some Negro children. This is his inspiration, and the result, according to a title, is "The Ku Klux Klan, the organization that saved the South from the anarchy of black rule . . ."

Initially the Klan proves ineffective. Then Flora, the Camerons' sunny-haired teenage daughter, jumps to her death in a ravine to escape from Gus, a former Cameron slave who has become what a title calls the "product of the vicious doctrines spread by the carpetbaggers." Flora's stumbling, terrified flight through the woods, Gus's hard-breathing, agitated pursuit, and her eventual suicide take nearly seven minutes. A Boston judge, Thomas Down, found this portion of the film "offensive and immoral," saying that "there is no question why the man is pursuing her, he is actuated by the lowest of human passions. The little girl to . . . preserve her honor has to bring about her own destruction." Gus is killed by the Klan, and his body thrown on Lynch's porch. Perhaps understandably, these events have hampered the course of true love: a distraught Margaret Cameron has rejected Phil Stoneman as a suitor and Elsie has broken with Ben, who has admitted to her his involvement with the Klan.

The film now moves forcefully and rapidly to a conclusion. Klansmen begin to gather in order to challenge the carpetbagger government in force. Dr. Cameron, Ben's father, is arrested for having harbored his Klansman son. The Camerons' faithful servants rescue the doctor with the aid of Phil Stoneman, who shoots a black militiaman. Dr. Cameron, his wife, Margaret, their servants, and Phil flee into the countryside pursued by black militiamen. Refuge is found in the cabin of two Union veterans, where "the former enemies of North and South are united again in common defense of their Aryan birthright." The black militia besieges the cabin.

Back in Piedmont, Lynch proposes marriage to Elsie, who has

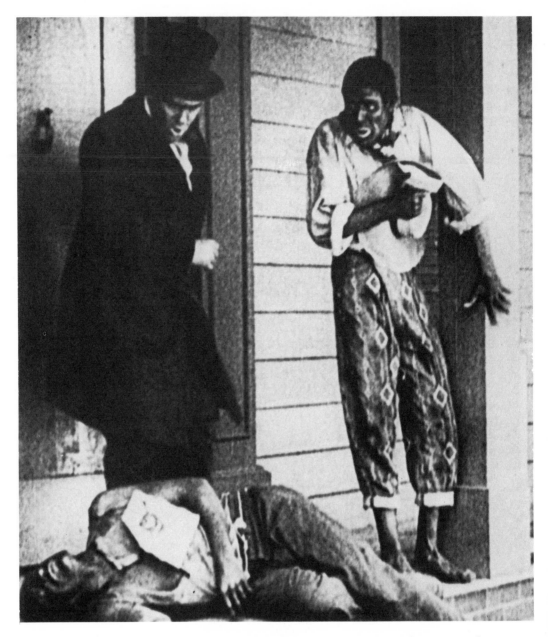

Silas Lynch, left, a mulatto carpetbagger, and a cohort (a white actor in blackface) discover a corpse, deposited as a warning by the Ku Klux Klan. (National Film Archive)

Lillian Gish, one of the white heroines of *The Birth of a Nation*, reacts to Lynch's proposal of marriage. (National Film Archive) come to see him in the hope of interceding for Ben Cameron. As the mulatto's black forces rampage through the streets of Piedmont, he tells her "I will build a black empire and you as my queen shall rule by my side." Horrified, she refuses, and he decides on a "forced marriage." Her attempts to escape fail and she sits tied and gagged in an inner room as her father, ignorant of the fate of his daughter, calls on the mulatto. Stoneman, told by Lynch that he wishes to marry a white woman, indicates approval until it becomes clear that the intended bride is Elsie. At this point Stoneman quickly makes clear that he no longer believes in absolute equality, but rage and storm as he will, the wedding preparations go forward. Ben — apprised of what is happening in the streets of Piedmont and to his beloved — leads the Klansmen to the rescue.

The last reel of the film is a masterpiece of quick cross-cutting

between the black mob in the Piedmont streets, Elsie bound and gagged, the siege at the cabin, and the Klan riding cross-country "as powerfully as Niagara pours over the cliff," as the poet Vachel Lindsay wrote in 1915. This "Anglo-Saxon Niagara" restores order in Piedmont, disarming the blacks after a short skirmish; thwarts Lynch's marriage plans; and rescues the group at the cabin at just about the last possible moment. During a preview showing in New York City, Dixon supposedly shouted to Griffith that "*The Clansman* is too tame, let's call it *The Birth of a Nation.*" In the film's few remaining minutes the Klan dominates the next election by barring blacks and their white supporters from the polls. Black rule is ended and Margaret and Phil and Elsie and Ben are shown on a double honeymoon, symbolic of the reunion of North and South. "The drama winds up," as critic Francis Hackett commented in 1915, "with a suggestion of 'Lincoln's solution' — back to Liberia — and then if you please, with a film representing Jesus Christ in 'the halls of brotherly love.' " However, the "City of Peace" as viewed by D. W. Griffith contained no blacks.[6]

Strange as it may seem, the guiding intelligence behind *The Birth of a Nation* did not consider himself antiblack. Quite the contrary, Griffith stated in one of the titles at the beginning of the second part of the film that it was not meant to reflect on "any race or people." And after the film's release he declared that if *The Birth of a Nation* attacked any group of persons it was the whites who had led the blacks astray during Reconstruction. Griffith and his supporters have also claimed that the film toned down substantially the racism inherent in Dixon's work. To be sure, there is nothing in the movie quite like Dixon's assertion that "for a thicklipped, flapnosed, spindleshaked negro, exuding his nauseating animal odour, to shout in derision over the hearths and homes of white men and women is an atrocity too monstrous for belief." To a limited extent Griffith did ameliorate Dixon's vicious prose, which portrayed the black as a degenerate incapable of civilization. But it should be remembered that the filmmaker did so by offsetting Dixon's brute image of the black with the comic and simplistically happy "faithful souls." It is also quite clear that the second and more controversial part of the movie does not differ substantially from Dixon's play. Griffith's defenders often point to the scene of Flora jumping to her death as being less inflammatory than a sequence in the novel in which Marion Lenoir is attacked by Gus in front of her mother, who has been tied by other blacks to a bedpost. But it was Dixon, not Griffith, who eliminated the Lenoirs from the dramatization of *The Clansman* and substituted the scene with Flora for the purpose of avoiding extraneous characters on stage.

Griffith was pained by the charge that *The Birth of a Nation* was antiblack. A Victorian idealist, he prided himself on his sympathy for the underdog, and many of his films had treated the poor sympathetically when derision or contempt were the cinematic style of the day. He had also presented the Indian on screen in a manner other than the prevalent "the only good Indian is a dead Indian" manner. Griffith told Lillian Gish (who portrayed Elsie) that to accuse him of being prejudiced against blacks "is like saying I am against children, as they were our children, whom we loved and cared for all our lives." Years later he described "the peculiarly close relationship between the whites and Negroes of the old regime." He related to an interviewer how, after "Uncle Henry, father's body servant" had cut his brother's hair badly, his Confederate veteran father had taken an old saber and, slashing away, had chased the black around the yard: "Uncle Henry laughed his fool head off as he ducked from tree to tree." For D. W. Griffith the black was either an Uncle Henry or a menace to white society. It was inconceivable to him that blacks could act independently, and he accepted Dixon's view of those who did. Griffith may have had genuine feelings for "the colored people" but as a product of his time and background he was a racist, a firm believer in the inferiority of the black.[7]

The Birth of a Nation vividly evidenced that belief, even in its publicity. One story about the making of the film recounted how a bunch of cowboys "representing the night raiders of the Ku Klux Klan" decided to "whoop it up." The black extras portraying the militia were supposed to flee before the white-uniformed riders, and did so. The "eager and hilarious cowboys" finding the chase "exciting," decided to "continue the hunt" and "pursued the colored troopers out of the scene." Supposedly one extra "in his fright outran his horse and failed to return, even on payday."[8]

Interestingly enough, many of the black roles in the film were played by whites. Griffith made use of real blacks only in the crowd scenes. When asked about this, Griffith said that "the matter was given consideration, and on careful weighing of every detail concerned the decision was to have no black blood among the principals." Griffith's defenders point to the absence of black performers on the West Coast at the time and argue that in any event "the type of work" then done by blacks in show business "was too limited, dramaturgically, to qualify them for . . . screen . . . work." It is true that Griffith was only following a common practice of the time. But in the 1920s, when others in the industry began to utilize black actors, he continued to use whites to play black roles.[9]

The Birth of a Nation was an enormous popular success. Although the precise financial details are hazy, it surely ranks as the all-time box office champion among American silent films. It had spectacular first runs in major American cities. At a time when a movie house normally held a film for only a few days, Griffith's work ran ten months in New York City and twenty-two weeks in Los Angeles. Contemporary estimates of the audience that saw the movie during its first year of release range upward from five million, or about 6 percent of the population of the United States in 1915. *The Birth of a Nation* was a well-received, aggressively promoted, exciting film. Nevertheless, much of its success depended on popular attitudes that crystallized around 1915 and lasted for over a generation.

The first decades of this century were hard ones for the black in the United States. Reconciliation of the sections was still being achieved at his expense. As the historian C. Vann Woodward has pointed out, "just as the Negro . . . gained emancipation and new rights through a falling out between white men, he now stood to lose his rights through the reconciliation of white men." The spreading Jim Crow system, which in the South as well as many other parts of the country consigned the black to separate and inferior public facilities, was extended to Federal agencies in Washington. Woodrow Wilson, the first Southerner elected president since the Civil War, was inaugurated on March 4, 1913, and not long after he wrote his old acquaintance Dixon that "we are handling . . . the colored people . . . in the departments in just the way they ought to be handled. We are trying — and by degrees — succeeding in a plan . . . which . . . will not in one bureau mix the races." The use of the black as a scapegoat for many of the problems facing the American people after the Civil

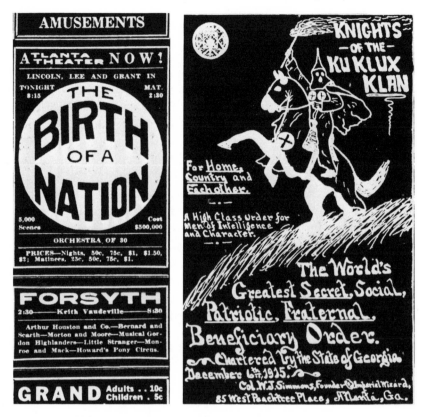

These advertisements appeared on facing pages of
the December 8, 1915 Atlanta *Constitution*.

War was already a familiar literary theme by the turn of the
century; now it began to find its way into the writing of history.
James Ford Rhodes, the author of an influential multivolume
work on the United States since 1850 and judged by his contemporaries as a leading historian of the period, described Reconstruction as "repressive" and "uncivilized," and argued that "no
large policy in our country has ever been so conspicuous a failure
as that of forcing universal Negro suffrage upon the South." William Dunning, a Columbia University professor who trained a
generation of scholars, wrote of "the struggle through which the
southern whites . . . thwarted the scheme which threatened
permanent subjection to another race." And the views expressed

by historians like Rhodes and Dunning soon permeated the school books of the day.[10]

Griffith's movie not only reflected this changing interpretation of what was still recent history but also reinforced it. For him, the view of the Civil War and Reconstruction put forth by *The Birth of a Nation* was "the truth about the South, with a touch of its eternal romance." And he made elaborate efforts to authenticate this truth for the audience. Interspersed throughout the film are what he called "historical facsimiles" of such actual events as President Lincoln signing the call for volunteers to fight secession, General Lee's surrender at Appomattox, and the assassination of the president. The opening shots of the sequence depicting the debate on the bill legalizing intermarriage are patterned, according to a title, "after a photograph by The Columbia State." The second part of *The Birth of a Nation* begins with nearly two minutes of titles justifying the film's view of the black role in Reconstruction. In the main, the source for these titles is Woodrow Wilson's *History of the American People* (published in 1902 to general acclaim from his fellow academics), and the direct quotes include his statement that "in the villages the Negroes were the office holders, men who knew none of the uses of authority, except its insolence."[11]

Griffith's efforts had a strong effect. Hearst columnist Dorothy Dix called the movie "history vitalized" and urged people to "go see it . . . for it will make better Americans of you." Novelist Booth Tarkington, Congressional Representative Claude Kitchin (D-NC), and other assorted literary and political figures also allowed themselves to be quoted in advertisements that proclaimed the educational value of *The Birth of a Nation*. A prominent Northern Protestant clergyman said that "a boy can learn more true history and get more of the atmosphere of the period by sitting for three hours before the film which Mr. Griffith has produced with such artistic skill than by weeks and months of study in the classroom."[12]

Many of these endorsements were garnered by Dixon, who had a significant financial interest in the film. Its detractors claimed that his strategy was to pass out cards asking for an affirmative statement during the intermission — that is, before the more controversial, and avowedly racist, second part of the film was shown. Whatever his technique, Dixon was indefatigable in

publicizing *The Birth of a Nation.* He even arranged an unprecedented screening at the White House, which was attended by the
president, members of the cabinet, and their families. Wilson was
supposedly quite moved, and he is reported to have said of the
film that "it is like writing history in lightning. My only regret is
that it is all so terribly true." Griffith and Dixon made use of this
friendly reception at the White House in defending the movie
against those who sought to censor or ban it. Dixon went so far as
to promote *The Birth of a Nation* as "federally endorsed." However, as controversy mounted, the president found it expedient to
allow his secretary to write a Massachusetts congressman that the
White House had never sanctioned the movie; later, during the
war, the president himself referred to the film as an "unfortunate
production."[13]

The Birth of a Nation very quickly became the subject of
strenuous controversy. The infant National Association for the
Advancement of Colored People, other black groups, and their
white allies tried to have the film banned in its entirety, or, failing
that, to have the more objectionable scenes eliminated. Opponents of the movie went to court or joined picket lines — and
occasionally expressed their disapproval by planting stink bombs
in theaters where it was being shown, or by throwing eggs at the
screen. But militant black activity was hampered by the fact that
even outside the South most movie houses would not admit Negroes. The many well-known figures who denounced the film
included Harvard University President-emeritus Charles Eliot,
black leaders such as William Monroe Trotter and Booker T.
Washington, Rabbi Stephen Wise, historian Albert Bushnell
Hart, and New York *Post* publisher Oswald Garrison Villard
(who refused to accept advertising for the movie). Some spoke
out more passionately than others but all echoed the judgment of
the noted social worker Jane Addams, who described Griffith's
film as "a gathering [of] the most vicious and grotesque individuals he could find among the colored people," whom he presented as being "representative of the . . . entire race."[14]

On the whole, the demonstrations proved unsuccessful. The
Massachusetts legislature was pressured into creating a censorship board, but that board proceeded to vote against banning the
film. After its initial showings the opponents of the movie did
manage to get removed the sequence in the epilogue showing

Lincoln advocating the deportation of blacks and their being loaded on boats in New York harbor. Some other scenes showing leering blacks also were cut. Seymour Stern, one of the most knowledgeable commentators on the film, estimates that a little over five hundred feet of the film's just over 13,000 feet were deleted.

Certainly Griffith's film stirred up race hatred. In periods of racial tension local authorities, who otherwise had proved unwilling to censor the film, prohibited theaters from showing it. In Omaha, during the summer of 1919, at a time when there was a rash of race riots across the country, the mayor offered a local movie house the choice of ceasing to show the film or closing. Well after its initial release, the black critic James Weldon Johnson expressed concern over "the power of *The Birth of a Nation* to do us damage" because it contained propaganda of "the most

THE VERDICT

This cartoon, part of the NAACP's vigorous campaign against *The Birth of a Nation,* appeared in the October, 1915 issue of its magazine, *The Crisis.*

insidious sort." Those who brought into being a revised Ku Klux Klan recognized that propaganda value, and made use of the film for Klan recruiting activities. At least one Atlanta newspaper carried the first public announcements soliciting membership for the new organization (which was started in Georgia in 1915) alongside theater notices advertising Griffith's film. As the historian George Tindall writes, "one could hardly exaggerate its significance . . . in preparing the way" for the Klan, which burgeoned so explosively in the 1920s. As late as 1931, tests of a group of white school children in a small Illinois town found them friendly to blacks before viewing *The Birth of a Nation* but "less favorable" afterward. Nor did this shift of attitude ebb with time, as was evidenced by a re-examination of the children's responses eight months later.[15]

For blacks, one of the more important consequences of *The Birth of a Nation* had to do with their image in the movies. The film critic Andrew Sarris has pointed out that "the outcries against *Birth of a Nation* served merely to drive racism underground," and indeed, until the introduction of sound movies, the black on screen was generally relegated to minor roles. Caricatures became more one-dimensional and limited than ever. If Griffith had emphasized the black as wrongdoer, at least he had presented him as a prominent one. For the remainder of the silent period the black on screen was presented not as a human being but as a cliché representing the lowest form of behavior, aspiration, motivation, and performance. In the same way as Jean Paul Sartre tells us that anti-Semites define the Jew to fit their prejudices, American society — and the movie industry in particular — defined the black to fit its racist attitudes.[16]

It once took only one drop of cinematic black blood to taint a lifetime, as the heroine of this 1917 tearjerker discovered. The ending, however, turned out happily — and lily white. (*The Moving Picture World,* June 2, 1917)

3

THE FREEZING
OF AN IMAGE

THOMAS EDISON invested about $25,000 in the development of
the Kinetoscope. In 1926 the total investment in the American
film industry was in excess of $1 billion. By 1922 there were over
16,000 movie theaters in the United States, many of them new
and luxurious. Three years earlier a report prepared for the
investment banking firm of Kuhn, Loeb had indicated that "the
gross annual return" from a somewhat smaller number of theaters
would be over $750 million. Movies were no longer just "a poor
man's show": by the beginning of the 1920's over fifty million
paid admissions a week were recorded. The cost of making
movies also went up substantially. The movie historian Benjamin
Hampton has noted that between 1914 and 1924 the cost of
"representative program offerings had advanced from an average
cost of $20,000 each to $300,000."[1]

Those in the movie studio who were responsible for meeting
increased costs wished to avoid any controversy that might cut
into profits; they stayed away from the image of the threatening
black — unless he were found in an exotic location such as the
jungle. The leaders of the film industry also claimed that Southern audiences would not pay to see a movie in which a black was
presented as other than a caricature. One director told a reporter
from the black press that the film "that turns Manhattan mad
with praise would meet with failure in the South . . ." These are
arguments that the historian Thomas Cripps has called "the myth
of the Southern box office." He points out that movie receipts in
the South were acknowledged by the industry to be notoriously

low: increased black patronage might have balanced any falling off of the Southern white audience caused by opposition to films treating the black fairly. Cripps makes a powerful case for his arguments that profits would not have been adversely affected and that "the myth," as he writes, ". . . must have been a rationalization for what Hollywood producers would have created anyway."[2]

Movie treatment of blacks ranged from their depiction as slaves brought over from Africa (*The Love Mart,* First National, 1927) to jazz musicians whose "hot rhythm" enhanced the seductive allure of a contemporary white temptress while their blackness presumably served to highlight her Caucasian sexual charm (*Circe the Enchantress,* Metro Goldwyn, 1924). If presented as natives in the jungle, blacks were crude, brutal, and superstitious. They might achieve some temporary success in their encounters with whites — and this initial success was often a vital part of the plot. Reviewing a 1923 Paramount film, *Drums of Fate,* part of which is set in the African jungle, the *Moving Picture World* commented on how "the usual story of the capture of a white man by the savages furnishes the suspense." Threatening black natives could also be found on screen in other exotic settings. D. W. Griffith's *The Idol Dancer,* a 1920 First National picture, was set in the South Seas, where, according to the caption on an advertising still, the senses of the heroine "reeled when the giant black caught her in his arms, for she felt all hope was past." She need not have feared: blacks never had their way with a white woman. This attitude also found expression in English movies of the time. For example, a description of the screenplay for *Palaver,* a 1926 British Instructional film made entirely on location in Nigeria, recounts "how the crowd of natives melts away" at the appearance of a young white political officer, "for his authority is known and respected."[3]

American films generally depicted blacks in a menial capacity. According to a survey based on films reviewed by *Variety* between 1915 and 1920, over 50 percent of the black characters were maids, stableboys, and the like. And during the 1920s more than 80 percent were some kind of subordinate help. Continuing the tradition that had developed in movies prior to *The Birth of a Nation,* most films touching on the South during the Civil War period had a "mammy" and/or what was called in

Gilbert Roland (right) was stoically calm, while his black servant, Raymond Turner, was stereotypically fearful in *The Love Mart* (1927).

the titles of one feature, "a faithful colored servitor." As always, the abolition of slavery meant nothing to an on-screen black. A typical situation was that outlined by Metro in its synopsis of *Marse Covington,* a 1915 film in which "Dan, as a boy given to Covington . . . refuses to take advantage of his legal right to freedom."

Occasionally a black did play some part in the story development of a film, as in the Williamson Brothers 1917 drama *The Submarine Eye,* where a black is called on to perform a Herculean physical feat, an action that intensifies his image as more animal than human. In this instance a black helper dives, knife in mouth, into the depths to rescue a young white inventor whose gear has become entangled. And in some movies, which only reinforced prevailing concepts of white superiority, a black would side with whites against his own race. Even black menials could come to the rescue. Chapter 7 of the 1916 Pathe serial *The Iron Claw* hinges on the fact, as the company synopsis indicates, that "Jemima Washington, a portly Negro matron, on her rounds of the local ash barrels finds the map that Davy dropped from the roof of the Central Tower Building . . ." Another white view of the black in action is presented in Metro's 1917 film *The Voice of Conscience,* in which a black woman employs voodoo incantations to force a half-witted black man to confess his deception, thus saving the hero from a murder charge. But blacks rarely show up to advantage. *The Headless Horseman* (Hodkinson, 1922) is an exception, for it is a young black boy's daring ride that saves schoolmaster Ichabod Crane from being tarred and feathered by villagers who believe that Crane has abused their children.[4]

Usually, however, the black was present on screen merely to provide comic relief. The laughs often came at the expense of a black male character, who is reduced to shivering wretchedness by thunderstorms, sliding panels, and ghostlike figures. He is the inevitably saucer-eyed fool, who hears a suspicious sound while inspecting a dimly lighted corridor. His eyes grow large, the pupils becoming dark dots frantically dashing about in a sea of white. His ears pick up. His mouth involuntarily grimaces. He makes a slow frightened turn to inspect the innocuous source of the sound. The black does a doubletake, his eyes seeming to leap from their sockets. His hair may stand on end or momentarily go white. Then he leaps out the window or flings himself down the stairs or bandy-leggedly runs away.

By the time the talkies were introduced, this image had become one of the more common movie caricatures of the black. This was not his only unredeeming feature, of course. The screen black never had an easy time with the English language. In *The Conqueror,* Fox's 1917 epic about Sam Houston, the future savior of Texas calls on a girl and is told by a mammy that her mistress could not see him until he "strained to be constable."

And so in this screen biography Houston plunges into a political career under a false impression — the mammy had been ordered to tell Houston that the girl was "constrainedly unable" to see him. Throughout the silent period filmmakers acted as though it were necessary for the black to say "dis," "dat," and the like in the titles in order to draw a clear distinction between the races.

This racist attitude manifested itself in endless ways. A black would be introduced by a title reading "the only thing fast about Ignition Jones was his color." Or a black woman would be presented as being sexually abandoned: a white viewer complained to the *Moving Picture World* about the vulgar way in which "a colored couple did the shimmy" in *His Darker Self* (Hodkinson, 1924). One Charles Lewis of Grand Gorge, New York, added that "the lady in the case is much more unstable from the hips up than nature and dignity intended her to be in public." In the stories they planted, the industry's corps of public relations men were fond of making the black a butt of inane jokes. A 1922 *Moving Picture World* item plugging the white comedian Larry Semon ended with this punch line:

> Two Darky extras were preparing to work on Semon's set the other day.
> "How come yo' got dat can o' shoe blackin'?" one asked the other
> "Ho, ho, pore fool, dat ain't shoe blackin' — dat's ma cold cream!"[5]

Probably the most unattractive presentation of the black was in one- or two-reel comedies. These shorts, which came to supplement the feature presentation, had to make their impact quickly because of their limited running time, and the comedies with black characters employed the prevailing stereotypes in much grosser form. The Sammy Johnsin cartoons (produced mainly in 1916) showed the antics of what the distributors called an "indolent colored boy." Young Sammy had many fantastic adventures, most of which took place in his dreams — he slept a great deal. He might imagine himself in the Fiji Islands with a cannibal girl. He tries to kiss her but instead winds up touching lips with a baboon. In 1918 the General Film Company advertised "Ebony Comedies" as a "new creation in screen style — real negro comedies with real negro players . . . every picture theater now can have a 'colored act' on its bill, just as every vaudeville house carries one as an indispensable feature." A good example of what a black newspaper called "two reel burlesques on the race" is *Mummy Love.* In this 1926 F. B. O. short the white protagonist gets his girl back from a libidinous sheik with the aid of a black porter. The porter wins the keys to the tomb in which the girl is held by cheating at craps with the black guards to the mummy vault.

For all that the comedy shorts lampooned blacks, one series did treat them as characters rather than objects. The "Our Gang" movies were launched in 1922 and continued into the late 1930s. They are regarded by many (including black critics) as "one of Hollywood's few attempts . . . to do better by the Negro." One or two black children appeared in each short. They were members of the group, sharing in its adventures and misadventures. It

The old year gets the message in this 1925 "Our Gang" comedy short. Blacks and whites could work together — as long as they remained children. (National Film Archive)

Frederick Ernest Morrison — known as Sunshine Sammy or Pickaninny Sammy — was the first black child star and part of the original "Our Gang" group.

is true that "Sunshine Sammy," "Pineapple," and "Farina" in the 1920s and later, "Stymie" and "Buckwheat" were frequently the butt of the other children's humor. But in many instances the black children shared in the hijinks directed at another member of the gang. In similar shorts made by other companies laughs were usually achieved at the expense of the black children involved. However, it was not unusual for this lampooning to be offset by a kind of roughhearted benevolence, as in the Vitagraph "Sonny Jim" series. Young Jim often did things accompanied by what company advertising called "his little colored friend Lilly." He rescues her in *The White and Black Snowball* (1915) from some rascally kids trying to steal her mittens. But before taking her home he tries to scrub her face white with snow: as Jim tells Lilly, he would never be allowed to come into the house with such a dirty face.[6]

Blacks fared no better in documentary films, though an occasional newsreel might treat them fairly. The August 1, 1917, issue of *Animated Weekly* included footage showing thousands of New York Negroes marching in a mass protest against racial violence. But more usual was a 1918 short showing New York State mounted police in action. It included a comedy sequence depicting the arrest of several blacks for a midnight raid on a chicken coop.

Disparaging movie stereotypes even found their way into newsreels and other supposedly factual films dealing with the black in the United States armed forces during World War I. Typical was the newsreel that first showed disciplined and battle-ready white Americans in the trenches — and then, a black soldier with a French lesson book in hand, scratching his head and gazing at the book in bewilderment. In another newsreel one black called another "niggah" during the course of an argument as to whether it would be safer to enlist in the army or the navy. The implication, as one black newspaperman bitterly pointed out, was that "the two colored men were figuring on the less dangerous way to serve their country." Thirteen months after the United States entered the war, the black journalist Lester Walton angrily declared in the New York *Age* that "AT NO TIME HAS THE COLORED SOLDIER BEEN SHOWN AS A MAN." In part the problem lay with a Jim Crow army that placed most of its 375,000 Negro recruits in segregated noncombat units. But there

Be it Hollywood or Europe, it helped to have some black jazz musicians around if you wanted to film an orgy. This scene is from the 1926 German *Der Prinz und die Tänzerin.*

were also thousands of black troops fighting in the front lines. Yet despite one of the most massive war propaganda efforts ever undertaken by a modern government, the considerable exploits of these black combat forces were almost totally neglected. The one official film dealing with black soldiers was not available until late in the war and apparently was shown only to black audiences. *Our Colored Fighters,* moreover, emphasized the labor role of the black soldier.[7]

One of the side effects of the war had been to hamper European film production and distribution. As one Hollywood spokesman boastfully put it years later: "the war delivered . . . the screens of the world to the American product." The black community understood only too well the harmful effects that the screen image of their race had abroad. A black nationalist convention called by Marcus Garvey in 1920 adopted "A Declaration of Rights of the Negro Peoples of the World" that included a protest against "picture films showing the Negro as a cannibal." In 1921 the New York *Age* carried a front-page report headed "Americans Use Movies in France to Belittle Negroes." Some years later a black foreign correspondent concluded his comments about the effect of American movies abroad with the question: "Is it any wonder that the majority of Europeans . . . think the American Negro . . . must be either a jazz musician or a servant after seeing how the race is misrepresented by the movies . . ."[8]

Some blacks argued openly for censorship of films defamatory to their race, but these protests, like those against *The Birth of a Nation*, were ineffective. Under pressure from church groups and community organizations outraged at what they considered the licentiousness of films and the loose morals of the movie makers, the industry during the 1920s did act to censor itself. But the resulting codes and formulas, which often were ignored by studios, made not even a *pro forma* difference to the portrayal of the black. The 1921 plan of self-regulation ignored the black entirely and a 1927 code of "Don'ts and Be Carefuls" mentioned only what was called "miscegenation (sex relationships between the white and black races)." But since the outburst over *The Birth of a Nation*, this had become taboo anyway.[9]

One thing did change: by the end of the silent period whites generally no longer played black roles. Still, it was a tradition that died hard. Well into the 1920s it was not unusual for more prominent black characters to be portrayed by whites hiding not too successfully behind a burnt-cork mask. Indeed, one of the last silent movies produced by Warner Brothers was a World War I comedy, *Ham and Eggs at the Front*. It was advertised by the company as "The Big Jazz Parade of Burnt-Cork Comedians in the Trenches" and as "Two darkies' hair raising adventures with girls, ghosts, and guns in No-Man's Land." Included in the cast of this 1927 production (based on a story by Darryl Zanuck) was Myrna Loy, who played a dusky Senegalese siren who tries to seduce information from the title characters, also played by whites in black-face makeup.

Why were white actors and actresses used to portray blacks? In the case of *Ham and Eggs at the Front* Jack Warner (according to his publicity department) "became imbued with the idea of a picture in which . . . characters would be in burnt cork." Other filmmakers such as D. W. Griffith simply preferred to cast whites in black roles. The black, it was argued, just did not have the necessary experience or talent. In 1922 Alexander Woollcott, then the drama critic for the *New York Times*, voiced a widely held belief when he wrote that, with very few exceptions, he "had not seen a Negro role acceptably played by a Negro." Though speaking about the stage, he gave voice to the belief of many in the movie industry.[10]

A number of white actors and actresses specialized in portraying blacks, though the one who probably made the most frequent appearances during these years was Tom Wilson. One of the leads in *Ham and Eggs at the Front,* he was over six feet tall and powerfully built. Born in Montana and raised in Illinois, he had appeared successfully on stage with such diverse troupers as Mrs. Fiske and Eva Tanguay before making his movie debut in comedy films during the early days of movies. Subsequently he had acted in many films, including *The Birth of a Nation* (in which he was Stoneman's Negro servant) and *The Kid* (in which he played the Irish cop who was Charlie Chaplin's nemesis).

Everybody but the dog appears to be cheating in *Ham and Eggs at the Front* (1927) — and even its paws are under the table. Tom Wilson is the burnt-cork comedian, second from left. (Courtesy United Artists International)

Between 1920 and 1927 Wilson appeared in over thirty-five films, and in many of them, he played black characters for comic relief. As one reviewer said of him, "Tom is excellent as always in a role of this kind and keeps you highly amused." Wilson became so identified with black roles that the movie column of one black newspaper once referred to him as "a colored star."[11]

Other white performers might take on a black role for a special performance. This was true of the actresses who played the black child Topsy in the various productions of *Uncle Tom's Cabin.* Marguerite Clark, a popular actress of the day, played both Little Eva and Topsy in the 1918 Paramount production. It was an artistic and public relations tour de force. The Duncan sisters, a popular musical comedy team of the 1920s, transformed the Harriet Beecher Stowe classic into a stage musical adapted to their own talents. The result was the vulgar and garish *Topsy and Eva,* which, according to one reviewer, "had much the same and inexplicable success as *Abie's Irish Rose.*" The Duncans' vehicle was disastrously transferred to the screen in 1927. In the absence of music, over half the footage of this film was devoted to Rosetta Duncan's boorish and silently boisterous portrayal of Topsy. As one film historian has pointed out, "Topsy is one of the most damning examples of racist portraiture in the American film: she is ignorant, thieving, superstitious, undisciplined, and given over to swearing and biting; she eats bugs . . . and butts heads with a goat."[12]

Black performers were beginning to find work in the movies, but almost always in peripheral roles. Tom Wilson played the relatively prominent part of "Sambo," a Negro valet who accompanies his employer on an automobile trip across the country in *California Straight Ahead* (Universal, 1925); the waiters they encountered at a roadside party en route were black performers. This kind of distinction was fairly typical. Black actors and actresses like Florence Miller Grant, Caroline Snowden, Raymond Turner, and Zack Williams portrayed natives (both the hostile and tame kinds), porters, maids, laborers, baggage handlers, musicians, slaves, janitors, and servants. They received considerably less money than their white counterparts, and quite often were not even given credits. Over and over again reviews would contain comments like: "the cast is more than adequate, especially a colored man who goes unnamed . . ."[13]

James Lowe (right), shown here in the 1927 *Uncle Tom's Cabin,* protested his studio's treatment of blacks; he never worked in Hollywood again. (Courtesy of Universal Pictures)

Other humiliations also were inflicted on black actors and actresses. They invariably played characters with names like "Smoke" or "Molasses," or simply "Nigger." Studio facilities were Jim-Crowed. Blacks who complained about discrimination found themselves out of work. James B. Lowe, who played Uncle Tom in the 1927 Universal version to considerable critical acclaim, tried during the course of the production to protest the studio's view of the black characters. Lowe had himself replaced Charles Gilpin, who had been fired in part because he had also protested against the way the character of Uncle Tom was presented. Lowe waited with his protests until considerable footage had been shot of him, but it made no difference. He never made another movie, and five years later he was found by a correspondent for a black weekly working as a tailor in Paris.

The reason why black performers accepted these humiliations and repeatedly accepted such demeaning roles is hardly a mystery. As a black newspaperman commented on the situation in 1927: "now the lady of color or the gentleman . . . needs the dough-re-me, or she or he says perhaps 'goodbye race pride' . . . and the movies have another colored individual in a role sponsored more by circumstance than desire." Behind this circumstance lay the continuing economic stranglehold of white society on the black community. Even at movie theaters in the heart of Harlem blacks were seated only in the balcony. And at these theaters the white management refused to utilize trained black projectionists and reportedly told a committee of blacks who protested this policy that "Negroes are not going to run this business."[14]

Blacks in the film industry were almost completely shut out of the production end of movie making. They were limited to performing or to employment in the studios as domestics or janitorial help. Moreover, as performers they never earned anything approaching the giant salaries made by a considerable number of whites. "Sunshine Sammy" in the early 1920s was paid $250 a week by the producers of the "Our Gang" series — at a time when equally popular white child actors earned five times as much. The desperate situation of the blacks in the movie industry was unintentionally highlighted by stories in the black press, which played up whatever favorable news there was. Thus the signing of an eighteen-year-old chorus girl to take a bit part as an Arab dancer was headlined in the Pittsburgh *Courier:* "*Chocolate Dandies* Dancer to Go to Africa as Film Star." The vast majority of black performers never advanced much beyond the four to seven dollars per day the studios paid extras of any race. But those who did advance, even in a minimal way, achieved a substantially better living than was otherwise open to most blacks at the time, despite the inequitable economic treatment meted out to them by the film industry.[15]

The most popular Negro actor of the early 1920s was a minor known by the name of the character he played. Few filmgoers had ever heard of Frederick Ernest Morrison, but they flocked to see "Sunshine Sammy." His screen career had begun in 1913, when he was still an infant. His father, a cook for a movie producer, overheard a conversation at dinner during which the filmmaker said that he was looking for a "colored comical baby"; Morrison suggested his infant son. After appearances in a number of one-reel comedies, the child attracted the attention of Hal Roach, who used him in support of comedians Harold Lloyd and Snub Pollard in their short films. The little black boy won favorable notices, even billing of a sort. And, for a time, the distributors gave prominent notice to "the funny little darky." When "Our Gang" was formed, the boy was one of the original group and as "Sunshine Sammy" rapidly became a popular screen figure. In the early 1920s he was earning $250 a week, which, according to one report in a black newspaper, "was the highest salary paid to any colored screen actor steadily employed in pictures." His parents managed his career carefully and their dissatisfaction with his salary resulted in the boy's accepting some vaudeville offers. Later he returned for a while to films, but he never achieved anything like his former success.[16]

Frederick Ernest Morrison not only received relatively high pay but also had an extended contractual relationship with a studio. It was rare for a black actor or actress to enjoy such a benefit at this time. Noble Johnson, one of the most active and highly paid black movie actors, worked for a variety of companies in the more than sixty films he made between World War I and the end of the silent period. Light-skinned, of athletic build, and projecting a powerful personality, Johnson had a career that lasted until the 1950s. He was steadily employed for thirty years, a record that no other black actor of his time matched. Although identified in the black press as a black actor, he was not identified with black roles. In the 1920s his parts included "Blackie Lopez" in a 1922 Hoot Gibson Western — *The Loaded Door* (Universal), a cannibal chief in a 1924 Jackie Coogan vehicle — *Little Robinson Crusoe* (Metro-Goldwyn), and Chief Sitting Bull in *The*

A light-skinned Noble Johnson, called "the race's daredevil movie star," drove a chariot in *King of Kings*. (National Film Archive)

Flaming Frontier, which was Paramount's 1926 retelling of Custer's last stand.

While patterns of discrimination remained largely unchanged, the black did become the object of a limited vogue during the 1920s. Certain authors came into their own and found a white reading public. Jazz and the musicians who played it achieved great popularity. The number of black performers active on the Broadway stage or "in the provinces" remained limited, but by the mid-1920s it was generally accepted that blacks had a certain "vitality" and "naturalness," and that there were parts they could and should play. A kind of circumscribed acceptance of mixed casts in stage shows even developed. Harlem and ghetto areas in other cities became playgrounds for prosperous white thrill-seekers, and intellectuals such as Carl Van Vechten — who based his novel *Nigger Heaven* on white misadventures and the clash of alien cultures in Harlem. But this pseudo-interest in black culture made no difference to the image of the black on screen. Indeed, to some degree, the fad for things black demanded acceptance of such aspects of that screen image as the supposed natural rhythm, sexual immorality, and animal vitality. As a black teenager wistfully commented on his movie-going experience during the years after World War I: "Most of the bad traits of unintelligent Negroes are used in many pictures and a loveable or educated character is rarely pictured." Going to the movies convinced him that injustice was being done to his race.[17]

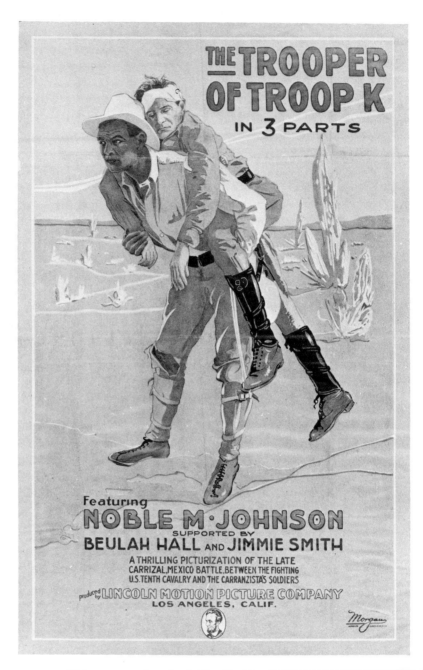

This poster advertised *The Trooper of Company K*, which starred Noble Johnson (here rescuing a white officer) and was produced by his black film company. (University Library, U.C.L.A.)

4

"ALL-COLORED" —BUT NOT VERY DIFFERENT

"THE MOVING PICTURE," said black showman William Foster in 1915, "is the Negro . . . man's only . . . chance to make money and put his race right with the world." And in Chicago during 1913, Foster had begun to put that precept into operation. Making use of "all-colored" casts, he made a number of short films portraying what the Chicago *Defender*, a black weekly newspaper, called "real Negro life." *The Railroad Porter*, one of Foster's first productions, was a comedy that does not seem to have been very different in style and content from the films depicting blacks that were turned out by the industry. But Foster also produced *The Butler* ("a detective kidnap movie") and *The Grafter and the Maid* (a melodrama), which at least attempted to be different from the usual product.[1]

Foster — described by *The Defender* as "one of the best informed men in theatricals hereabouts" — was no starry-eyed crusader. He genuinely believed that a black movie company utilizing blacks and making films about blacks for black audiences would be a commercially viable endeavor. But the Foster Photoplay Company had to rely on white financing because it could not obtain sufficient black support. In the main, the company seems to have been virtually a one-man operation, with Foster writing, directing, and filming some of the productions. Notwithstanding his well-thought-out plans, the company soon foundered for lack of funds, technical know-how, and distribution outlets.[2]

Despite the Foster Photoplay Company's lack of success with

the black movies it produced, Foster, in the column he wrote for a black newspaper under the name Juli Jones, Jr., continued to argue that blacks should make movies with black performers for black audiences, saying that there was a market waiting for such films and that the black entrepreneur would profit financially. To show "the Negro side of it . . . nothing can beat a moving picture . . ." But, as might be expected, when movies with "all-colored" casts were financed by white businessmen or made by companies that they owned, there was absolutely no interest in the image of the Negro beyond what would sell tickets.[3]

What was probably the first attempt by blacks to produce a feature film grew out of the desire to challenge the image of the black presented in *The Birth of a Nation*. The result was both a stock swindle and a cinematic disaster. Much of the initiative for the project seems to have come from Emmett J. Scott, who served as Booker T. Washington's confidential secretary until the black leader's death in November, 1915. In this sensitive position, which Scott held for eighteen years, he participated in the administration of organizations that Washington had helped to establish, including the National Negro Business League. The initial plans for the movie called for working through the film industry. A professional writer was hired to put together a scenario, and he turned out *Lincoln's Dream*, described by one scholar as an "optimistic prophecy of Negro fortunes." Not unsurprisingly, the industry failed to express any interest in the scenario. Scott and his group (which included both blacks and whites) then decided to raise the necessary money and to produce on their own what was now known as *The Birth of a Race*. Scott apparently believed that funding could be obtained through sale of stock in the producing company to the many blacks with whom he had contact through such organizations as the League.[4]

Although headquartered in Chicago, the Birth of a Race Photoplay Corporation was incorporated in Delaware in July, 1916. The pressure of events soon caused the attention of Scott and many of the original supporters of the project to be directed elsewhere. Scott became involved with the plight of black draftees in the army, and in October, 1917, he was named a special adviser to the Secretary of War. Meanwhile, the film project continued. Such eminent members of both races as former president William Howard Taft, philanthropist Julius

Rosenwald, African Methodist Episcopal Zion Church Bishop Isaiah B. Scott, and Mrs. Booker T. Washington had endorsed the idea behind the film, and they were unpleasantly surprised to find themselves touted as endorsing the purchase of stock in the corporation. Then, in March, 1918, some of the salesmen were indicted in Illinois under a law designed to prevent stock fraud.

Certainly there had been some irregularities. On incorporation 100,000 shares had been issued, each with a par value of $10. The entire issue — valued at $1 million — had been turned over to one Edwin L. Barker and his associates. In return Barker, a minor film distributor who was president of the Birth of a Race Photoplay Corporation, gave the corporation the rights to a revised script of *The Birth of a Race* and other assets. He also turned back to the corporation 80,000 shares of the stock, which were to be sold to finance production of the film. By the time of the indictment, over 50,000 of these shares had been sold to about 7000 investors, "largely to colored folk on South State Street in Chicago," said *Variety*. Because some stock had been sold at a considerable discount, only about $350,000 were realized. And the net after commissions, advertising, and other overhead expenses were deducted was just over $264,000.[5]

The elaborate efforts undertaken to sell the stock included the printing of a handsome prospectus that not only listed the prominent persons "interested and assisting," but also promised great financial rewards. It appealed to blacks to support "an entertaining motion picture of racial understanding" and predicted that the finished movie would be "the true story of the Negro — his life in Africa, his transportation to America, his enslavement, his freedom, his achievements, together with his past, present, and future relations to his white neighbor and to the world in which both live and labor." Barker and his associates mounted an extensive newspaper advertising campaign, taking care not to mention outside of the black weeklies the film's origins or its purpose. *The Birth of a Race* was made to seem an alluring investment. The reader was asked: "Do you know that dividends of 1000 percent are not unusual in the big feature film business?" and was told that "each $100 invested in *The Million Dollar Mystery* made $700; that $100 in *The Birth of a Nation* made $1800; that $100 in *The Spoilers* made $1000; and that $100 in *Traffic in Souls* made $3000." Hundreds of postcards were sent out with the same

message as well as a warning that "the stock will positively be
withdrawn from the market within 30 days, so no matter whether
you have $50 or $5000 to invest, sign the attached card and mail
now — today. A delay of a single day means the loss of several
hundred dollars." When it seemed that the black market had
been exhausted, the stock promoters concentrated their efforts on
the Jewish community. But despite the proposed addition of
scenes opposing anti-Semitism and what one newspaper called
"gorgeous declamations on the brotherhood of democracy," the
promoters had little success.[6]

The energy put into selling stock did not carry over into production of the film, which suffered innumerable delays and false
starts. And each new development brought further deviations
from the original idea of celebrating black achievement and
countering the image of the black set forth in *The Birth of a
Nation*. Initially the Selig company had agreed to handle production, but it soon dropped out, supposedly because it objected
to "the character" of the proposed film. After the scenario had
been altered somewhat, the Frohman Amusement Company
agreed to make the picture. When the trouble with the Illinois
law arose, the president of Frohman announced reassuringly that
"the contract which we have entered into for the production of
The Birth of a Race carries with it more than a business arrangement. It carries our largest interest and enthusiasm." But a few
weeks later Frohman, too, abandoned the production. By this
time scenes from the Creation, the Flood, and the time of Christ
had been filmed at a cost of about $140,000. In attempting to
justify what was for the time an exorbitant outlay, a spokesman
for Edwin L. Barker explained that "the greatest expense of the
picture, of course, is in making the prologue, which required a
large expenditure for research work." The corporation changed
the film into a war story. Most of the material dealing with
blacks was eliminated. Shortly after the Armistice was signed on
November 11, 1918, it was announced, according to *Variety*, that
the movie henceforth would be called *The Story of a Great
Peace*. But in the end the original title was retained.[7]

The Birth of a Race premiered Sunday evening, December 1,
1918, at the Blackstone Theater in Chicago. Then considered one
of the most fashionable theaters in the United States, the Blackstone had been rented for a month by the corporation, reportedly

Announcement for the 1918 premiere of *The Birth of a Race*.

at a cost of $6,000, to provide a first-rate showcase for the movie. About the only good review the movie got was the Chicago *Post's*, which called it "clean" and "sincere." The Chicago *Tribune* said "the picture tires you"; *Billboard* characterized it as "perhaps the worst conglomeration of mixed purposes and attempts ever thrown together"; and *Variety* described the production as "a ghastly example of terrific waste. Magnificent, gorgeous settings run alongside of shoddy drops . . . Stock battle cut-ins are used in a manner which advertise their 'stockness.'" Subsequent advertising in the black press emphasized what the producer seemed to feel were the picture's saleable qualities, for instance, "the Story of Sin . . . Conceived in the Spirit of Truth and Dedicated to All of the Races of the World." But the final twelve-reel product had little to do with the project outlined some years earlier. To the extent that blacks appeared at all, they were the usual stereotyped figures. Indeed, in one scene a white boy is seen trouncing a black lad.[8]

The Birth of a Race begins with the Kaiser and his counsellors discussing when to open hostilities. A workman, meant, it seems, to represent Christ, breaks in on the meeting and for over an hour relates the history of the world since the Creation, including such unrelated episodes as the expulsion from the Garden of Eden, the Jewish flight from Egypt, the Crucifixion, and the discovery of America by Columbus. This first part of the movie lacked, in one reviewer's words, "any tangible reason and was about as easy to follow as the dictionary is to read." The second part, also over an hour long, is set in the World War I period and deals in extremely melodramatic fashion with sabotage, suicide, murder, and the divided loyalties of a family of German-Americans.[9]

At about the same time that the plan to produce *The Birth of a Race* was first formulated, a group of blacks in Los Angeles organized the Lincoln Motion Picture Company. This company must rank among the very first black movie producers to turn out serious films with black performers for black audiences. The company was organized in 1915 in the hope of providing a showcase for black talent and of tapping what was considered to be potentially a very profitable black market. The only white person formally involved in the operation was Harry Gant, a cameraman at the Universal Film Company, who filmed the Lincoln productions and later produced such black-oriented movies on his own. The blacks participating included Clarence Brooks, an actor; James T. Smith, a reasonably well-off Los Angeles druggist; and Noble Johnson, who was to enjoy such an extensive career in the industry. His brother, George Perry Johnson, became involved in the company's operations shortly after its first film was produced, and later became one of its officers.

Noble Johnson, who was the original president of the Lincoln Motion Picture Company, was raised in Colorado. At the age of fifteen he had struck out on the travels that in the next few years saw him wander over the western part of the United States and work at jobs ranging from cowboy to cook. In 1914, while still in his early twenties, he began his film career by filling in for an injured actor; he portrayed an Indian chief in a Lubin production that was filming on location. The company used him to play Mexicans or Indians. In 1915 the light-skinned Johnson went to

Hollywood, where, while working as a stunt man, extra, and bit player, he became involved in the formation of the Lincoln Motion Picture Company and starred in its first three productions.

Johnson did not fit the usual image of a black, nor did many of the other light-complexioned performers who appeared in Lincoln productions. The casting of light-complexioned blacks was common practice among companies who advertised "all-colored casts" or "race performers." But for the advertising it would often have been difficult for a viewer to know that many of the actors and actresses were black. To a remarkable degree the films of Lincoln and those of other companies are visual evidence of an attitude that many blacks themselves accepted. As a popular verse of the period went:

> If you're light, you're all right;
> If you're brown, stick aroun';
> But if you're black, stand back.

Both in the silent period and later, the heroic leads, the lovers, and even the "bad women" in movies with black performers were played by light-complexioned performers.[10]

The Lincoln company's first venture was a two reeler, *The Realization of a Negro's Ambition.* Like all the company's films it was made on a shoestring; almost no money was available for salaries and some performers appeared free of charge. The plot of *The Realization of a Negro's Ambition* was little more than a black version of the kind of Horatio Alger success story that the industry turned out by the dozen at this time. The hero, a Tuskegee Institute engineering graduate (Noble Johnson) leaves the family farm, bids a sad farewell to his southern "country sweetheart," and goes to California to make his fortune. While looking for work in the oil fields, he sees a runaway carriage. Leaping on a convenient horse, he gives chase, stops the runaway, and saves the daughter of a rich white oilman. Rewarded with a job, the young engineer soon proves himself and obtains the oilman's backing to prospect for oil on the family farm. He brings in a gusher and marries the girl back home. The last scenes show him "in later years, with ambition realized, home and family, a nice place to live in and nice people to live and enjoy it with him," to quote the plot synopsis. As clumsy and simple-minded as it was, the movie did find some favor with its intended audience. The owner of one Chicago movie house that catered primarily to blacks later declared that "our patrons were surprised and delighted" by the film.[11]

A second film, *The Trooper of Company K*, was built around the fact that during General Pershing's pursuit of Pancho Villa in northern Mexico, the black Tenth Cavalry regiment had taken part in a bloody fight at Carrizal in June, 1916. This movie, too, suffered from financial and technical deficiencies, but the Lincoln company did stage quite an exciting battle, featuring a large number of black ex-cavalry troopers in the Los Angeles area. The

A home, family (Noble Johnson holds the baby), and a secure place in the middle class were, as the title of this all-black movie proclaimed, *The Realization of a Negro's Ambition*. (University Library, U.C.L.A.)

company also obtained the services of enough Mexicans to portray "Montezuma's murderous horde" and rented guns, horses, and costumes.

If *The Trooper of Company K* reached a much wider audience than *The Realization of a Negro's Ambition,* it was because the Lincoln company had managed to work out a system of distribution. George Johnson persuaded Tony Langston, who edited the amusement section of the Chicago *Defender* and was involved in other show business activities, to handle *The Trooper of Company K* and other Lincoln productions on a commission basis in Illinois, Indiana, and Ohio. Through Langston, it was possible for Johnson to contact and make similar distribution arrangements with weekly entertainment editors who were active in black show business, including Romeo Daugherty of the New York *Amsterdam News* and W. H. King of the St. Louis *Argus.*

Because such arrangements sometimes were temporary and because representatives could not be found in many areas, an alternative distribution system was evolved in which George Johnson also was very active. Since it was unusual even in a large city for a movie theater to venture, sight unseen, the $25 or $50 per showing that the Lincoln company charged, and since in many smaller communities the money for payment in advance just was not available, a salesman with a print of a Lincoln film would call on the theater owner or manager and show the movie. Should it find favor, a booking for one or a number of days was made for three or four weeks later — on a percentage basis. Normally, 60 percent of the gross receipts would go to the Lincoln company. A sharp eye was kept on the number of tickets sold (often the Lincoln agent collected them to ensure an accurate count), for the commissions earned by the travelers came from the company's share of the receipts. Heavy rains or an unforeseen church social could severely cut a day's take, which, at the going rate of ten or twenty cents a head for a black audience, was never great in any event. (Even when a black movie-maker did get an established company to distribute his film, as happened occasionally, there were problems. The white-owned L-KO Comedy Company agreed to distribute a seven-reel drama, *Injustice,* made by a black group, but then edited it into "a five-reel comedy" and added titles in dialect.)[12]

Underfinanced from the beginning, the Lincoln company continued to operate on a narrow margin. Unlike most of the white-owned companies in the industry (including those that later made films for the ghetto market), Lincoln could neither obtain financing in advance of production nor borrow large sums on finished films; the money came in solely from the showing of the movies. The Lincoln company, like other black film ventures, also suffered from the unwillingness of a white industry to handle movies made by blacks that did not conform to the usual stereotypes. Moreover, most of the movie houses catering to black audiences were owned and managed by whites, the majority of whom thought they knew the tastes of their patrons. One manager said that he used "white pictures because Negroes preferred to see white faces on the screen or funny colored pictures."[13]

The Lincoln Motion Picture Company also faced other problems. Noble Johnson, its leading player and star attraction, appeared in only one more movie for the company. *The Law of Nature* (1918) was a three-reel drama about a girl who marries an attractive, hard-working Western ranch foreman (Johnson), persuades him to go East, has a child, finds the Westerner less appealing in the city, and takes up with another man. She abandons her husband and child, who return to the West. Soon abandoned in her turn, she "realizes her folly" and returns to the ranch where her husband has re-established himself. Enfeebled by dissipation, she dies "heartbroken and repentant," with her child clasped in her arms — but not before she receives "the blessing of her husband as she passes into the care of God." *The Law of Nature*, in one exhibitor's words, was "a good box-office attraction."[14]

As a result, Johnson, who had achieved feature billing in Universal's more important serials (the black press referred to him as "the race's daredevil movie star"), was now advised by Universal that he must choose between it or Lincoln. Universal officials told Johnson that exhibitors had complained because his Lincoln movies were doing better with black audiences than their white-made competition; the company claimed that the success of the black films was a result of the buildup given the black actor in the serials. For all his interest in black filmmaking, Johnson did not want to risk his hard-won position in the industry for a most uncertain future with the underfinanced, struggling Lincoln Motion Picture Company. He resigned as Lincoln's president and

Albertine Pickens, who could have passed for white, played the female lead in *The Law of Nature*. Even in all-black films, light skins were the rule.

ended active participation in its affairs. Clarence Brooks, who replaced him as Lincoln's leading actor, would in time also carve a niche for himself in the industry; but in 1918 he was still too inexperienced and too little known to carry a film the way Johnson could.[15]

Brooks starred in two six-reel features for Lincoln, *A Man's Duty* (1919) and *By Right of Birth* (1921); the later film was a most ambitious project that made some interesting comments on the California social scene from a black point of view. For example, the villain is one Romero, a Mexican-American stockbroker who is cheating blacks and Indians out of valuable oil lands. (The film also contained an unfortunate concession to what was presumed to be popular taste: comic relief was provided by the villain's black chauffeur, "Pinky.")

The response of the black press was favorable, as was, surprisingly, that of those white magazines and newspapers that bothered to take note of the film. *Billboard* called *By Right of Birth* "powerful" and Hearst's Los Angeles *Examiner,* although its review was tinged with condescension, declared that the film had "crude strength" and offered proof that colored players could develop histrionic talent above that required for straight comedy.[16]

But the lack of any kind of solid financial support, aggravated by the continuing difficulties of distribution as well as Noble Johnson's unavailability, forced the disbanding of the Lincoln Motion Picture Company in 1923. The closing down of the enterprise had less to do with the imperfections of its films than with the almost insurmountable obstacles facing blacks interested in producing movies, especially movies that did not treat the black as a stereotype.

A similar venture at this time on the East Coast fared no better. Initially spurred on by the desire to respond to "the antagonistic propaganda against the race" in *The Birth of a Nation,* the Frederick Douglass Film Company premiered its first film, *The Colored American Winning His Suit,* in Jersey City on July 14, 1916. But the Douglass company, too, suffered from lack of funds, and except for some outdoor scenes, the movie had to be filmed in "homes of members of the race." The company also had to make use of amateurs. The cast was made up almost entirely of "young men and women of the race from . . . the best families in New Jersey," and the producers stated that, as a result, "no attempt had been made at strong dramatic action." The quality of this six-reel production may be judged by the fact that a review of a later Douglass film stated that "another big improvement is that the pictures are plainly seen." The Douglass company also found it expedient to cut *The Colored American Winning His Suit* to four reels after its first showing.[17]

Financing for the Douglass operation came from a small group, most of whom belonged to what the black leader W. E. B. DuBois had some years earlier dubbed "the talented tenth . . . of the race," that is, the educated professional men. The first Douglass production in many ways represented DuBois's views on how to improve the image and condition of the black (views that were in sharp contrast to Booker T. Washington's idea of "industrial training" that was accepted by most whites). Indeed *The Colored American Winning His Suit* is something of an allegory. The black protagonist was "Bob Winall." His rival in romance was a clean-cut young black building contractor and businessman called "Jim Sample." Representing the "white man North or South ready and willing to lend a helping hand to the deserving Negro" was "Colonel Goodwill," while the white villain was "Mister Hinderus."[18]

The screenplay, written by the Negro pastor of Jersey City's Monumental Baptist Church, was set in Virginia. Bob Winhall and his sister Bessie are the children of a former slave who makes good and buys his one-time master's homestead. Great emphasis is placed on the children's education: Bessie attends Spelman Seminary in Atlanta and Bob goes to Howard University (scenes were filmed on the campus). Bob meets Bessie's roommate Alma and falls in love with her. But her parents favor Sample, the son of wealthy farmers, and are opposed to Bob's opening a law practice in Upton where Alma has become the principal of the black high school. All is resolved, however, when Bob wins an acquittal for Alma's father after Hinderus, his unsuccessful rival in the express business, brings a criminal charge against him. Bob has taken a case that white lawyers would not handle, and the successful termination of the court action means that he "wins his suit for Alma's hand in marriage."

In its second production Douglass, under partially new management, made use of such professionals as Abbie Mitchell, who had appeared in Bert Williams shows and who was to have a long and successful career in the theater and on the concert stage. *The Scapegoat*, a three reeler that premiered in May, 1917, was based on a story by the noted black writer Paul Laurence Dunbar. Although a considerable improvement over the first Douglass production, *The Scapegoat* was still on the rudimentary side. Titles were misspelled and "their" was used for "there." The New York *Age* critic, though responding favorably on the whole, complained of a tendency to thrust characters "into new environments and new conditions with startling abruptness." One black exhibitor's response to the presentation of black policemen points up a problem that faced Douglass and other film companies that did not make use of the accepted movie stereotypes. The exhibitor said that his patrons liked *The Scapegoat* but that he "did not relish the idea of portraying colored police officers as . . . the white people in . . . town might not like it." In 1920 the head of the Frederick Douglass Film Company told a reporter that "prospects were never so bright in the colored motion picture industry." However, hampered as it was by lack of financing and skilled personnel, Douglass did not survive to test these prospects.[19]

Other filmmaking organizations formed "by business and professional men of both races" also tried and failed. In 1920 the Royal Gardens Film Company of Chicago presented *In the Depths of Our Hearts*, a six-reel drama that revolved around the trials suffered by a brother and sister, both light-skinned blacks, who had been taught by their equally light-skinned mother to "believe that anybody of a darker hue is unfit as an associate." In the same year, the Maurice Film Company presented *Nobody's Children*, about a brother and sister who, because of the cruelty of "an unnatural stepfather," become involved with the underworld.

Occasionally companies hired well-known black athletes in an effort to take advantage of their popularity with ghetto audiences. In 1921 the ex-heavyweight champion Jack Johnson starred in a seven-reel feature, *As the World Rolls On*, for Andlauer Productions of Kansas City, Missouri. Johnson is shown laying out some bullies as well as instructing the hero, Joe Walker, "a small but industrious youth subject to sudden heart attacks." Under Johnson's tutelage Joe learns to defend himself, to give up smoking, and to build up his sickly body. In the end he wins the girl and severely thrashes his bigger rival, "a ne'er do well bully." But this movie, which tried to cut costs by incorporating actual black organizations in its plot, is less interesting as a story than as a social document. The Kansas City Monarchs baseball team plays other teams of the National Colored League, and (thanks to Johnson's training) Joe saves one game with late-inning pitching heroics. There is also footage of a Negro Elks meeting. And as the movie closes, Joe and his family are seen at a "parade of the National Bi-Annual Conclave of Knights of Pytheans of North Am., South Am., Europe, Asia, and Australia."[20]

Another company that presented its first feature at this time was the Reol Motion Picture Corporation, which lasted for a few years and produced at least six features and some shorts as well. This venture was headed by a white man, Robert J. Levy, who had theatrical interests in Harlem and who, according to one scholar, "was encouraged by their success to start the film company." A typical Reol film was the 1921 production, *The Call of His People.* The protagonist is an ambitious, increasingly successful Negro business executive who has passed for white. He is given his big chance and makes good, but under the influence of a childhood sweetheart who has helped him to triumph he confesses his race to the head of the company. The movie ends happily as the hero is assured that "it is the man and not the color that counts."[21]

Movies for black audiences were made by several other companies during this period. Ben Strasser Productions in 1923 filmed *A Shot in the Night* and *His Great Chance;* the latter, described as a five-reel dramatic comedy, featured Tim Moore, who became famous on television many years later as Kingfish on the *Amos 'n' Andy Show.* The Colored Players Film Corporation, owned, according to one black newsman, by "a wealthy Jewish syndicate which several race men are affiliated with," presented its first feature, *A Prince of His Race,* in 1926. That same year the company gave Charles Gilpin his first chance in the movies, playing the lead in an all-black version of *Ten Nights in a Barroom.* Gilpin, who had created the title role in Eugene O'Neill's *The Emperor Jones,* has been described by one black critic as "the first modern American Negro to establish himself as a serious actor of first quality." Even in *Ten Nights,* that feeble old melodrama of alcoholic downfall and prohibitionist redemption, there is no mistaking his extraordinarily fine talents. He was brought to Hollywood in the same year to play Uncle Tom. But Gilpin's own drinking problem (partly a result of his bitter frustration at having to work frequently as a porter or elevator operator because so few roles were available to blacks) as well as his unwillingness to portray Uncle Tom in what he considered a demeaning way led to his being fired. *Ten Nights in a Barroom* seems to have been Gilpin's only movie appearance.[22]

Another Colored Players Film Production movie is among the last silents made for black audiences. *The Scar of Shame*, an eight-reel drama filmed in 1927, deals with a music student who falls in love with an attractive working girl named Louise, marries her out of pity, and then keeps her apart from his well-off and cultured family (whose black butler would even look down on his new wife). Louise, understandably upset, yields to the blandishments of her drunkard stepfather and his racketeer friend to become a saloon entertainer. Through a ruse the husband is temporarily removed from the scene. He returns just as Louise is about to leave with the racketeer, there is a struggle, and she is wounded and disfigured. Her husband goes to jail but breaks out, assumes a new identity, and becomes a music teacher. Soon he falls in love with a proper young girl, proposes, and is accepted. Meanwhile, his prospective father-in-law has taken up with Louise, who has become a speakeasy entertainer who hides her "scar of shame" with a silk scarf. One day Louise and her former husband meet. She tries to blackmail him, but fails because he decides to confess all to his fiancée and her family. Louise commits suicide, leaving a note exonerating her husband; he is free to marry the "right" girl. "If only she had turned her mind to the higher things in life" is his moralistic, and surprisingly shameless, comment on her fate.

This film was reasonably well made technically, and it had something of a visual style, although it was decidedly inferior to similar films turned out by the white industry. But *The Scar of Shame* cannot be said to have been seriously concerned with the black image: what makes it at all unusual for a black film of the time is the fact that (in one scholar's words), "it justifies its dramatic action with a Darwinian universe," the girl's base instincts leading to her destruction.[23]

Perhaps the best known black filmmaker and certainly the most prolific producer of movies using black performers was Oscar Micheaux, who made more than twenty silent features (and later a considerable number of sound features as well) primarily for the ghetto trade. Born on a farm near Metropolis, Illinois, in 1884, he was the fifth child of parents who were former slaves. By his own account "his larger education began when as a Pullman car porter, on a run from Chicago to Portland, Oregon, he saw an advertisement in an Omaha, Nebraska newspaper regarding the famous Rosebud Indian Reservation in South Dakota, which was being opened for settlement." He decided to invest his savings and become a homesteader. Ultimately he lost his land, and always claimed that this loss was caused by the financial chicanery of his father-in-law, a minister. He now decided to turn to writing. By 1917, in less than seven years, he had written two novels and an autobiography describing what he called "his life of Hell." Micheaux's stories, which drew heavily on his own experiences, were very much like the pulp fiction of the day but with the one significant difference — the main characters were blacks. But Micheaux made his living less from writing books than from publishing them. A very convincing talker (according to George Johnson, who had dealings with him), Micheaux peddled stock in the companies he organized to publish his books to white farmers in Iowa, South Dakota, and Nebraska on the promise that sale of the books would result in a very profitable return on a small investment. Johnson believes that few of the stock purchasers ever saw any return whatsoever.[24]

Toward the end of 1917 or the beginning of 1918 Micheaux's semi-autobiographical novel *The Homesteader* came to the attention of Johnson, who thought it would be a good work for the Lincoln company to film. He contacted Micheaux, some rather torturous negotiations ensued but no deal resulted. Johnson recalls that the Lincoln company — or rather, his brother Noble — would not agree to Micheaux's demand that he be brought to Los Angeles to supervise the filming of the story. Micheaux then decided to film the book himself even though he had virtually no experience in making or distributing motion pictures. But one thing he did know was how to raise money, and he soon came up with the necessary capital by selling stock at $75 a share in a newly organized film company; most of his customers were, as usual, midwestern farmers. The movie was staged by Jerry Mills, who had appeared in the Foster Photoplay films; and it featured both inexperienced unknowns such as Charles Lucas, who portrayed the title role, and somewhat more veteran performers such as Evelyn Preer.

The resulting eight-reel drama, which was highly emotional in style if crude in technique, premiered in Chicago at the begin-

ning of 1919. Micheaux had to overcome some opposition to the
licensing of the film because of the manner in which he presented
the homesteader's minister father-in-law, who was, to quote the
plot synopsis supplied the press, "narrow, spiteful, envious . . .
the embodiment of vanity, deceit, and hypocrisy." *The Homesteader* was advertised as "a powerful drama of the Indian Reservation of the Great Northwest into which has been deftly woven
the most subtle of all America's problems — THE RACE QUES-
TION." The story is about Jean Baptiste, the homesteader of the
title who lives in the Dakotas where "he alone is black." Baptiste
meets Agnes, the motherless daughter of Scotsman Jack Stewart.
Baptiste and Agnes fall in love, but because she is apparently
white they must stifle their feelings. Baptiste then marries the
daughter of the venomously depicted black preacher. Difficulties
arise between Baptiste and his father-in-law. The wife, Orlean,
described as sweet, but without the strength of her convictions,
fails the homesteader. Her "evil" sister Ethel joins with the
preacher in his "base intrigues" against Baptiste and his property.
The stress of the quarrel drives Orlean insane and one night in a
trance she stabs her father to death and then commits suicide.
Baptiste returns to the Dakotas and discovers that Agnes is not
white, and "the story has a beautiful ending after a life of storm
and misery."[25]

Micheaux spent only about $15,000 in making *The Home-
steader*, and managed to turn a profit despite a makeshift distribution system similar to that utilized by Lincoln. For the next
decade Micheaux ground out as many as two or three movies a
year. He did not direct them all, but they carried his stamp:
complex, often controversial plots, stalwart heroes undaunted by
adversity, heroines faced with extraordinary dangers. Micheaux
was very cost-conscious, and his economies were often a bit too
apparent. His films were barely adequate technically and the
photography tended to be either too dark or too light, although in
time some of the more egregious defects were corrected.
Micheaux, who hated to waste either time or film, demanded a
great deal from his performers. Evelyn Preer, a nonswimmer,
recalled being nearly drowned on one occasion when she had to
wade through a pond; the water was supposed to come up to her
waist, but it turned out to be over her head. She expressed great
admiration for Micheaux but maintained that "colored actors

Oscar Micheaux (Schomburg Collection/New York Public Library)

Charles Lucas and Evelyn Preer agonize over her apparently undiluted — and invincible — white blood in Micheaux's *The Homesteader*.

would get their best chances from white directors." However, although she eventually reached Broadway, she never appeared in any Hollywood films because, with her light skin, she did not look like Hollywood's idea of a black. However, Micheaux, like most producers of "race productions," made extensive use of light-complexioned performers. Indeed he even used them to play white roles such as Stewart in *The Homesteader* or a murder victim in *Within Our Gates* (1920).[26]

Micheaux even attempted to reach out beyond the limited ghetto audience. *The Dungeon* (1922) dealt in part with residential segregation and a campaign for a black seat in Congress, but, as a Chicago. *Defender* columnist commented, this production has "nothing to indicate that the feature is colored, as the characters are . . . almost white"; the writer conjectured that "the producer was after bookings in white theaters." But these Micheaux did not obtain.[27]

Micheaux had a knack of turning every situation to his advantage. He was a superb promoter. But instead of selling shares in a publishing company, he now pushed stock in his film corporation. While on a money-raising trip to Baltimore in 1926 he found that "several scenes had to be re-taken" on *The Spider's Web*, and he persuaded two of the city's prominent black businessmen to play parts in the film. They both invested in it, of course. On another such trip he made a visit to a home in Shelton, Pennsylvania, where he saw a picture of the young daughter of a successful black businessman. According to the New York *Age* report, her "screen possibilities struck Micheaux at once as being far above the average," and so Shingzie Howard came to act ingenue roles in a number of his films.[28]

Paul Robeson also made his movie debut in a Micheaux film, *Body and Soul,* released in 1925. Robeson, who was already well known to the black community from his football-playing days as an All-American end on the Rutgers University team, had recently turned his back on the legal profession. Though his concert career was not yet fully launched, he had just scored a great personal triumph as an actor in two Eugene O'Neill plays off-Broadway. Micheaux seized the opportunity to make use of him and managed to place a ten-line item on *Variety*'s front page announcing the pairing of Robeson with Julia Theresa Russell, described as "one of the most beautiful colored women anywhere." (She was soon to become Micheaux's sister-in-law.) Robeson, as one biographer suggests, "probably took his first role simply to make a little money and to get work." Apparently Robeson later regretted his involvement with Micheaux because the producer and the film receive no mention either in an early biography by Robeson's wife or a later one by a close family friend. More recently, too, Anatol Schlosser's massive doctoral dissertation, which was written with Robeson's cooperation and which goes into nearly every detail of the performer's life, makes no mention of Micheaux or of *Body and Soul*.[29]

The same instinct that had led Micheaux to use Robeson must have influenced the choice of many of the stories he filmed. He had a keen sense of the topical as well as a real feeling for the tastes of his audience. *The House Behind the Cedars* (1923), based on a work by the black novelist Charles Chestnutt, dealt with marriage between the races. In *The Spider's Web* (1926), Micheaux showed that even respectable people play the numbers. *The Devil's Disciple* (1926) touched on compulsory prostitution in New York City. The black hero of *The Symbol of the Unconquered* (1920) braves the Ku Klux Klan, which attempts to drive another black off valuable oil lands. *The Gunsaulus Mystery* (1921) was a fictional reworking of the Leo Frank case in Georgia. Myrtle Gunsaulus's body is found in the basement of the factory where she worked, and it is obvious that she had been assaulted before her death. Her body is discovered by a black night watchman, who is accused of the crime but is proved innocent by his black lawyer; the lawyer pins the guilt on the manager of the factory, who is then unmasked as "a sexual pervert."

Micheaux initially received high praise from the black press for his endeavors and his enterprise. But in time critics began to take him to task for his depiction of the life of the black community. As early as 1920 Lester Walton, though he praised a Micheaux movie called *The Brute* (starring the black prizefighter Sam Langford), commented at length on the scenes of crap games, black dives, wife-beating, and women congregating to gamble. These scenes, Walton said, were "not any too pleasing to those of us who desire to see the better side of Negro life portrayed"; they reminded him of "the attitude of the daily press, which magnifies our vices and minimizes our virtues." In 1925 Sylvester Russell of the Pittsburgh *Courier* reported on his arguments with Micheaux about "the objectionable race features" in the producer's films. Other black newspapers also criticized Micheaux, but seemingly their objections made little impression on him.[30]

Although Micheaux could and did ignore his critics in the black press, he could not disregard his film company's deteriorating financial condition. The return on even the most successful black film was relatively small. There were about 20,000 movie theaters in the United States in 1926, but only a few hundred of these would play an all-black production, and theaters that catered to ghetto audiences charged reduced admission prices. Even if one includes the Southern theaters that had special midnight showings for blacks, the potential earnings were severely limited. And rarely did a black producer reach all the possible exhibitors, given his necessarily makeshift system of distribution. Micheaux was a clever businessman, but he was no exception.

Moreover, the novelty of the all-black movie was beginning to wear thin. In 1917 the New York *Age*, although acknowledging the drawbacks of a Douglass company movie, still praised it as "a racial business venture which ought to be encouraged." But, already by 1920 the *Age* was pointing out that "the day of expecting charitable consideration in business even of our own people just because we are Negroes is past." Though Micheaux's films

In *The Brute* (1920), a character named Aunt Clara warns the villain not to abuse her niece: "The next time you lay a finger on her, I'll use this."

did improve technically, they still remained amateurish by comparison with Hollywood's products. Ghetto audiences began to stay away from "race productions," and as one black newspaperman noted, "the worst enemy of the race production is the race movie fan himself." In February 1928, the Micheaux Film Corporation filed a voluntary petition of bankruptcy. It should be noted that Micheaux, ever the careful businessman, had seen to it that most of the corporation's films were legally the property of his wife.[31]

Oscar Micheaux's silent motion picture works cannot be considered outstanding. He is significant, however, because he was one of the first independent black producers making popular and for a time profitable movies with black actors and actresses for ghetto audiences. Despite his public utterances, Micheaux's films were not designed to uplift or to enlighten. They were meant to entertain, to appeal to his concept of black popular taste, and to make money. The marginal nature of his enterprise is highlighted by the details of the bankruptcy petition. The corporation had assets of $1400 and liabilities of $7837, including $132 owed in back taxes to the state of Delaware and $1125 due to performers who had appeared in movies but who had not been paid.

The sad fact was that the white film industry had made it impossible for blacks like Micheaux to acquire the necessary technical and distribution fundamentals. With no experienced personnel available and with few sources of financing, black production companies found that all the facilities for improving their products were in the hands of people who were indifferent if not hostile. They had to hire such help as was available to them, invariably, as one black filmmaker put it, "the most inefficient, inexperienced, and least skilled." Moreover, the segregated theaters in the black ghetto played the white industry's movies as well as the black companies' films, and the latter could not help but suffer by comparison. To expect the black movie producers to compete with the industry was like asking a local auto body shop supplied by General Motors to compete with it. At the close of the silent period the ideas set forth by William Foster in 1915 about "Negro-produced movies" making a profit as well as improving the screen image of the black were farther than ever from realization.[32]

Stepin Fetchit, here taking a cuff from the young massa (Robert Young) in *Carolina*, seemed to sum up for the 1930s the ludicrous image of the white man's black. (The Museum of Modern Art/Courtesy Twentieth Century–Fox. © 1934 Twentieth Century–Fox Film Corporation)

5

SHUFFLIN'
INTO SOUND

THE MOVIES began to talk at the end of the 1920s. For blacks on screen this meant only that their "yasshuhs" could now be heard rather than read. Sound added a new "reality" to the movies; the ears reinforcing what the eyes saw. But the more complete the illusion of real life became, the more difficult it was to change the screen image of the black. Though the period from the advent of sound until the beginning of World War II has been referred to as the "Golden Age of the American Cinema," for blacks in film those years were mostly the same old dross.

From the earliest days of the movies filmmakers had been experimenting with the use of sound. (Indeed Lee De Forest, a pioneer radio inventor, making use of his phonofilm system, had made a number of shorts in the early 1920s including one that featured "those colored vaudevillians" Noble Sissle and Eubie Blake singing "Snappy Songs.") But not until the mid-1920s was there the necessary merger of advanced technology and entrepreneurial enterprise that made possible the rapid success of the "talkie," first in the United States and soon all over the world. About 150 American movie houses had been wired for sound by the end of 1927, and two years later that number had increased to over 8700. During 1929 the American movie industry produced some 700 features, of which more than 500 made some use of sound — either in dialogue, music, or effects.[1]

For blacks there is a bitter irony in the movie that symbolizes the introduction of sound: its hero is a white entertainer who sings in burnt-cork makeup. Warner Brothers' *The Jazz Singer* premiered in New York City on October 6, 1927. It featured the Vitaphone system, which utilized record disks synchronized with the images on the screen, though the use of sound was limited to a few songs and some brief snatches of dialogue. Critics hailed the new invention, but otherwise found the film to be trite and lachrymose. As one remarked, "it would be sad to think of what would happen to the picture without the Vitaphone . . . songs." The story told of Cantor Rabinowitz's son Jakie, who defies his Orthodox father's wishes; instead of following the family tradition of being a cantor in a synagogue, he becomes a "jazz singer." After some travail Jack Robin (as the son calls himself) achieves great success as an entertainer and is reconciled with his father as the old man lies on his deathbed. Al Jolson played "The Jazz Singer": along with some other white performers such as Eddie Cantor, he had continued to use blackface makeup even though minstrel shows had virtually died out by the 1920s.[2]

The Jazz Singer was actually not the first Vitaphone movie. In August 1926 Warners had presented at their New York theater the feature *Don Juan,* which had a synchronized score and sound effects, as well as a number of accompanying shorts also making use of the Vitaphone system. The program, introduced from the screen by Will Hays, head of the industry trade organization, had an extraordinary impact. In the next months Warners produced a number of Vitaphone shorts, including one with Jolson. At the same time Fox Films also made some sound shorts, most of them newsreels, in which the sound was recorded directly on the film, running on a track along the edge. This system of sound-on-film quickly superseded Vitaphone's sound-on-a-disc and with refinements is still being used today. What made *The Jazz Singer* so significant, however, was that it brought together for the first time in a feature film a synchronized score, musical numbers, and some dialogue — especially Jolson's first spoken words, which came well after the movie had started and which in hindsight have become symbolic: "Wait a minute, wait a minute, folks, you ain't heard nothin' yet."

Jolson went on to make other films but none so noteworthy as *The Jazz Singer.* However, in the 1934 movie *Wonder Bar* (also a Warner Brothers' film) he did earn the further distinction of appearing in one of the most tasteless production sequences that ever caricatured black men and women. The movie was set in

Al Jolson displays a chicken-eatin' grin for *The Singing Kid* (1936). Hollywood still saw nothing distasteful in surrounding a performer in burnt-cork makeup with real blacks. (The Museum of Modern Art/Courtesy United Artists)

Paris and dealt with the romance and tragedies of one night in a Montmartre cabaret. Jolson portrayed Al Wonder, owner of the establishment and its chief entertainer. In the musical sequence "Goin' to Heaven on a Mule" (staged by Busby Berkeley), the cabaret's dance floor becomes a giant stage on which Jolson in blackface, joined by what seems like a small army of dancers and singers, wends his way to a black heaven, a place of eternal watermelon feasts, gambling, chicken thieving, and choral syncopation.

This *Wonder Bar* sequence is only a more blatant manifestation of the continued caricaturing of the black on screen, a caricaturing that some blacks rather naively hoped the "talkies" would restrain. One black writer went so far as to argue that sound would bring a "recognition of the Negro as movie material." But the more pessimistic views of such people as Urban League official Elmer Anderson Carter proved correct. As he predicted in 1929, "motion picture producers will hesitate long before they attempt anything in the nature of a new evaluation of the Negro."[3]

Much of Carter's pessimism stemmed from his viewing of the 1929 Fox film *Hearts in Dixie.* Described by the company as "a musical drama of the South," this film with its almost all-black cast, rarely strayed from the condescending cliché. It told the story of a black farmer called Nappus and his family. His daughter Chloe is married to Gummy, described by one critic as a "languid, shiftless husband whose 'mysery' in his feet prevents him from being of any earthly good as far as work is concerned, although once away from his wife's eye he can shuffle with the tirelessness and lanky abandon of a jumping jack." Gummy and Chloe have a girl and a boy, Trailia and Chinquapin. When Nappus's daughter and granddaughter become ill with swamp fever, the voodoo woman comes and a gathering of neighbors tries to restore the health of the sick by singing spirituals — but to no avail. By the time Nappus decides to send for the white doctor (the only non-black in the film), it is too late. Gummy remarries, but his new wife is a shrew — mainly, it seems, because she makes him work. Meanwhile the worthy Nappus sells his farm and mule to pay for his young grandson's education, hoping that one day he may return and help his people. The film ends with a sad but resolute Nappus bidding farewell to Chinquapin, who then boards the riverboat that carries him north to his destiny.[4]

This episodic plot line served as little more than an excuse for singing, dancing, and comedy. Among the many songs performed in *Hearts in Dixie* — and the titles are a good indication of the attitude of the film toward its subject — were "Ring, Ring de Banjo," "Go Ring Dem Bells," "Deep River," and "Swing Low, Sweet Chariot." The dances included the inevitable cakewalk as well as a solo jig by Gummy. And much of the comedy centered

Clarence Muse (right) played the lead in *Hearts in Dixie* (1929). The stereotypes of this all-black feature were designed to delight white audiences only. (National Film Archive/Courtesy Twentieth Century–Fox)

about Gummy's attempts to avoid work or manifested itself in such bits of dialogue as "I ain't asking you is you ain't. I is asking you is you is." Even by the standards of its time *Hearts in Dixie* is a crude movie, a series of barely related incidents that serve, as NAACP official Walter White pointed out, as a "minstrel show, 'befo' de war' type."[5]

The reaction of white reviewers such as Louella Parsons, writing for the Los Angeles *Examiner,* was typical. She professed to find *Hearts in Dixie* a "remarkable talking picture" in which "one glimpses the real soul of the Negro." Like many of her colleagues, Parsons discerned "nothing in *Hearts in Dixie* . . . at which either race can take offense, it is such a true and sympathetic picture of the colored folk." Black critics, although delighted that entertainers of their race had been given a chance to perform on screen, inevitably were more realistic in their appraisals. As the reviewer for the Chicago *Whip* noted: "Fact is I was expecting that type of minstrelsy [,] having long since become familiar with 'colored hits' for white consumption."[6]

Whatever their opinion of the film, most critics praised the cast, which included such veteran black performers as Gertrude Howard and Zack Willams. Chinquapin was played by Eugene Jackson, who had appeared in the *Our Gang* series and whose show business career continued on into television in the 1960s. Clarence Muse ably portrayed Nappus. Originally Charles Gilpin was signed for this role, but was released. His replacement was also fired, and Muse got the part. Then in his late thirties, Muse was an erstwhile "song-and-dance man" who had an LL.B. degree and who had worked as an actor, director, writer, and producer in the ghetto theater in New York and Chicago. When Fox Films approached him about playing Nappus, he was appearing with a stock company in Columbus, Ohio. After *Hearts in Dixie,* Muse went on to a highly successful career in films, appearing in more than fifty movies in the next twenty-five years. However, given the roles blacks were asked to play, few of these films made great demands on his obvious talent.

The actor who won the most acclaim for his performance in *Hearts in Dixie* was Stepin Fetchit, who played Gummy. Fetchit was the first adult major black film personality whose career lasted beyond one or two movies, and during the 1930s became the best known film actor of his race. He achieved that renown by playing what was essentially the Gummy role over and over again, in everything from a vehicle for the singer Lawrence Tibbett called *The Prodigal* (MGM, 1931), and the mystery *Charlie Chan in Egypt* (Fox, 1935), to the Oliver Hardy-Harry Langdon comedy *Zenobia* (Hal Roach, 1939). Fetchit became identified in the popular imagination as a dialect-speaking, slump-shouldered, slack-jawed character who walked, talked, and apparently thought in slow motion. The Fetchit character overcame this lethargy only when he thought that a ghost or some nameless terror might be present; and then he moved very quickly indeed. One film critic wrote that the actor "shuffled through identical performances . . . bent on demonstrating the descent of the Negro from a lower order of the animal kingdom."[7]

Stepin Fetchit's real name was Lincoln Perry, and he was born in Florida. Little more is known about his early years. He made varying statements about his birthdate — he was in either his late twenties or early thirties when he played Gummy — and about the origin of the name Stepin Fetchit. According to an interview in *Ebony* he came to Hollywood in the 1920s as part of a comedy team known as "Step and Fetch It." He told another interviewer that the name was that of a race horse, but "no big time race hawse . . . just one of the inmates of a Texas track . . . that was gettin' venerable." In any event, his first featured movie role under that name was in 1927 when he played a stable boy in MGM's *In Old Kentucky*. He had appeared in a number of movies before scoring a hit as a "lazy darky" in *Hearts in Dixie*. He was to make this image part of his personal publicity. According to a Fox Films release of the early 1930s, Fetchit's advice was to "take your time — time ain't gonna take you." And in the early 1930s he placed the following advertisement in an industry trade paper:

> Calafurnia here I'se am,
> Right from sunny Alabam
> De lan' ob cotton, corn, un moonshine
> Dat taste jus' lak dis moobin pitcher gib ob dine.
>
> I'se lak Dixie, deed I do,
> But you'se raise watter mullons, too,
> An' your chickens jus' as grand —
> Calafurnia, here I'se am!
>
> > Yours fo' de axin,
> > Stepin Fetchit

Although he started out in 1927 earning $75 a day, Fetchit probably earned over $1 million before he went bankrupt in the 1940s. At the height of his career he had six houses, a staff of Oriental servants, and a fleet of limousines, including a pink one. When criticized for the roles he played, Fetchit insisted that he had never done anything in the movies to hurt blacks. "I'm a comedian, not a clown," he told one interviewer. And in 1970 he sued CBS, charging that the network's 1968 television documentary series on black history had libeled him by saying that he was "the symbol of the white man's Negro." The suit was subsequently dismissed.[8]

Hearts in Dixie was not the only all-black feature produced by a major studio in 1929. A few months after that film's release MGM began distributing *Hallelujah,* based on a story by King Vidor and directed by him. Vidor had won acclaim for his imaginative craftsmanship in films such as *The Big Parade,* a 1925 romantic drama about American soldiers in World War I, and his reputation led many of those who deplored the movie image of the black to hope that for once black characters would be represented accurately.

Technically *Hallelujah* was a very impressive film. At the time when most filmmakers were prisoners of the stationary microphones and heavy cameras needed for shooting synchronized sound, Vidor retained the fluidity of style that characterized the best silent movies by dubbing in much of the sound after shooting. But for all of Vidor's pronouncements about filming "a dramatic tale of Negro life in the South," *Hallelujah* fell back on familiar stereotypes.[9]

Just consider the scenario.

The film begins with a group of blacks picking cotton and singing "Swanee River." We are then introduced to Parson Johnson and his family: Mammy, his wife; Missy Rose, his adopted daughter; the younger boys; and Zeke, who (like Gummy in *Hearts in Dixie*) prefers loafing to working and whose antics distract the rest of the family from their chores. Zeke is the pivotal character. Accompanied by one of his younger brothers he takes the cotton crop to market and sells it for a good price. But he is enticed by the seductive Chick into a crooked game of craps with her current lover, Hot Shot. Zeke loses his money, becomes wise to the loaded dice, and gets into a fight with the

Daniel Haynes, playing the shiftless but well-mean-
ing hero of King Vidor's all-black extravaganza,
Hallelujah, is vamped at the crap table. (From the
MGM release "Hallelujah" © 1929 Metro-Goldwyn-
Mayer Distributing Corporation. © renewed 1957
Loew's Incorporated)

gambler, who draws a gun on him. Although Zeke manages to
wrestle the weapon away from Hot Shot, he accidentally wounds
his brother, who dies on the way home. A repentant Zeke finds
God during the wake, is forgiven by his parson father, and becomes an evangelist "saving souls." At one of his revival meetings
Zeke meets Chick again and convinces her to jump off "the Black
Diamond Express to Hell." The momentarily repentant Chick,
enamored of Zeke and unable to distinguish between love and

religious zeal, deserts Hot Shot. When the gambler attempts to force himself on her she beats him on the head with a poker, saying "Ain't no one goin' to stand in my path to glory." But she soon backslides. Zeke, although he is pledged to his foster sister Missy Rose, succumbs to Chick's blandishments and gives up preaching to work in a sawmill. It is all to no avail. Chick deserts him to run off with Hot Shot, and he pursues them. The chase ends with an accident on the road in which Chick dies. Zeke trails Hot Shot into a swamp and kills him. He serves time on the chain gang, and — once more filled with faith — returns home. One of the last shots in the movie shows Zeke with his head on Mammy's breast, surrounded by the younger children, exchanging looks of tender affection with the faithful Missy Rose, as the Parson lays a hand of blessing on his older boy's head.

Hallelujah was cast with much publicity and fanfare. Vidor undertook a search (extensively reported in the black press) for black actors, the intention being, he said, "to do for Negro talent what we did for the doughboy in *The Big Parade*." The part of Zeke went to Daniel Haynes, a college graduate, most of whose theater experience had been in all-black shows, and who had a powerful physique and a rich voice. Parson Johnson was played by Harry Gray, a former slave who in his late eighties still worked as a janitor at the New York *Amsterdam News*. Fanny Belle De Knight — well known, according to the New York *Age*, "as a dramatic reader and elocutionist" — was cast as Mammy. The role of Missy Rose was entrusted to blues singer Victoria Spivey, who had made many recordings for Okeh Records, a firm that directed its product at black audiences. The brother who gets shot was played by Everett McGarrity, a recruit from vaudeville. Another vaudevillian was William Fountaine, who played Hot Shot. Sixteen-year-old Nina Mae McKinney, a sexy and extraordinarily good-looking chorus girl from Lew Leslie's *Blackbirds of 1928*, was Chick. Much of the movie was shot on location around Memphis, Tennessee, and the extras were local black people, some of whom also played bit parts. The interiors were filmed in Hollywood, and extras there included members of the Dixie Jubilee Chorus, which sang the spirituals and other musical numbers that were liberally interspersed through the movie.[10]

There can be no doubt that Vidor's intentions were high-minded, and that he sincerely wanted to make a movie that would treat the black seriously. Vidor, however, proved unable to escape either his Texas upbringing or the then-common beliefs about blacks. As he said, it was the "sincerity and fervor of their religious expression" that had attracted him, as had "the honest simplicity of their sexual drives": he had concluded that "the intermingling of these two activities seemed to offer strikingly dramatic content." The result was *Hallelujah*. Before pleading his case with the studio bosses, Vidor made a point of listing what seemed to him "scenes suitable for an all-Negro sound film — river baptisms, prayer meetings accompanied by spirituals, Negro preaching, banjo playing, dancing the blues." If his presentation of the black was less crude than those in films such as *Hearts in Dixie,* the difference was one of sophistication rather than content, for he succeeded merely in dressing up the old image rather than in creating black human beings. As the British critic John Grierson later remarked: "I note from a publicity puff that Vidor freed the Negro from misunderstanding just as Abe Lincoln freed him from slavery. Both statements are exaggerated."[11]

Vidor's film was actually a lumpy mixture of naive sentimentality and hackneyed melodrama. The musical numbers can be exhilarating, but there is something incongruous about the juxtaposition of music traditionally identified as black with the special material composed by Irving Berlin, including "Swanee Shuffle" and "Waitin' at the End of the Road." Moreover, because the characters were presented as living in a community that was self-contained and entirely black, their erratic behavior appeared to arise out of their own peculiarities and shortcomings rather than from any pressures or limitations imposed by white society. But *Hallelujah* was presented as a serious view of black experience in America. It was an experience that most white moviegoers knew next to nothing about, and the Vidor film only reinforced their fantasies.

Not surprisingly, this misrepresentation aroused hostile comment in the black community. The Pittsburgh *Courier* reported that black moviegoers "who belong to what one might tap as the middle and upper classes" viewed *Hallelujah* as "representing conditions in which they had no pride." One letter to the editor of a black paper charged that King Vidor's "filthy hands [were] reeking with prejudice." Another writer referred to the movie's "insulting niggerisms." *Hallelujah*'s treatment of the Negro church came under especially heavy attack. Paul Robeson claimed that the movie was spoiled for him because "they took the Negro and his church services and made them funny." A Harlem leader called *Hallelujah* "an insult to the religious ideal of the colored race of today." W. E. B. DuBois was a notable exception, possibly because of his negative feelings about organized religion. He found *Hallelujah* "beautifully staged under severe limitations" and "epochmaking."[12]

DuBois, however, reported feeling somewhat "Jim-Crowed" at the theater where he saw the movie, and this was understandable. In many areas of the United States, and not just the South, blacks were restricted to certain sections of movie theaters until after World War II. (In Harlem, even into the early 1930s, the Loew's movie houses attempted to maintain a policy of seating black patrons in the balcony even when they paid for orchestra seats.) In Southern theaters, blacks frequently had to enter through "an alley or a back way" and the physical condition inside was inevitably disgraceful. Many theaters on both sides of the Mason-Dixon line simply refused to admit blacks. Such policies of exclusion or segregation were enforced by law in the South; elsewhere the situation was more ambiguous, although not necessarily more beneficial to blacks. In 1928 a group of Montclair, New Jersey, black citizens protested against arrests arising from a local theater's segregation policy. The town attorney spoke out against discrimination but stated that "an amusement place" could refuse to admit a person (and therefore could seat him where it wished), even "for such reasons as dislike of the way a patron's hair is combed or the kind of necktie worn."[13]

The producers of *Hallelujah* (and of *Hearts in Dixie*) apparently realized that the discriminatory policies of exhibitors had to be taken into consideration. *Hallelujah* was given a joint world premiere. One opening took place in midtown Manhattan, the other, at the Lafayette Theater in Harlem: it featured spotlights, hoopla, celebrities such as Oscar De Priest of Chicago, the only black Congressman of the time, and what was described as the "colored socially elect." The noted black entertainer Bill "Bojangles" Robinson served as master of ceremonies. Despite this well-publicized Harlem premiere some blacks did venture downtown to see the movie on Broadway. Three who did were informed, after a long wait in line, that seats were no longer available for the performance but that "tickets could be secured at the Lafayette" in Harlem. As they walked away from the box office they saw whites purchasing the supposedly unavailable tickets. The blacks filed suit under a New York civil rights law and the resulting publicity brought forth other blacks who had been similarly rebuffed, but the legal action proved unproductive.[14]

The techniques used to keep black and white viewers of *Hallelujah* separate varied from place to place. In Pittsburgh the film did not play at the first-run Loew's theater used by most MGM productions but at a smaller movie house that, according to the local black weekly, had "an understood policy . . . that Negroes are not welcome." Another technique was to refrain from advertising the film in the black press until the movie played a theater there. Vidor has recalled that *Hallelujah* encountered distribution problems because exhibitors worried about "attracting a large percentage of Negro patrons," especially in the Northern states where legalized segregation did not exist. In discussing the response of moviegoers to *Hearts in Dixie, Billboard* raised the question of whether the "negro picture fans . . . will be willing to wait until the film is shown in their own neighborhood houses," and a Fox Films official indicated that after the completion of the movie "it was realized that its release might result in complications."[15]

Much was also said at the time about the resistance of Southern exhibitors to all-black films. Harry Levette, who wrote a Hollywood column that appeared in a number of black newspapers, reported that "there will be no more all-colored-cast films made" because the South was "not quite ready for dark stars in the real sense of the word." And a movie company executive told a black newspaperman that "it does not suffice that the East, West, and North accept Negro pictures . . . the South refuses to accept pictures wherein Negroes are starred." But it was fear of "complications" and the attempts to avoid them that contributed as much as anything to the lukewarm box-office response to *Hearts in Dixie* and *Hallelujah.* The failure of these films to make a substantial profit meant that the industry had little reason to experiment further with black leads. Black performers were once again relegated to supporting and minor roles.[16]

There would be only one more major all-black film before the

The Great Fish Fry in the Sky: "De Lawd," played by Rex Ingram (left), receives some distressing reports about the state of the world, in *The Green Pastures* (1936). (National Film Archive/Courtesy United Artists)

end of the decade, and predictably, it would be one in which the condescendingly sentimentalized white view of blacks and the resulting stereotypes found full expression. The movie was the screen version of Marc Connelly's Pulitzer Prize-winning play *The Green Pastures*, which was filmed by Warner Brothers in 1936. Connelly, a white newspaperman, playwright, and director, had drawn the inspiration for his play from a collection of short stories, *Ol' Man Adam An' His Chillun*. Written by Roark Bradford, who was also white, these stories were in turn based on Old Testament narratives. They told about "Eve and That Snake,"

"Mrs. Lot," "Old King Pharaoh's Daughter," and "Crossing Jordan." In Connelly's play, written in dialect for an all-black cast, these stories are supposedly visualized in the minds of black children being taught the Bible in a back-country Louisiana Sunday school by an old preacher. Connelly showed Heaven as a fish fry. "De Lawd" enjoyed his "ten cent seegars" and when creating the world spoke of "a place to dreen off dis firmament." Both as a play and as a film *The Green Pastures* won acclaim. Even black newspapers found the stage production "loveable" and "enjoyable" when it opened on Broadway in February, 1930. But some black critics did blast the film. Roi Ottley called it "the phoniest panorama of hocus pocus that has yet come out of Hollywood."[17]

The movie, which Connelly co-directed, only made the play's one-dimensional view of the black more pronounced. Noah's home (in the words of an industry press release) "is a typical shack of a Louisiana Negro," and just before the Flood, Noah attempts to talk De Lawd into allowing an additional barrel of whiskey on the Ark "for snake bite." At one point a black boy rides a cloud shaped like a horse, joyously proclaiming "I'se an Indian." Film made it possible to turn theatrical illusions into cinematic images. Sin in Babylon was depicted in a nightclub scene, with "a bevy of black beauties" dancing in an abandoned fashion. When De Lawd decides to "r'ar back and pass a miracle," a whirling mist gradually assumes the shape of the earth while the white-robed blacks inhabiting Heaven indulge in an orgy of eye-rolling. Indeed, no caricature of the black seemed too grotesque for the Great Fish Fry in the Sky.[18]

It is possible that if more all-black films had been made by the industry, fairer characterizations might have emerged. But as it was, not until the 1940s did the industry begin to depart significantly from the stereotypes with their "insulting niggerisms."

Much of the public not only accepted but welcomed these "niggerisms," which found expression outside the movies as well. A hit radio show of the 1930s was *Amos 'n' Andy*, which centered around the comic adventures of black characters in a mythical section of Harlem. It was the creation of two white men, who also played the lead roles. Although basically a situation comedy, in its early days the program emphasized the caricature aspects of the characters, and among the running dialect jokes was "I'se regusted," not to mention "unlax." *Amos 'n' Andy* reached the peak of its popularity in the early 1930s when, according to one show business history, "phones fell silent and people stopped eating" during the dinnertime broadcasts. Another example of the role of the black in American culture at this time are the Aunt Jemima Pancake Mix advertisements. These showed a broad-bosomed, fat, handkerchief-headed, gingham-dressed, black mammy who told worried housewives: "Don' yo' fret none, honey . . . Jus' follow dese directions for de world's mos' delicious pancakes." *Life* revolutionized magazine journalism in the late 1930s, but its treatment of the black was strictly traditional. A photo essay on watermelons, for example, included a picture of a black baby sucking at its mother's breast while she chews a piece of watermelon. The caption reads: "Nothing makes a Negro's mouth water like a luscious, fresh-picked melon. Any colored 'mammy' can hold a huge slice in one hand while holding her offspring in the other."[19]

Such racial views permeated American society even as that Depression-ridden society was being transformed by the New Deal. Despite all that the New Deal did for blacks, many of its noted alphabet agencies practiced segregation. President Franklin D. Roosevelt, though certainly more responsive to black demands and desires than his predecessors, agreed in 1941 to a weak Fair Employment Practices Committee to deal with discrimination in defense industries — but did so only when faced with the threat of a black march on Washington.

It is hardly surprising, then, that the American film industry continued to caricature and denigrate the black. Like their silent predecessors, those sound movies that were set in the South during the Civil War hardly acknowledged the abolition of slavery. The mammy in *Rainbow on the River* (RKO, 1936) was typical of many black film characters who indicated that they had never wanted to be free. *So Red the Rose* (Paramount, 1935) so aroused the exasperation of one reviewer that his critique was entitled "Uncle Tom, Will You Never Die?" This film shows blacks cheering the Confederacy as their masters ride off to fight. And a noisy revolt by emancipated blacks is quelled by the daughter of the dying plantation owner and her young brother. She simply slaps one of the ringleaders and she and her little brother shame the rest into silence with some sloppily sentimental speechmaking. Her father dies undisturbed and only then do the blacks quietly leave the plantation. The Southern white's supposed ability to handle the black received its most exaggerated tribute in the 1936 Twentieth Century-Fox production, *Prisoner of Shark Island*. This film dealt with the ordeal of Dr. Samuel Mudd, the Maryland physician who was imprisoned after unwittingly setting John Wilkes Booth's leg during the assassin's attempted flight. At one point Mudd is forced to face rioting black troops in the Florida fortress where he is imprisoned. When he peremptorily orders one of the blacks to "put that gun down, Nigrah," another black says, "Dat am no Yankee talkin' jus' to hear himself talk. Dat's a Southern man 'n he means it!"[20]

The most extravagant and outrageous portrait of the black in the Old South was, of course, the one painted in *Gone With the Wind*, a movie that in this respect has to rank with *The Birth of a Nation*. As with the Griffith film, many moviegoers accepted David O. Selznick's 1939 movie as historical and social truth even though *Gone With the Wind* merely repeated many of the earlier movie's caricatures in a more up-to-date style — and in Technicolor. The one major difference was that *Gone With the Wind* emphasized not the blacks' supposed viciousness but the faithfulness, ignorance, and servility of what one character in the film called "the simple-minded darkies." Plantation life before the war was shown as idyllic for the blacks, who are depicted as being treated kindly and magnanimously. But the film also depicts the black as belonging in the fields and in the servants' quarters. The most faithful of faithful souls is Scarlett O'Hara's ever scolding but ever loyal mammy, who stays with her mistress through good times and bad, through the Civil War and after. Hattie McDaniel, who played this role, won an Oscar for best supporting actress, the first black to win an Academy Award. A former radio vocalist, she had enjoyed a long career but one with little variety. Most of the roles she played in the more than forty movies she appeared in between the early 1930s and her death in 1952 were variations on the same part that won her the Oscar. She was obviously unhappy with this type-casting, but she also recognized if she did not play the role on screen, she would end up playing it in real life.

Gone With the Wind was permeated with antiblack sentiment, some of it rather outrageous by the standards of our day. While Scarlett drives through the slum quarter of Reconstruction At-

Hattie McDaniel, the archetypal movie mammy, informs
Scarlett O'Hara (Vivian Leigh) that she should cut down
on the hominy. For this role in *Gone With the Wind*,
Miss McDaniel became the first black to win an Oscar.
(From the MGM release "Gone With the Wind" © 1939
Selznick International Pictures, Inc. © renewed 1968
Metro-Goldwyn-Mayer Inc., successor in interest to Selz-
nick International Pictures, Inc.)

lanta, she is attacked by a black and a white renegade. Big Sam,
a one-time slave on her father's plantation who just happens to be
nearby, comes to her rescue. As the black columnist Dan Burley
angrily pointed out, "in some mysterious hocus-pocus at which
Hollywood is peculiarly adept, the white renegade is disposed of
without Big Sam's black hands ever touching him, but a Negro is
allowed to kill a Negro . . ." Even less subtle is the scene that
takes place during the siege and evacuation of wartime Atlanta.
The black servant girl Prissy, who previously had claimed experi-

ence in delivering babies, admits to Scarlett just as Melanie Wilkes is about to have her child with no doctor available that she knows nothing about being a midwife. In a whining, almost incomprehensible dialect she hysterically chatters out her fears of the Union siege guns, of the atmosphere in the dying city, and of participating in the birth of a baby. Scarlett slaps Prissy, the force of the blow nearly knocking the girl down, and after issuing some orders goes on to deliver the baby herself.[21]

Except for some left-wing organizations such as the National Negro Congress there was surprisingly little public outcry against *Gone With the Wind* from black groups. In large part the "clever elimination of the blatantly objectionable parts of the book," as one black newspaperman put it, accounted for this mild reaction. The NAACP had led the fight to cut or soften some of the more offensive scenes in the novel, and it was the organization's relative success in the pre-production phases of the movie that undoubtedly led to its near silence after the film's release. Given the popularity of the novel and the ineffectiveness of the few protests staged against the film, there was little else that the NAACP and other groups could have accomplished.[22]

But those sound films that were set outside of the South were scarcely an improvement. In the main, the black men on screen continued to be presented as emasculated, easily frightened semi-literates while the women were shown as fat, excessively jolly menials. Blacks of both sexes were to be found cleaning, cooking, or carrying suitcases; their place was in the fields, the kitchen, the stable, or the train station. Director Fritz Lang recalls that MGM head Louis B. Mayer "at that time was convinced that Negroes should be shown only as . . . menials of some description." Other studio heads shared this view. The situation is typified by the fact that the only casting call blacks received for Warners' 1940 football epic *Knute Rockne — All American* was for six performers to play porters in a depot scene.[23]

But by and large, in the movies dealing with the American scene, blacks hardly seemed to exist. About the only films, outside of those set in the South, in which a black could be assured of a part, were prison films, a popular genre for much of the 1930s. There even was a black woman among the *Ladies of the Big House* (Paramount, 1932). Typically, one of the condemned men on Death Row would be a black prisoner, who would comment in song (usually singing a spiritual) on the torment of prison life. Daniel Haynes, for instance, played a variation on such a role in the 1932 World Wide production *The Last Mile*.

The introduction of sound created a new movie form, the musical, which did benefit black performers to some small extent. It must be noted, however, that their appearances on screen as singers, dancers, and musicians were very carefully defined. Typical was the musical tour of New York night life in the Walter Wanger production *Vogues of 1938*, at a segregated club, a white audience enjoys a black production number. As usual in

The races could mingle as equals under special circumstances. Here, Miss Beavers (top center) appears as one of the *Ladies of the Big House*. (National Film Archive/ Courtesy of Universal Pictures)

the movies, a tiny stage expands into a giant set to accommodate intricate and exciting song and dance numbers. The emphasis is on the primitiveness and inherent rhythm of the blacks, who shed formal garments and manners for more abbreviated dress. They play no other part in the development of the plot. Better-known black performers received billing in such movies but the listing in the credits was invariably "as themselves." In 1937, for example, appearances by black artists in specialty numbers included brief stints by Louis Armstrong (*Artists and Models,* Paramount) and Duke Ellington (*The Hit Parade,* Republic). Among other black stars who so appeared in feature films were Ethel Waters, the Mills Brothers, and Cab Calloway — who in Paramount's *International House* (1933) sang a song in praise of marijuana. A recent survey has found that such casting accounted for about 15 percent of all the movie roles credited to the blacks in the 1930s. These black entertainers were cast for their presumed drawing power, but their presence was otherwise incidental.

Movie blacks may have seemed benign enough in an old South or a New York nightclub setting, but once transported to an exotic place they were still likely to be portrayed as threats. Thus, in *Nagana* (Universal, 1937) the white heroine faces death at the hands of black natives. Tied to a stake, she watches helplessly as the natives dance around her: at the last possible moment she is saved. The classic African melodrama of the period was MGM's *Trader Horn* (1931), which featured a blond jungle queen attired in wisps of monkey fur. She gives up her suzerainty for one of the whites who has come crashing into her domain. In this film, unusual for the time because portions were shot on location, the blacks are inevitably depicted as ignorant savages, except for those serving white masters.

But the blacks were never depicted as being *too* savage. The battle scenes between the Zulus and the whites in *Rhodes of Africa* (Gaumont, 1935) were, according to one of the filmmakers who helped shoot them, cut to a minimum since "it was not thought wise . . . to show in full scale such a realistic battle between black and white . . ." Even in supposedly factual films such as Columbia's 1930 release *Africa Speaks*, a condescending attitude prevailed: when the roar of lions is heard, the whites stand their ground but the blacks bolt helter-skelter for cover. Many of these movies staged rather than genuinely recorded native life, and the emphasis even in the better films was on the strangeness of the blacks. Highlights in *Dark Rapture,* a 1937 Universal release, include a wild native dance and a tribal flagellation ceremony.[24]

Such views also found their way into the "selected short subjects" which were so much a part of the movie scene of the 1930s and 1940s. For instance, a Movietone News sequence showing a game between two black football teams was treated as comedy and reported in dialect. Even *The March of Time,* which was relatively enlightened, treated the black shabbily, so much so that the New York *Age* charged that "Time Marches Backward." During its first two years *The March of Time* directly touched on black activities only twice. Once it showed Father Divine, and in March, 1937, part of the regular issue dealt with "Harlem Black Magic." The population of the area was characterized as being primitive, ignorant, and superstitious, and the script stated that one-third of Harlem's blacks were voodoo worshippers. A white critic of a later *March of Time* short, "Dixie, 1940," commented that in it "the Negro retainers cringe amongst the ancient bric-a-brac as if they had never heard of Abraham Lincoln."[25]

The Hollywood stereotyping of the black was so effective that it also influenced filmmaking in Europe — when attention was paid to them at all. An occasional German film might utilize blacks to set a scene: jazz musicians in a night club, for instance. Indeed, the American view of the black was so pervasive that even as well meaning a project as the 1931 pacifist film *Niemands Land* (called *Hell on Earth* for English language distribution), in depicting how various national types reacted when trapped in No-Man's Land, presented a French black soldier as a happy-go-lucky tap dancer. In the operatic process of showing the grandeur that was Rome — and that would be Fascist Italy — Italian films of the period inevitably presented blacks as exotics or as slaves. The French, in their war movies, liked to include a black as a symbol of the colonial troops who comprised a significant portion of their armed forces. And one of the early French sound films starred the American black entertainer Josephine Baker, who had become a stellar attraction in Paris during the 1920s. Called *Siren of the Tropics* in English, it was periodically distributed to ghetto theaters in the United States.

In 1932 the Russians did announce plans for what was described as a serious attempt to portray black life in the United States. Twenty-two young American blacks were invited to the Soviet Union to participate in a film called *Black and White;* only two of them were professional actors. From the moment the group arrived salaries were paid, even though shooting of the film was delayed. They were wined and dined. One of their number reported in the black press about an outing in the country: "Home was never like this was the . . . opinion of everyone of us who has spent this . . . day . . . with Russian people, playing tennis with them, dining with them, and swimming with them in the nude in the placid river that skirts the Kalinin Rest Home."[26]

Unfortunately the film was never made, but the Soviets made propaganda capital out of it anyway. The blacks had arrived in Moscow at the end of June. At the beginning of August they were taken on a tour of the Ukraine and Crimea. While they were away, it was announced by Mescharaboom, the production company, that the project had been abandoned; news of the decision appeared in the Western press before the blacks were formally notified. Some of the group later issued a statement charging that representatives of "American capitalism" had managed to "turn thumbs down on a Soviet project designed to aid in the liberation of the Negro masses." But the probable reason for the abandonment of *Black and White* seems to have been the failure to piece together an adequate script. According to Langston Hughes, who had been hired to work on the dialogue, the proposed script that had been authored by a well-known Russian writer "was impossible to the point of ludicrousness." Hughes recalls laughing out loud while reading the script, which "was so interwoven with major and minor impossibilities and improbabilities that it would have seemed like a burlesque on screen." In one scene, a poor but honest young black girl is serving drinks at a fancy party. The music starts and a wealthy young white man comes up to her and says, "Honey, put down your tray; come on, let's dance," and proceeds to seduce her. The director was a young German who hardly spoke either Russian or English, and who had been chosen because he had successfully directed a travelogue on Africa.[27]

Meanwhile, only a handful of Hollywood films attempted to bestow some dignity on their black characters or to present them in an active role. In Samuel Goldwyn's 1931 production of the

Sinclair Lewis novel *Arrowsmith*, Clarence Brooks portrayed a
black physician on a Caribbean island who worked with the title
character and his white associates to combat an outbreak of
disease. The protagonist of *I Am a Fugitive from a Chain Gang*
(Warner Brothers, 1932) is aided in his escape by a friendly and
sympathetic black convict. And the wise-cracking gangster portrayed by Slim Thompson in both the stage and screen versions of
The Petrified Forest (which was filmed by Warner Brothers in
1936) is no Uncle Tom; indeed, he chides the black chauffeur for
Tomism. Leigh Whipper's role in the movie version of Steinbeck's
Of Mice and Men (a Hal Roach production released by United
Artists in 1940) also managed to escape the usual stereotyping.
But such film portrayals were rarities.

Occasionally, too, a Hollywood feature film would touch on a
subject that had special meaning for blacks or would treat, however imperfectly, some aspect of black life in the United States.
One such movie was Warners' *They Won't Forget* (1937), a
reworking of the Leo Frank case and an eloquent protest against
lynching, which had taken some four thousand black lives since
the Civil War. The film deals with a northern teacher in a
southern state who, on the flimsiest of evidence, is convicted of
killing one of his teenage pupils. The governor commutes the
death sentence passed on the teacher, who is then lynched by a
mob. At one point, however, authorities work to force a statement of guilt from the black man who has discovered the girl's
body. This process stops only when the politically ambitious
district attorney (who sees a chance to use the case as a stepping-
stone to the governorship) lets the black go because "anybody
can convict a nigger."

Fury, a 1936 MGM movie directed by Fritz Lang, also took a
stand against lynching — although there, too, the person involved
was white. Lang recalls that the studio cut from the final version
a shot of some blacks listening to a radio broadcast of the prosecutor's summation of his case against members of a lynch mob. In
this short scene (the only appearance by blacks in the film) the
prosecutor comments on the large number of lynchings each year
in the United States, and an old black silently and sadly nods his
head. Even that, apparently, was too strong for Hollywood.

The subject of "passing" was another touchy racial matter that
at least one major motion picture, the 1934 Universal production

The tragic mulatto, 1934-style: In one of the great three-handkerchief jobs of all time, *Imitation of Life*, a light-skinned daughter (Fredi Washington) tells her mother (Louise Beavers) that she is leaving home to "pass." (National Film Archive/Courtesy of Universal Pictures)

Imitation of Life, dealt with — if only in a sub-plot. Based on a Fannie Hurst novel, this cinematic tear-jerker recounted the woes of two Atlantic City widows, one white and one black, as over a span of years they attempt to provide for their daughters. The principal character is the white widow, Beatrice Pullman, who becomes a business success but a romantic failure. Her success stems from the merchandizing of her black maid's secret recipe for tasty pancakes. But Delilah expresses no interest in the business; she wants only to continue serving "Miss Bea" and her daughter Jessie. Moreover, she refuses a share of the profits even though her formula serves as the cornerstone of the food empire Miss Bea has built. This modern-day mammy figure, when given the opportunity to have a place of her own, responds like the mythical Southern slaves who renounced freedom in many a movie: "My own house. You gonna send me away? Don' do that to me. How I gonna take care of you and Miss Jessie if I'se away?" Indeed, Delilah seems to care more for Jessie Pullman that for her own daughter, Peola.

If Miss Bea's tragedy lies in her frustrated love life, Delilah's is tied to her daughter's light skin, which allows Peola to pass for white. While Peola and Jessie are still children they attend one of Atlantic City's segregated public schools together. On a stormy day Delilah comes to the school to bring her daughter a raincoat and galoshes. A teacher kindly tells Delilah that there are "no colored children in the school," but Delilah points out Peola, who runs out of the classroom screaming, "I hate you, I hate you." Over the years the daughter comes to resent and then reject her mother. At a grand party in the Pullman home at which the two are present, Peola asks why she can't dance with the other guests: "Mother, look at me. I'm white. I'm not colored at all. I'm white." When Delilah's response proves unsatisfactory, Peola runs away from home. After a brief reconciliation, she leaves again, telling her mother: "Don't come for me. If you see me in the street, don't speak to me. From this moment on I'm white. I am not colored. You have to give me up."

In the novel Peola passes, meets a white engineer, has herself sterilized, marries him, and goes off with her husband to the wilds of South America. An anguished and heartbroken Delilah dies some time later. Though Peola never does get to meet the engineer in the movie, she does come to accept her heritage. As Delilah's coffin is being carried to the hearse at a grand funeral in Harlem, Peola is seen at the edge of the large crowd, distraught and in tears. Accepting what she is at last, Peola has come back to her mother; she joins the Pullmans in a limousine that will take them all to the cemetery, not really separate, not really equal.

The movie Peola is simply an updated version of the tragic mulatto of nineteenth-century melodrama and early silent film. As was the case with her predecessors, mixed blood can bring nothing but sorrow. And the movie delineates Peola in the same terms that had always defined the mulatto stereotype. While Delilah's mammy figure is treated sympathetically if condescendingly, the character of Peola has virtually no redeeming features.

The reaction of black moviegoers to *Imitation of Life* varied. The singer Bobby Short saw the movie when he was a boy, and remembers that it made a great impression on him and his friends. They thought it "a dilly" but considered it a "classic example of the colored world as interpreted by whites." But apparently many blacks did accept the characters as they were presented. A New York *Age* columnist reporting on the reaction of Harlem audiences to the movie angrily noted that blacks laughed at Delilah "for being so dumb and illiterate" and "sneered" at Peola without understanding what it was she really wanted.

But a great many black people strongly criticized the film. Howard University faculty member Emmett Dorsey expressed dismay that "Negroes applaud and acclaim this picture," which he characterized as a "rationalization of racial prejudice." Black critic Sterling Brown, attacked by Fannie Hurst as "ungrateful" for his critical review, argued that the story of Delilah and Peola was "incredible" and that it reinforced "the stereotypes that Hollywood holds to firmly."[28]

Although the actresses who portrayed Delilah and Peola received considerable critical acclaim, their Hollywood careers benefitted little. As was the custom for white Hollywood actresses, Louise Beavers (Delilah) attempted to obtain larger and better-paying roles, but with no success. In order to keep on working in the movies she was forced to continue playing what she described as "maid roles — just pleasant, likeable Negro maids — plump and happy and quick to laugh." The actress who played Peola faced a different kind of barrier. Fredi Washington was so fair that it was difficult to cast her as a black; at the same time, no acknowledged black was allowed to play a white. Rumor had it that studio makeup artists had even darkened Miss Washington's skin coloring for *Imitation of Life* so that she would not photograph too white.[29]

Industry restrictions on the roles available to blacks also hampered the more important and well-known Negro performers. The exuberant Bill Robinson achieved great success in a number of movies, most notably in the Fox production, *The Little Colonel* (1935), in which (cast as Lionel Barrymore's butler) he did his famous dance on the stairs with Shirley Temple. The result was enormous publicity and much favorable comment about opportunities for the black in the United States. (There was little discussion of the fact that the black children in the film were utilized as comedy stooges for Shirley Temple.) Despite Robinson's popularity in Hollywood, he made relatively few movies there; according to one black source, "he did not fit the Hollywood stereotype." But his personality and talent could not be imprisoned in a stereotyped character; they shone through even when he played the servant roles for which he would be harshly criticized by some in his own community.[30]

Even so well known and able a performer as Paul Robeson had a hard time finding proper vehicles for his great talents. Between

Shirley Temple and Bill Robinson trip the light fantastic in *The Littlest Rebel* (1935). The slack-jawed onlooker, right, is Willie ("Sleeps 'n Eats") Best. (National Film Archive/Courtesy Twentieth Century–Fox. © 1935 Twentieth Century–Fox Film Corporation)

1929 and 1942 he played important roles in nine feature films, but he never fully realized his ambition of presenting the movie-going masses with a realistic image of the black. Unfortunately, most of his movie roles — as the black separatist leader Marcus Garvey pointed out — tended "to dishonor, mimic, discredit, and abase the . . . attainments of the Black Race . . ."[31]

In 1929, some years after Robeson's appearance in the Micheaux movie *Body and Soul*, he played one of the leads in *Borderline*. It was an experimental film made in Switzerland by the group that published the intellectual cinema journal *Close Up*, and it examined the complex personal relations among four people, two of whom are not white. *Borderline* gave Robeson the chance to play a black character rather than to act a stereotype. But this self-conscious and arty film, which had an extremely limited appeal in any event, suffered distribution problems and was seen by very few people. Robeson's next film, *The Emperor Jones*, produced in 1933 by John Krimsky and Gifford Cochran in New York City, reached a wider audience. Robeson played a part in which he had won great acclaim on the stage — the brutal black ruler who disintegrates emotionally as he flees from his rebellious subjects through the jungle. The movie version of the Eugene O'Neill play expanded it to show in detail the rise of Brutus Jones from Pullman porter to emperor of an island kingdom of blacks. Among the additional scenes were ones set in a Harlem night club and on a chain gang in the South. Robeson was compelling as Jones and presented a picture of strength, especially in his dealings with the white trader who deferred to him. But the film is uneven, revealing the producers' limited resources and suffering from the attempt to expand the stage work. Nor did the film deviate too far from the conventional stereotypes. As one black newspaperman pointed out, "crap-shooting, gin-guzzling, immorality, cutting, killing, fear of ghosts and other supposed Negro characteristics are dragged in[,] in heavier quantities than usual."[32]

Robeson fared no better in his next two movies. Hoping that in England (where he had achieved great popularity as a stage and concert performer) it would be possible for him to play a non-stereotyped role, he had crossed the Atlantic to film *Sanders of the River*. Robeson's friend Nancy Cunard described this 1935 Alexander Korda production as "pure Nordic bunk." Robeson played Bosambo, an enlightened native chief but one whose position is clearly dependent on the good will of Sanders, the colonial district commissioner. Bosambo is clearly Sanders's man and subservient to "the lord Sandi . . . the man who gives the law." When the movie was severely criticized in the black press, Robeson responded by stating that his growing interest in Africa and its culture had influenced him to accept the part and that the tenor of the movie had been changed "during the cutting of the picture after it was filmed." The English film critic Paul Rotha reported that Robeson, after seeing the complete movie for the first time on the night of the world premiere in London, locked himself into a dressing room and refused to make an appearance on the stage.[33]

When approached by Universal the next year to appear in the musical *Show Boat,* Robeson attempted to gain a final say over his scenes in order to avoid a repetition of his experience with Korda. Universal refused, but Robeson decided nonetheless to go to Hollywood and play the role of Joe, one which he had already acted in the London stage production: Such appearances, he believed, would strengthen his bargaining position in the future. Publicity releases for the film describe him as the "lazy, easygoing husband" of the showboat's cook, Queenie (Hattie McDaniel). In one scene Queenie shouts at him: "You don't work like me, you don' act like the show folks, you don' work on the tow boat . . ." But he merely replies that "no matter what you say, ah still likes me." And he proceeds to sing a song that defends his laziness. Robeson's other number was the famous "Ol' Man River." He was much praised for his singing and acting, but he received strong criticism for the role itself, especially in the black press.[34]

As *The Emperor Jones,* Paul Robeson (at left) might bark out orders to a white man, but black hubris had its price in those days: his life. If Robeson thought that he could find roles more to his liking on the other side of the Atlantic, he was mistaken. Above, he played Bosambo, an enlightened African chief, in the British *Sanders of the River*. But the 'Bo' might as well have been silent. (The Museum of Modern Art/Film Stills Library) (National Film Archive)

Between 1936 and 1940 Robeson appeared in four other English films: *Song of Freedom, Big Fella, King Solomon's Mines,* and *The Proud Valley*. Although they were an improvement in terms of the characters he portrayed, only *King Solomon's Mines* (Gaumont British, 1937) achieved wide distribution. In this screen version of H. Rider Haggard's novel Robeson portrayed Umbopa, the white hunter's servant who turns out to be the rightful king of the country where they discover the legendary mines. Robeson saw to it that the character was more than just a splendid savage, and black critics did find the character a refreshing alternative to the usual movie African. But the same cannot be said of the lesser black characters in *King Solomon's Mines:* one critic indicated, "Robeson's ideals were lost in the rough and tumble of the film studio."[35]

Robeson's last English film was *The Proud Valley,* produced by Michael Balcon in 1940; as he later stated, "it was the one film I could be proud of having played in." His role was that of David Goliath, a one-time American miner and ship's stoker whose quest for work takes him to Wales. He finds a job in the mines, becomes an important member of the local community, helps the village choir to win a singing prize, and assists the family he boards with when the father is killed in an accident. In a subsequent disaster he sacrifices his life to save his fellow miners. The film suffers by comparison with some of the other films about life in Welsh mining communities produced at the time, but for all its crudeness, staginess, and excessive sentimentality, *The Proud Valley* was a powerful drama and one that did give Robeson a unique chance to play a role significantly different from the usual stereotype.[36]

Robeson returned to the United States when the war broke out, and in his last feature film, he once again found himself imprisoned in a stereotyped character and setting. *Tales of Manhattan* (Twentieth Century-Fox, 1942) was a multi-episode film about a dress suit and what happens to those who come into contact with it. In the film's final sequence the now-tattered suit, its pockets bulging with loot from a robbery, is thrown out of an airplane. Luke (Robeson), a black sharecropper, and his wife find the money, which they regard as manna from heaven. They take the money to the black parson of the wretchedly poor black community they live in; he declares that "de good Lawd done sent it fo' a

Christmas present fo' all de people in dis heah place." Part of the money is used to fulfill the prayers of the poor blacks for shoes, "good vittles," and "a blanket wat ain't got no holes." Luke suggests that the bulk of the windfall be used to buy the land they all work so that "dere won't be no rich an' no mo' po'." The chance to speak out about economic security apparently had induced the socially conscious Robeson to accept the role after turning down many other Hollywood offers since his return from Europe. But the character's brave words notwithstanding, various black groups attacked Robeson so violently that he volunteered to picket theaters showing the movie.

Other actors tried, but largely failed, to alter the stereotypes that had so restricted Robeson. Eddie Anderson, for one,

Eddie Anderson played Jack Benny's valet Rochester. Benny might be the star on radio, but in the movies the feeling persisted that the black supporting actor was the real drawing card. (From the motion picture *Man About Town.* /Courtesy of Universal Pictures)

achieved considerable prominence in the late 1930s as Jack
Benny's sassy valet-chauffeur, Rochester. He occasionally out-
smarted his boss and was obviously no Uncle Tom, but Rochester
was still a servant and there were limits to how far he could go.
Anderson led a checkered show-business career before becoming
Rochester. He had played in vaudeville, worked in nightclubs,
and appeared in a number of movies. His most notable role had
been Noah in *The Green Pastures*. In 1937, when Jack Benny
traveled to Hollywood to make a movie, he decided to build his
regular Sunday night radio show around his train trip west.
Anderson took the part of Rochester Van Jones, a porter on the
train. The "Van Jones" was dropped when the Pullman porter
was transformed into a valet-chauffeur, a role that Anderson
played for years both on the radio and in the movies. Paramount
quickly recognized how much Rochester bolstered the weak box-
office draw of Benny, who was not at his best in the movies. In
1940 the studio premiered *Buck Benny Rides Again* at a Harlem
theater the day before it opened at the New York Paramount.
One movie exhibitor echoed the feelings of many in the business
when he reported that "I don't think Benny has enough on the
ball to carry a show without . . . Rochester."[37]

One thing can be said for this period: the practice of having
whites play black roles died out almost completely. There were a
few instances such as *Big Boy*, a 1930 Warners' production in
which Al Jolson played a faithful Negro jockey. But Jolson's
desire to play De Lawd in *The Green Pastures* came to nothing,
perhaps because of black opposition. As the drama critic Burns
Mantle commented, if Jolson were cast in the role then Eddie
Cantor should play Gabriel, Amos 'n' Andy should be Noah and
Moses, and Texas Guinan should be Eve "with her girls doubling
as the angels and the heavenly choir."[38]

But an end to whites being cast in black roles did not result in
any real economic benefits for black actors and actresses. There
were simply too few black roles, and they paid relatively little.
Eddie Anderson and Paul Robeson commanded good salaries for
their movie work, and so did some other blacks such as Rex
Ingram, who reported receiving $2,500 a week for playing the
Genie of the Lamp in Alexander Korda's production of *The Thief
of Bagdad* (1940). But Harry Gray, who played the old preacher
in *Hallelujah*, initially refused to accept the part because he was

offered a salary of only $60 a week, less than he earned from his job as a janitor. Eventually this offer was more than doubled, but it was only a fraction of what a white actor would have received for a comparable part. The black performers brought to Hollywood for *The Green Pastures* received such small salaries that their pay became an object of public discussion; the New York *Amsterdam News* reported that some black talent in that film was being paid as low as $3.50 a day. The total paid to black movie performers in 1935 amounted to less than $75,000.

In most other respects blacks also continued to receive shabby treatment from the industry. Few received billing for their parts. Credits meant money in Hollywood, but except for the musical entertainers appearing "as themselves," most black players remained anonymous. At the studios, moreover, Jim Crow policies were the rule. Not until 1939, for instance, were the "white" and "colored" signs removed from the Selznick and Universal studios. This attitude also manifested itself among studio employees. On the MGM lot a white laborer told the actress Nina Mae Mc-Kinney not to forget her place and to "remember you are a nigger . . ."[39]

Blacks gained little from the introduction of sound. True, there was some additional work available for black performers, especially those who could sing, dance, or play jazz. And a few blacks did manage to achieve some kind of second-class standing in the industry. But this limited distinction came in stereotyped roles. In 1935 the New York *Age* in a despairing editorial on "Negro movie characters" asked when the motion picture industry would have the "guts and moral courage" to stop pandering to society's "prejudices and fanaticism." That question would not even begin to be answered positively for many years.[40]

In the interests of the war effort, Hollywood occasionally deigned to tip a helmet to racial harmony. The token black in *Bataan* (1943), played by Kenneth Spencer (front row, center) fought bravely but spent a lot of time humming "The St. Louis Blues." (From the MGM release "Bataan" © 1943 Loew's Incorporated. © renewed 1970 Metro-Goldwyn-Mayer Inc.)

6

A LIMITED RESPONSE

ALTHOUGH HOLLYWOOD FILMS before Pearl Harbor tended to be cautious in their treatment of World War II, once the country was formally involved the industry unstintingly backed the war effort and its announced goals. For the coming four years, the on-screen population of the United States would fight a heroic battle to preserve democracy's "Four Freedoms." If there were few black participants in these films, the industry did at least try to heed the advice of the Office of War Information to "stress national unity" and to "show colored soldiers in crowd scenes."[1]

Yet even as American propaganda castigated Axis racism, the traditional stereotypes of the movie black failed to disappear. Producer David O. Selznick's approach to publicizing *Since You Went Away* typified the industry's attitude toward the black during the war years. In March, 1944, his public relations staff released a statement to the black press about the film, which was scheduled to premiere shortly. According to the release, *Since You Went Away* would show the home front activities of "all" Americans. Selznick, it continued, felt that "not enough attention had been paid to the colored Americans who fight and die for their country and work and live in it." The movie proved to be a banal and melodramatic view of the effects of the war upon an American family called the Hiltons while the man is away in the armed forces. The only prominent black role was played by Hattie McDaniel, as the Hilton cook, Fidelia: she "satisfied all that anyone could possibly desire of a Negro in . . . restive times," James Agee ironically noted. For not only did Fidelia "keep strict union hours on the job she takes when Mrs. Hilton can no longer afford her," she then hustled back to the Hiltons' to get in her day's measure of malapropisms, comic relief, mother wit, and free labor.[2]

The Selznick organization may have been cynical in publicizing this film as they did, though it is true that *Since You Went Away* did contain shots of a black working alongside Mrs. Hilton as she did her welding work. But for the most part, the industry continued to demean blacks whenever it bothered to take note of them, making, in Dalton Trumbo's words, "tarts of the Negro's daughters, crap shooters of his sons, obsequious Uncle Toms of his fathers, superstitious and grotesque crones of his mothers, strutting peacocks of his successful men, psalm-singing mountebanks of his priests, and Barnum and Bailey side-shows of his religion."[3]

Veteran black performers like Clarence Muse (who offered an inconsequential comic relief in Columbia's 1944 *Jam Session*) had no option but to accept such parts if they wanted to work. Less well-established black actors and actresses began to lose even that option during the war years. Avenelle Harris, for example, had appeared as dancer, extra, and chorus girl in numerous movies after her first screen appearance in 1936 as one of a group standing behind a black-face Al Jolson in Warners' *The Singing Kid*. When the movie industry turned to war themes, the type of film she had appeared in stopped being made. Along with many other black extras and bit players, the sexy, good-looking Harris found it almost impossible to find work in films. Before the war over three hundred black performers had paid dues regularly to the Screen Actors Guild and to the extras union. By mid-1946 this number had dwindled to less than half that, and Harris had not received a casting call for two years.

One of the last films Avenelle Harris appeared in was the 1943 MGM film version of the successful all-black musical *Cabin in the Sky*, which had been a smash hit on Broadway. Much of the superb John Latouche-Vernon Duke score was retained, and several new numbers by E. Y. Harburg and Harold Arlen were added, including "Happiness Is a Thing Called Joe," which was marvelously rendered by Ethel Waters. The music remains the most winning aspect of the movie, which has little plot to speak of. *Cabin in the Sky* is the story of Little Joe Jackson, a weak-willed but loveable sinner. He fantasizes that the forces of Heaven and Hell in the persons of the Lord's General and Lucifer, Jr., are competing for his soul. That Little Joe has any chance at all for heavenly grace is due to the "powerful" praying of his wife Petunia. For a while the devil's minions seem to have the edge, especially after Lucifer, Jr., arranges for Joe to win a large sum gambling and for the seductive Georgia Brown to work her wiles on him. Petunia's love falters briefly and Joe seems lost for eternity. But in the end, Petunia does a little vamping of her own, and the forces of right carry the day.

The director, Vincente Minnelli, did manage to soften some of the more outrageous stereotypes of the stage show: for instance, the line "eating fried chicken all the time" was deleted from the title song. In the brawl scenes the razors traditionally flashed by screen blacks were absent. Though years later a black film critic could describe *Cabin in the Sky* as "the most acceptable all-Negro movie musical ever made," it is also not difficult to agree with the contemporary critic who called the movie "a stale insult." The foreword to the film may have proclaimed that "The folklore of America has origins . . . in all races, all colors. This story . . . seeks to capture these values." But in fact the values caught were ones that had exasperated blacks for decades. The movie contained the standard sequences of ecstatic psalm-shouting and jubilant crap-shooting. Black women were either old and dowdy or young and lascivious. The aides of Lucifer, Jr., (played by Mantan Moreland, Willie Best, Fletcher "Monk" Rivers, and Leon "Poke" James) spoke in ungrammatical dialect. In emphasizing the superstitious aspects of black religion, the movie was reminiscent of the inanities of *The Green Pastures*. And so one black reviewer complained at the time, there was the usual patronizing approach to the problem of "what filmdom thinks the colored vein of happiness should be."[4]

In addition to Ethel Waters as Petunia, the leads included Eddie Anderson as Joe, Rex Ingram as Lucifer, Jr., Kenneth Spencer as the Lord's General, and Lena Horne as Georgia Brown. Although comparatively well known at the time, Horne was far from being the established star that she has since become. As a teenager in the early 1930s, she had sung and danced in the chorus line of Harlem's Cotton Club; she had later worked as a vocalist with various orchestras, and had gone on to score enormous successes as a nightclub performer. In 1938, she had appeared in an obscure all-black film, *The Duke is Tops,* made for ghetto audiences only. Four years later, MGM, the most important studio in the industry, had signed her to a long-term contract: she thus attained a degree of security rare among black performers.

At MGM Lena Horne encountered many of the same difficulties that even the most notable black performers had to face until well after the end of the war. The studio first tested the light-skinned, stunningly beautiful singer for a maid's role opposite Eddie Anderson in a comedy melodrama. To make her skin color as dark as Anderson's, she recalled, she was smeared with so much makeup that she looked like "some white person trying to do a part in blackface." Ultimately the makeup department worked out a shade dubbed "Light Egyptian." Horne did not "feel too good or too proud" for such roles but felt it "essential . . . to try to establish a different kind of image for Negro women."[5]

She did not plead for special privileges. "All we ask," she said in 1943, "is that the Negro be portrayed as a normal person." Her efforts in this regard were as futile as they were strenuous. In her first MGM movie, *Panama Hattie* (1942), she did a rumba number that had nothing to do with the plot. The bulk of Miss Horne's movie work consisted of such cameo numbers. (Not until 1969, in fact, years after her MGM contract had ended, did she get to play a purely dramatic role. In the Universal western *Death of a Gunfighter* she played a madam who was the mistress of an ill-fated white marshal; no mention was made of her race.)[6]

Lena Horne played only one other role that was not merely the standard cameo bit for black entertainers. That was in *Stormy Weather*, released by Twentieth Century-Fox in 1943. This film was the story of a black dancer, engagingly portrayed by Bill Robinson (whose career between the wars the story line somewhat paralleled). It was Lena Horne whom Robinson wooed for most of the movie, finally winning and wedding her. The plot was unexceptional, but this show business cavalcade splendidly displayed the talents of such performers as Fats Waller, Cab Calloway, Katherine Dunham, Ada Brown, and the Nicholas Brothers. Inevitably, there were aspects of the movie that verged on the ridiculous and the patronizing. William Grant Still, a

Lena Horne's long-term contract with MGM gave her a degree of security rare among black performers. Still, her roles involved more singing, as here in *The Ziegfeld Follies,* than acting. (From the MGM release "Ziegfeld Follies" © 1946 Loew's Incorporated. © renewed 1973 Metro-Goldwyn-Mayer Inc.)

"Play it again, Sam": As Humphrey Bogart's musical sidekick in *Casablanca* (1942), Dooley Wilson gave one of the few memorable movie performances by a black during the 1940s. Sidney Greenstreet peers over Wilson's shoulder, right. (National Film Archive/Courtesy United Artists)

black composer of stature whose works included a well-received symphony, resigned as the film's music supervisor in protest against studio attitudes that, he said, "degraded colored people." Still charged that some of his orchestrations for post–World War I music were thrown out because, according to the studio's white music director, "Negro bands didn't play that well then."

Still also assailed the studio for emphasizing "crude" black music and "erotic" black dancing, and for frustrating attempts to counter the "Hollywood stereotype as regards colored people."[7]

And yet, that stereotype was beginning to be occasionally shattered. In the 1943 Twentieth Century-Fox film *The Ox-Bow Incident,* for example, a black man (sensitively played by Leigh Whipper) is one of the few members of a posse who unsuccessfully oppose the lynching of three supposed cattle-rustling murderers, all of whom later turn out to be innocent. And in *Casablanca* (Warners, 1942), Humphrey Bogart's piano-playing black companion, Sam (well enacted by Dooley Wilson), is by the standards of the day a refreshing alternative to the usual shuffling movie black. Another Warners film, *In This Our Life* (1942), for the most part a typical Bette Davis melodrama, is extraordinary for one unexpected reason — its presentation of black characters. Although *In This Our Life* had the predictable accoutrements of the cinematic South, including Hattie Mc-Daniel in her usual mammy role, the film made some very frank references to the kind of injustice that often was legally meted out to blacks. The potential victim, moreover, was presented as an intelligent and ambitious young black (Ernest Anderson), who is attending night school to become a lawyer. When a spoiled and selfish woman, played by Davis, runs down and kills someone with her car, she claims that the black law student was driving. In a confrontation at the jail she tells him that since no one will take his word against that of a white woman, he might as well "take the rap." Ultimately the Davis character gets her just desserts and the innocent young man is freed. For perhaps the first time, *In This Our Life* had brought to the screen what one enthusiastic black newspaperwoman called "the formerly taboo subject of a white girl framing a colored boy."[8]

It was in the war movies, however, that the portrayal of the black differed most sharply from the usual caricatures. To be sure, the industry slavishly followed the policy of segregation then practiced by the military, and it was rare to find a black among the roster of minorities who seemed to form the Hollywood version of the American fighting forces. Yet the cycle of war movies did not completely overlook blacks. One interesting example was *Crash Dive* (Twentieth Century-Fox, 1943), in which Ben Carter played a messman on a submarine — official

Navy policy early in the war limiting blacks to menial tasks. Even though the character retained many of the movie black's less attractive characteristics, he did get a chance to show his mettle against the enemy and to save the life of the star, Tyrone Power. A somewhat different example is the character Rex Ingram portrayed in the 1943 Columbia movie *Sahara*. Tambul was presented as a non-com in one of the Allied colonial units fighting in the North African desert, but he finds himself joining a small contingent of Americans, British, and a Frenchman who have banded together in an attempt to get through the Axis lines. During their fight to hold a key oasis against a much larger German force, Tambul is mortally wounded. He dies, but not before he has chased and killed in hand-to-hand combat an arrogant Nazi captive who was trying to inform his compatriots that the oasis was dry and not worth a fight.

An inordinate amount of public-relations hoopla was made of any black participation in a war film during these years. And while it was true that black characters were generally endowed with various noble and indubitably patriotic virtues, the roles also contained features of the caricatures that had so long demeaned the race on screen. In *Bataan* (MGM, 1943) a black soldier is one of a group of thirteen who die one by one as they fight a holding action against a much larger force of Japanese. The black soldier fires away as stalwartly as the others; indeed, he is the workhorse of the group. Yet he is clearly in a junior, and inferior, position at all times. He places explosive charges under instruction from his partner, who wires them and pushes the plunger. He is present during discussions about whether to continue fighting or to withdraw, but speaks out only once — to reaffirm his faith in the United States. And he spends a good part of his on-screen time humming "St. Louis Blues." The black in *Bataan* is as much a stereotyped symbol as any of the other thirteen (who include a Filipino, a Pole, etc.), but still there is something different about him.

Alfred Hitchcock's *Lifeboat* (released by Twentieth Century-Fox in 1944) is another war movie in which a black is treated as part of a cross-section of humanity, which in this case includes a capitalist, a communist stoker, and a famous woman correspondent, and the black crewman, Joe. The setting for the entire film is a lifeboat containing eight survivors from a torpedoed vessel, as

Canada Lee, playing the cook in Alfred Hitchcock's *Lifeboat* (1943), passes out hardtack to one of the survivors of his torpedoed ship. (National Film Archive/Courtesy Twentieth Century–Fox. © 1944 Twentieth Century–Fox Film Corporation)

well as the commander of the U-boat that sank their ship, the U-boat having been sunk in return. In such confined quarters Joe should logically be seen on screen more than he is. Well played by Canada Lee (a boxer who successfully turned actor), Joe is never really part of the group. When the suvivors vote on various decisions, Joe abstains for no discernible reason. He is made "head of commissary," which, as one scholar has pointed out, is a "janitorial position": "On a nearly barren life-boat that is to say that he has been given no job at all." Moreover, Joe is presented as an adept if reformed pickpocket.[9]

This somewhat dualistic approach was also evident in *The Negro Soldier* (1944), an army orientation film that was also distributed to the public. It was produced by the noted Hollywood director Frank Capra as one of the many wartime propaganda films he made for the army. Carlton Moss, a young black radio writer who, according to Capra, "wore his blackness as conspicuously as a bandaged head," researched and wrote *The Negro Soldier*. Though most of Moss's anguished fervor was lost in the finished product, the movie did point out, even if somewhat superficially, that blacks had played a role in the development of the United States. The film begins with closeups of various churches, until finally the audience sees one that black worshipers are entering. In preaching to his congregation, the black minister, played by Moss, narrates much of the film and talks about how black Americans have defended liberty since the death of Crispus Attucks in the Boston Massacre. Also highlighted are the contributions of notable blacks, ranging from scientist George Washington Carver to track star Jesse Owens, to the culture of the United States. A substantial portion of the film described the accomplishments of black troops in World War II. Capra smoothed the transition into this footage through a neat, if somewhat glib, device: a mother at the church service reads a letter from her son detailing his situation from induction through preparation for Officers' Candidate School.[10]

The Negro Soldier treated the black with more respect than commercial movies ever had. Instead of the handkerchief-headed, dialect-crooning mammy there was a black mother (no different in dress or demeanor from her white counterpart) who expressed concern and pride about her GI son. Instead of the usual popeyed, superstitious buffoon there was an intelligent young black recruit who qualifies for officer training. Capra was understandably proud of this film. But for all its merits, *The Negro Soldier* was, as one critic said, "pitifully, painfully mild." It was a Jim Crow film, reflecting the segregation practiced by the Army. None of the real problems faced by blacks in military service were touched on. Relations between the races, whether in the armed forces or in civilian life, received no real examination. No doubt to avoid bruising Southern feelings, *The Negro Soldier* barely touched on the Civil War, in which over two hundred thousand blacks fought in the Union army. Moreover, the War Department allowed the industry to handle the distribution of the film in the most gingerly way possible. Instead of being distributed by a major studio, it was parceled out to a number of distributors in various regions of the country; the film then was made available to those exhibitors who requested it.[11]

Meanwhile, in many other nonfeature films, the old caricatures persisted. As in World War I, the newsreels used black troops for comic relief, if they showed them at all. And this attitude also found expression in the films made for agencies such as the Red Cross. Its 1944 fund-raising short *At Their Side* presented war as a serious business for everybody except the clownish black troops.

During the war years and immediately afterward the National Association for the Advancement of Colored People periodically intensified its continuing campaign to break such stereotypes. The organization strove to win for blacks "roles in motion pictures more in keeping with their status and contribution to American life and culture." Perhaps its most dramatic effort came in 1942 during the organization's annual meeting, held that year in Los Angeles. The California location made possible private conferences between NAACP executive secretary Walter White and industry executives, and these talks were climaxed by what White recalled as "a magnificent luncheon" (which was formally hosted by Walter Wanger and Darryl Zanuck) on the Twentieth Century-Fox lot. White's friend Wendell Willkie, who was counsel to the industry as well as one of the principal speakers at the annual meeting, helped arrange the talks. At the luncheon White and Willkie addressed a select group of seventy producers, directors, and other important filmland figures. White pointed out that the NAACP "did not ask that Negroes be pictured as superhuman heroes"; all that it asked was that "Hollywood . . . have courage enough to shake off . . . fears and taboos and . . . depict the Negro in films as a normal human being and an integral part" of American life. Willkie took a much tougher stand. He castigated the film industry for fostering anti-Americanism abroad through its caricaturing of nonwhites, and he declared that the industry had to give the black "a better break." Willkie bluntly concluded his remarks by asserting that "many of the persons responsible for Hollywood films" belonged to "a racial and religious group which had been the target of Hitler" and argued that "they should be the last to be guilty of doing to another minority the things which had been done to them."[12]

Immediately after the luncheon the NAACP was given assurances by industry figures that blacks would receive fairer treatment on screen. Zanuck, then a vice president of Twentieth

Century-Fox, publicly urged that "the program of casting colored persons in more normal roles be put into effect at an early date." Will Hays, head of the industry's trade organization, expressed complete agreement with such a program, as did producers Sam Goldwyn and Sol Lesser. In expressing his support, MGM vice president Al Lichtman asserted that "I will do my utmost in whatever way I can in helping this cause." Jack Warner stated that his studio had scheduled several films for production in which "we will definately portray the colored . . . the same as any other human being is portrayed."[13]

But what really could be expected of an industry that still passed out studio publicity releases that had Ella Fitzgerald supposedly responding to a compliment on a performance with: "I'se glad I done okay, this job sho am going to change my mode of livin"? An industry where a director for the musical *This Is The Army* (Warners, 1943) could shout "Okay, bring on the white soldiers! Bring on the nigger troops!" Before long, many industry figures hardly wanted to be reminded of the assurances they had given. A survey taken some months after the luncheon for White and Willkie by a member of the black press found the heads of MGM, Twentieth Century-Fox, Universal, and RKO unavailable for comment. Sam Goldwyn referred all inquiries to the head of his public-relations staff. Paramount executives carefully hedged their answers. Perhaps the most interesting response came from an unidentified Columbia Pictures spokesman. He pointed to *Sahara* and *None Shall Escape* (a 1944 movie in which a black was one of the judges in a war crimes trial) as instances of the studio's good faith, but admitted that Columbia's record was "not perfect." He added that "as long as there are colored persons . . . willing to play Uncle Tom roles or through buffoonery . . . to barter the dignity of their race, it seems likely that Uncle Toms and buffoonery will continue."[14]

It was not surprising that the actors who played such "Tom" roles strongly resented the NAACP efforts. In January, 1943, the Baltimore *Afro-American* held a round-table discussion at Ben Carter's home in Hollywood on the role of the black in the industry. Some of the more prominent black actors and actresses attended. The participants all agreed that "the NAACP and other pressure groups should keep their noses out of Hollywood." Clarence Muse called the NAACP approach "wrong and ill-advised." He did admit that "colored should have better roles" but argued that if the NAACP was "sincere it would first have consulted the performers." Comparing their situation to that of Booker T. Washington and other black leaders in disfavor, Muse concluded that "those whom the race would destroy they first call Uncle Tom." Most of the participants were more restrained in their comments. Hattie McDaniel, for example, said that "I know there is much room for improvement but having been part and parcel of this industry I have seen great strides made." Carter asserted that "there is less discrimination in the motion picture industry than in any other profession including the government, as far as established actors are concerned." He then related how, while on location in New England for *Crash Dive,* the company manager had insisted that he be given accommodations "equal to any member of the cast."[15]

There was an understandable element of fear in these remarks, fear that the NAACP effort to upgrade characterizations might result in less work. Lillian Randolph, who had become known for her maid parts in the movies, and who was featured as a housekeeper in the radio comedy series *The Great Gildersleeve,* declared that the NAACP effort to end the stereotyping of blacks as servants had nearly resulted in her replacement by a white actress in a movie based on the radio show: "I was given the role . . . only when the star of the radio show who had worked with me for years refused to work with a white . . . because it completely changed his conception of the role . . ."[16]

Resentment was also expressed against those black performers who accepted or supported the NAACP campaign. Lena Horne was one. Because of her outspokenness and her friendship with White and other militant blacks, she was labeled "a tool of the NAACP" and "an Eastern upstart." At one point Hattie McDaniel invited Horne to her home, and made a point of telling the young entertainer how difficult it had been until then for blacks who worked in the industry. Though McDaniel expressed sympathy and understanding for her position, Horne later recalled that "in a large part of the Hollywood Negro community I was never warmly received."[17]

Segments of the established black acting community also spoke out strongly against White and the NAACP when he renewed his efforts immediately after the war. In early 1946 White talked

with studio executives and revealed plans for an NAACP Hollywood office that would consult in an advisory capacity with filmmakers on scripts before production. White and other NAACP officials, aware that the organization lacked the strength to censor films, hoped that the prospect of an endorsement of those movies that did not demean Negro characters would induce producers "to treat the Negro in a fair and sensible way."[18]

While in Hollywood White held a dinner for Carter, Muse, McDaniel, Beavers, and other black performers to tell them about the proposed new office and its purpose. (The ineffectuality of this type of action became clear five years later in 1951, when the NAACP issued a twelve-point protest against the establishment of the *Amos 'n' Andy* television series. The protest had absolutely no effect, and the program retained its prime-time niche; not until 1966 did CBS stop syndicating reruns of *Amos 'n' Andy*.) Many of those present asserted that such an office would place their livelihood in jeopardy and that White should have consulted them before initiating any action. Charles Butler, who was described by the black press as "the only Negro casting director" and who for years had handled almost all calls for black extras and bit parts, declared that the NAACP attitude would result in black roles being cut from films. Butler, who obviously had a great personal stake in the matter, pontificated that "Hollywood is a place for commercializing, not social propagandizing." Such statements helped to stall the NAACP proposal and played into the hands of those who opposed any change in the on-screen image of the black. In defending the industry, Charles Metzger, a white lawyer and a member of the Production Code administration, referred to these anti-NAACP statements. He spoke of "the previous harmonious and profitable relationship" between black performers and the studios and argued that "producers have exercised extreme care as to the proper showing of racial groups."

Mantan Moreland, above, makes ready to bolt from a morgue in a Charlie Chan mystery. Below, an unremembered black actor is one of death's slaves in *I Walked with a Zombie* (1942). Grotesque stereotypes like these were at last beginning to draw protests. (Courtesy RKO General, Inc.)

White's answer was that "employment at any cost" was a mistake. The NAACP, he declared, did not take the position that blacks should never be shown as servants or clowns. On the contrary, the organization's position was only that they should not be limited to such roles and "should be pictured as normal human beings playing an integral . . . role in the life of America."[19]

White's statements seemed in fact to be representative of a growing sentiment in the black community. The mail response to the 1943 *Afro-American* round-table discussion had been both heavy and hostile to the attitudes expressed by the performers. The tenor of much of this mail is exemplified by a letter from a Washington, D. C., resident who said that "if Clarence Muse, Hattie McDaniel, and others can't make a living any other way than accepting roles reflecting adversely on the race, then let 'em get on relief." A wartime poll by the *Negro Digest* found that while 53 percent of whites queried said that the movies were fair to the black, 93 percent of the blacks questioned thought otherwise. In New Guinea during the summer of 1945 large numbers of black troops walked out of movies that they felt depicted their race unfairly.[20]

During these years comment of a different sort came from some Southern censorship boards. These boards always had been sensitive to any movie in which blacks were shown in other than a servile or comic position, and they had prevented some movies from being exhibited, while requiring cuts in others. In the more relaxed postwar atmosphere most of these boards did ease their restrictions. An exception was the Memphis board, whose outrageous rulings may have done as much to highlight the problem of how blacks should be depicted as any NAACP campaign. Under the direction of Lloyd T. Binford, an energetic octogenarian who had been its chairman since 1928, the Memphis board required the deletion of Lena Horne sequences from various MGM musicals because, in Binford's words, "there are plenty of good white singers." Cab Calloway and his band were excised from a 1945 film in which they appeared because Binford considered them "inimical to public health, safety, morals, and welfare." The Memphis censor also ordered cut from MGM's *The Sailor Takes a Wife* (1946) a scene in which a white actor tips his hat to a black. Sometimes the cuts ordered by Binford's board were so extensive that the distributor decided against showing the incomprehensible footage that remained. Alternatively, as with the revival of *Imitation of Life* (which had been approved when first exhibited in the Memphis area) Binford simply had the film banned. Another typical example of Binfordism is the case of the 1947 Hal Roach film *Curly,* an innocuous little comedy about a schoolteacher, which had been approved without a single cut by boards throughout the country. The distributor was notified by Binford that the Memphis board was "unable to approve your picture with the little negroes as the South does not permit negroes in white schools nor recognize social equality among the races even in children."[21]

Caught between the rulings of censorship boards like that of Memphis and the proddings of the NAACP, industry executives became increasingly aware that a new approach to the depiction of the black was needed. But exactly what that new approach should be proved difficult to define, and in time-honored Hollywood fashion producers met the problem head on by ignoring it completely. Rather than cast blacks as ordinary people doing ordinary jobs, the studio executives gave orders to "write out" black characters as far as possible. As a result, there was a further drop in the employment of black actors and actresses in the postwar period. Appearing on a radio program with an NAACP official early in 1952, Dore Schary, then MGM production head, spoke with pride of what he called "the job that Hollywood had done in ridding most films of objectionable casting of Negroes." He did, however, remark that an unfortunate side effect of this had been the number of black performers thrown out of work.[22]

Probably the best-documented instance of "writing out" occurred in 1947 at Paramount and concerned a movie called *Hazard.* This film was based on a novel by Roy Chanslor, who also wrote the screen adaptation. According to Chanslor, he was asked by the studio to change a black character to a white one. This character, a porter who was also a Sunday-school teacher, was presented in the novel as a person of perception and education far above his employment. Chanslor told the *New York Times* that Paramount had ordered the change because the studio's "New York office feared southern censorship." The studio replied that the rulings of Binford and others had nothing to do with the matter and that the change had been ordered "because Negroes have objected . . . to depiction of members of the race as menials in films."[23]

Meanwhile many of the traditional stereotypes continued to find their way onto the screen until well into the 1950s. Blacks continued to be presented as maids and menials. Leigh Whipper was a caretaker in MGM's *Undercurrent* (1946) and a convict in *The Young Don't Cry* (Columbia, 1957); Clarence Muse played Whitey — a familiar groom role — in Paramount's horseracing musical *Riding High* (1950), and Louis Armstrong was used as comic relief in *Glory Alley* (MGM, 1952), when he was not playing his horn. Black actors continued to portray street vendors and servants. In films such as the Tarzan series, which were set in more exotic locales, blacks were once again cast as ignorant and superstitious savages who could not stand up to whites; in the Abbott and Costello vehicle *Africa Screams* (produced in 1949 by Huntington Hartford) they appear as inept comic menaces. And in costume pictures blacks were invariably shown as slaves. The dancer Carmen De Lavallande played a series of unbilled bits as a slave maiden or dancing girl in movies such as the Grade B Caribbean pirate drama *The Golden Hawk* (Columbia, 1950) and the Cinemascope epic *The Egyptian* (Twentieth Century-Fox, 1954). For all the much-vaunted end to stereotyped casting there were still black maids in such diverse movies as the comedy *Mr. Blandings Builds His Dream House* (RKO, 1948) and the Martin and Lewis *That's My Boy* (Paramount, 1951). The major studios no longer made use of Stepin Fetchit types in feature films, but until the early 1950s such characters appeared in animated shorts. Paramount's *Jasper* series dealt with a young black boy with a wide, white mouth and popeyes. He romped through adventures such as *Jasper and the Watermelons* and *Jasper and the Haunted House* with a scarecrow and a black crow who were braggarts in dialect, caricatures at their worst. In some of the Tom and Jerry cartoons released by MGM in the late 1940s and early 1950s there was a black maid who spoke an ungrammatical dialect: "Thomas," she says to the cat, who has once again failed to capture the mouse Jerry, "if you is a mouse catcher I is Lana Turner, which I ain't."

Perhaps the most blatant example of the use of an older stereotype was Walt Disney's *Song of the South* (1946). A central figure in this film was Uncle Remus, attacked in an angry *Ebony* editorial as an "Uncle Tom-Aunt Jemima caricature complete with all the fawning standard equipment thereof: the toothy smile, battered hat, grey beard, and a profusion of 'dis' and 'dat' talk." A combination of live action and cartoon, the production dealt with a lonely little white boy who comes to spend a summer in the 1870s with his grandmother on her plantation. His parents are estranged and he is troubled. Uncle Remus with his tales of Brers Rabbit, Fox, and Bear helps the boy to face his problems, which finally are resolved happily. Blacks strongly condemned the glorification of Uncle Remus. Clarence Muse, who had been hired to help prepare the story, quit after his suggestions for upgrading the image of the black in this film were rejected. The man who had once called the NAACP approach "ill-advised" now spoke out against the Disney movie as "detrimental to the cultural advancement of the Negro people." Another black performer turned down the proffered role on the grounds that the film would "set back my people many years." Once it was released *Song of the South* was picketed more heavily than any film since *The Birth of a Nation* and was the subject of much criticism. All the agitation was to no avail. The movie was a substantial profit-maker for Disney. And James Baskett, who portrayed Uncle Remus, was awarded a special Oscar in 1947 "for his able and heart warming characterization."[24]

The industry also continued to grind out films in which blacks were used in specialty numbers only. For instance, singer Billy Eckstine made his movie debut in the 1952 MGM film *Skirts Ahoy* playing himself in a nightclub scene. This film also had a snappy drill number performed by sixteen black women who were cast as a crack Navy WAVE precision marching team. "The story of the WAVES," said the film's producer, "would be incomplete without the colored girls who serve their country," yet this segregated drill sequence was made at the very time that the Navy was integrating its units.[25]

The immediate postwar years also saw the production of a handful of movies whose treatment of the black began to diverge from the traditional stereotypes. Among the more unusual was *Till the End of Time* (RKO, 1946), a well-intentioned but weak movie that attempted to deal with the problems faced by war veterans. At one point two Marine veterans are in a bar playing a pinball machine with a black soldier when they are approached by an organizer for a veterans group. From his line of talk it becomes clear that the group is fascist and racist, and a fight ensues. The point that the movie tried to make somewhat mawkishly was that postwar America had no room for racial or religious prejudice. The 1947 Enterprise production *Body and Soul* dealt with boxing and the rackets. Probably the most sympathetic male role was that played by Canada Lee. Of the role and the actor the *New York Times* movie reviewer wrote: "As a Negro exchamp who is meanly shoved aside, until one night he finally goes beserk and dies slugging in a deserted ring, he shows through great dignity and reticence the full measure of his inar-

In *Till the End of Time,* a 1946 film about the problems of returning veterans, Ernest Anderson (left) is befriended by another ex-Marine, Guy Madison (right). Meanwhile, Robert Mitchum prepares to make trouble. (Courtesy RKO General, Inc.)

A confident young black fighter (James Edwards) stops to wish an aging pugilist (Robert Ryan) good luck in *Set-up* (1949). (Courtesy RKO General, Inc.)

ticulate scorn for the greed of shrewder men who have enslaved him, sapped his strength, and then tossed him out to die."[26]

Another boxing film was a 1949 RKO release, the *Set-Up,* a downbeat movie about an aging fighter. One of the subsidiary characters was a young black boxer who was presented as splendidly confident and vital. Leaving the ring victorious as the older man arrives for his fight, the black pauses and wishes the aging fighter good luck. This action is in deliberate and highly effective contrast to the general tone of unpleasantness and corruption that pervades the film's background.

However, it was in postwar Europe, most notably in Italy, where the black image on screen first received a markedly different treatment. A number of films produced in Italy right after the war presented blacks very sympathetically. The most distinctive portrayal was to be found in *Paisan,* a film made during the winter of 1945-46 by Roberto Rossellini. This film (which achieved worldwide distribution) told of the effects of the Allied advance through Italy in six separate episodes. One episode dealt with a drunken black MP and a Naples street urchin. The boy takes the soldier to a street puppet show in which a Moor is the villain. The GI intervenes and tries to help the black puppet. Later the boy takes the GI across the rubble of Naples to a spot where the black can be robbed. The GI is full of tipsy idealizations of home and boasts how wonderful things are in America, but suddenly he ashamedly admits his home is a dirty shack in Mississippi, and he begins to fall asleep longing for that home. The boy, having come to like the GI, warns him that he will steal the soldier's boots if he falls asleep. The GI passes out and the boy takes the boots. The next day the GI catches the boy stealing goods from a truck and demands to be taken to the urchin's parents only to discover that the boy is a war orphan living in total squalor with hundreds of others in caves on the outskirts to the city. A crowd collects, and one of them offers the GI his boots. The black looks at the boy and the others in the crowd with rags around their feet. "Those are not my boots," he says, and drives away. The GI was played by Dots Johnson, an American black actor of limited experience, who was one of a group brought to Italy from the United States to play the roles of Americans in the film.

An Italian movie that painted a very different portrait of a black was *Without Pity,* filmed in 1948 by Alberto Lattuda. The film is set in and around the Italian city of Leghorn immediately after the war. A port of entry for American army supplies, it was a black market center that suffered from prostitution and crime. The main characters are Angela and Jerry, who first meet on a train going to the port. She has left her home in the country to look after her brother; he is a black GI attempting to desert. After being captured and tormented in jail by white MPs, he escapes and meets Angela again. By this time she has fallen victim to the corruption of the city and has become a prostitute. Their love transforms both their lives, and they plan to escape to Latin America, where they believe an interracial couple can survive. Jerry's attempt to obtain the necessary wherewithal involves him with the gangsters in the black market. Angela is killed shielding Jerry from the gangsters, and he in despair kills himself by driving a truck containing her body over a cliff. Although Jerry is presented as a forceful and attractive figure, the interracial romance is handled very delicately — there are no passionate scenes between Jerry and Angela. Jerry was played by John Kitzmiller, who became an actor while on occupation duty in Italy in 1946. He was playing poker in a sidewalk cafe when he was spotted by two Italians who thought him physically perfect for a war movie they were casting. So began a career that ended only with his death in 1965 and that included a part in the James Bond movie, *Goldfinger,* and the lead role in the 1960s German film production of *Uncle Tom's Cabin.*

A thoughtful but somewhat unsatisfactory English attempt to deal with the situation of the educated African who returns to his people ran into unfortunate distribution problems in the United States. Filmed both on location and in a studio, the Two Cities film *Men of Two Worlds* was released in Great Britain early in 1946. It was concerned with Kisenga, a talented composer and pianist who returns to his native Tanganyika, where he agrees to assist the English district commissioner in persuading his tribe to leave their disease-ridden traditional home region for a healthier area. Magole, the tribe's witch doctor, threatens disaster in the event of a move. Magole's power is heightened when, as he has predicted, Kisenga's father dies after being treated by white doctors. Kisenga remains contemptuous of the witch doctor and challenges his authority. The educated African finds himself engaged in a war of nerves with Magole. As the drums beat night after night and as Magole's followers chant and dance, Kisenga falls prey to the power of suggestion. Weakened by a touch of malaria, he takes to his bed and begins to express doubts and fears about his own methods. He finally snaps out of his decline when he hears some native children (whom he had taught) singing one of his choral compositions. Magole is defeated, and his hold on the people broken. The tribe moves and Kisenga determines to spend his life among them and work on their behalf.

Men of Two Worlds received a generally favorable reception among British critics, but it ran into problems in the United States. At the request of the NAACP, Universal, which had

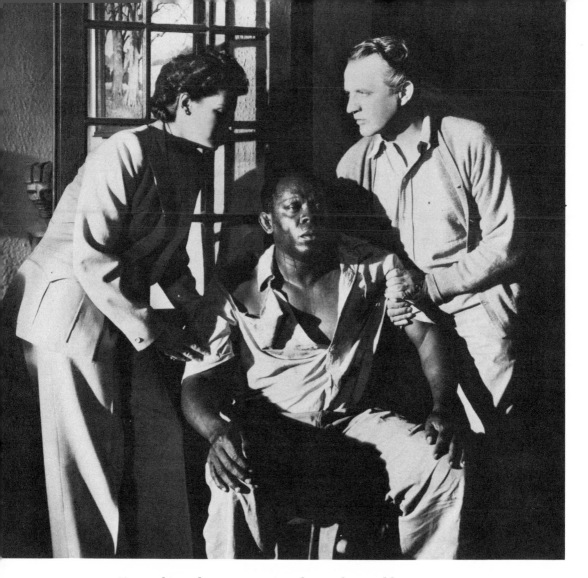

Two white characters assist the malaria-ridden black hero (Robert Adams) of the English *Men of Two Worlds* (1946). The film, retitled *Kisenga, Man of Africa*, was not released in America until 1952, for fear of offending southern audiences. (National Film Archive)

agreed to distribute the movie, held a private screening of the film for Eleanor Roosevelt as well as for representatives of the NAACP and other antidiscrimination groups. The Baltimore *Afro-American* reported that Mrs. Roosevelt and the others "condemned the final part of the film because it depicted . . .

Kisenga relapsing into elementary voodooism." The consensus was that the film (in *Variety*'s words) "would be objectionable to Negroes." *Variety* reported that probably "southern white sentiment would also have been unfavorable" because a black man was depicted as a crusader. The film was shelved, and it was not released in the United States until 1952 when International Releasing Corporation distributed it without fanfare as *Kisenga, Man of Africa*. It received few notices and did little business either under that title or as *Witch Doctor*.[27]

A much harsher foreign view of the situation of the black was presented in a Soviet film, *Harlem, U.S.A.* This movie, dubbed into English, found its way to the United States in 1952. It never achieved wide distribution but it did play to small groups. Harlem was shown as a black ghetto guarded by white police. According to *Variety*, the film had the "residents . . . beaten and not permitted to leave the area. Pets are prohibited. White merchants own all the retail establishments and all food sold has been condemned elsewhere."[28]

However outrageously exaggerated the premises of this film, it contained just enough truth to shed an uncomfortable light on Hollywood's treatment of blacks between the beginning of World War II and the desegregation decisions of the mid-1950s. Here the dishonesty of foreign propaganda serves to illuminate the dishonesty of American prejudice and timidity. Despite important if limited changes in the social, economic, and political situation of blacks in the United States and Africa during those years, the movie industry with few exceptions continued to relegate blacks to the same old inferior positions in its on-screen version of society. To be sure, the industry was in the business of making commercially successful movies and not in the profession of social reform. Nevertheless, it should have been able to accomplish more than the mere softening of degrading stereotypes, although even that action was a step forward. The older and more debasing stereotypes may have begun to disappear or change, but the movie industry generally continued to treat blacks — whether the movie was set in past or present, in the United States, Africa, or elsewhere — as objects rather than people. This proved true even of the films made in the late 1940s and early 1950s that claimed to deal with the problems of being black in the United States.

7

GLIMMERS
OF CHANGE

BY THE 1950s the film industry had considerably muted the
coarser, more unattractive image of the black. True, the same old
demeaning caricatures still did turn up. Take the 1957 Twentieth
Century-Fox production *The Enemy Below*, which dealt with a
duel between an American destroyer and a U-boat. A black is
shown only once: coming out of the galley to dump garbage
overboard, he sees a torpedo passing the ship. His eyes grow
large; he makes some strange noises, and, flinging the garbage
into the air, runs back into the galley. But on the whole, the
industry, which was increasingly concerned with maintaining its
audience in the face of competition from television, responded to
the mounting pressure from outspoken individuals and from such
organizations as the NAACP.

One manifestation of this changing attitude — it could almost
be called a milestone — was a cycle of "racially aware" pictures
made in 1949 and 1950, which at least touched on the problem of
being black in the United States. These movies, however, presented no real solutions to the questions that they somewhat
artificially raised. Nor did the industry produce them out of any
genuine sympathy with the civil-rights movement then gaining
strength — it was in 1948, after all, that the inclusion of a civil-
rights plank in the Democratic platform split the party in a
Presidential election year and that the Supreme Court ruled that
racially restrictive covenants violated the 14th Amendment to the
Constitution. Rather, the studios were attempting to capitalize

Birth of a superstar: In 1950 Sidney Poitier made his
debut as a young intern in *No Way Out*. (National
Film Archive/Courtesy Twentieth Century–Fox. ©
1950 Twentieth Century–Fox Film Corporation)

on a situation summed up by a *Variety* headline: "More Adult Pix Key To Top Coin." The industry was beginning to feel the first impact of TV; between 1946 and 1949, its profits slid 45 percent. Movies with so-called "adult" themes such as anti-Semitism, juvenile delinquency, and mental health did well at the box office, and the race problem seemed a topic ideal for raising profitable controversy. Various producers vied to be the first to cash in on the issue. Within the industry the competition was open and fierce. One of several *Variety* stories about this trend began: "1949 is definitely lining up as the year of the Negro problem pic; result has been the development of a race to be first on the screen with the subject."[1]

The winner proved to be neither the major studios nor the well-known independent filmmakers who had announced forthcoming movies on the subject of race relations. *Home of the Brave,* released by United Artists in the spring of 1949, was the work of a small independent company. The film was the third production of 35-year-old Stanley Kramer, a promotion-minded former film cutter and script editor, and his young partners, writer Carl Foreman and agent George Glass. Their first venture in 1947, a slight comedy called *So This Is New York,* had fared badly. But their second feature, *Champion* (1949), an adaptation of a Ring Lardner short story about a great prizefighter who is a heel, had been a critical and financial success. *Home of the Brave* was produced on a very low budget and was shot in less than a month under the deliberately misleading title "High Noon." The cast and everyone else connected with the film were pledged to secrecy until it was ready for release. Kramer and his partners rightly believed that the first picture on the theme of race was going to make money, and they did not want to alert the competition.

Home of the Brave was based on a none-too-successful play by Arthur Laurents that dealt with anti-Semitism. Kramer's first attempts to film the story after the play's Broadway run ended had proved futile. In 1946, the industry was not ready for controversy. Later, the success of movies dealing with anti-Semitism (including the award winning *Gentleman's Agreement*) made Kramer's project seem redundant until the idea of switching the main character from a Jew to a black was proposed. Kramer reacted enthusiastically; as he reasoned, "an audience could see the difference in terms of color rather than having one white man

saying he was Jewish, another saying he was Christian." Foreman, who wrote the screenplay, was "tense" as well as "excited"
at the prospect of breaking new ground.[2]

Home of the Brave had an enormous impact. But how much
new ground it broke is questionable, and in retrospect the film
seems stilted and naive. The story is about a black GI named
Peter Moss, who is suffering from partial amnesia and hysterical
paralysis. A sympathetic psychiatrist at the field hospital tries to
help Moss by making him relive the reconnaissance mission from
which he returned unable to walk. The bulk of the film deals
with this mission and is told in a series of flashbacks. The other
members of the reconnaissance group were a harried twenty-six-
year-old officer; Finch, a high-school chum of Moss; Mingo, a
sergeant who loses his arm; and T. J., a tough, bigoted corporal
who resents having to work with "some boogie" and continually
baits Moss. Their task is to map a Japanese-held island. The
selection of Moss as a surveying specialist discomfits all except
Finch, who is delighted to see his old friend. (Finch later trades
punches with T. J. over racial slurs and offers to open a bar and
restaurant together with Moss when the war is over.) As the
group prepares to leave the island after completing their mission,
they are fired on by a sniper. Finch loses the all-important map
case. Later he and Moss go back to look for it. When they fail to
find it, Moss urges that they return, but Finch wants to keep on
looking. They argue. Finch starts to call Moss a "yellow bellied
ni–" but catches himself to amend the phrase to "nit-wit." He
finds the map case, is shot by another sniper, gives the case to
Moss, and tells Moss to go ahead. Finch, however, is caught and
tortured by the Japanese, and Moss, hearing the screams, is restrained by the others from going back to help him. A boat comes
to pick them up, and Moss is standing guard when Finch crawls
up and dies in his arms. Moss now finds that he cannot walk, and
has to be carried to the boat.

The doctor fails to overcome Moss's paralysis until as a form of
shock treatment he calls the black GI "a dirty nigger." Having
tricked Moss into walking, the doctor proceeds to give an explanation that is typical of the film's platitudinous treatment of a
very complex subject. Every soldier who sees another get shot,
the doctor says, feels glad that it happened to somebody else, but
Moss has special guilt because Finch was shot just after calling

him a nigger. The doctor continues: "It's not your fault . . . It's a legacy. A hundred years of slavery, second-class citizenship, of being different. You had that feeling of difference pounded into you when you were a child, and being a child you turned it into a feeling of guilt. You've always had that guilt inside you. That's why it was so easy for you to feel guilty about Finch." As for those who try to make Moss feel "different," — "they need help as much as you do — maybe more."

The final scene of *Home of the Brave* takes place in the orderly room. T. J. baits Moss until the one-armed Mingo orders him from the room. The sergeant then tells Moss that T. J. has also made cracks about Mingo's disability: "To that crud and all cruds like him, it's the same thing. We're easy targets for 'em to take pot shots at." Mingo then offers to replace Finch in the proposed restaurant partnership. He refuses to take Moss's weak no for an answer. A jeep horn sounds; it is time for them to go to the airport. Moss helps Mingo to shoulder his bag, and the crippled white and the psychologically scarred black walk out together. While this ending does signify some sort of resolution, its implications are not altogether happy ones.

Some critics found *Home of the Brave* "contrived" and "spurious" but the general reaction echoed the judgment offered by *Newsweek*'s reviewer, who found faults in the movie but called it an "unusually fine film." Yet for all its excellences, the film fell short of dealing adequately with any of the problems it raised. Moss is tormented by T. J., but the film's manifestation of prejudice is far less ugly and physical than anything that would have occurred in similar situations in real life. Even T. J.'s words of hate are soft. Moreover, in times of stress there always seems to be someone like Finch or the doctor around to defend or to soothe Moss. Indeed, the film expresses a kind of cheap tolerance. At one point during the mission, for instance, the officer says to Mingo: "It's funny, ever since we got on this island I never think of Moss as being black." And the sergeant replies "Yeah it is funny. I never think of you as being white." Nor can Moss be said to be presented as a human being. He functions as a passive, not-much-more-than-symbolic character with overtones of nobility. In that sense, it is true, a new and unusual dimension is added to the movie black: here the black is not like the white, but better. Only once does Moss really lash out verbally, shouting "I

A white psychoanalyst (Jeff Corey) helps a black soldier (James Edwards) to overcome hysterical paralysis in the 1949 *Home of the Brave*. Race "problem" films were a brief rage at the time. (National Film Archive/Courtesy Stanley Kramer)

had to get beat a couple . . . times before I learned that if you're colored, you stink. You're not like other people . . . You're alone. You're something strange, different." But there is something odd about this outburst and about Moss's situation in general. Why were the guilt feelings of a black GI made the central theme of the industry's first "serious" film about the question of the black in American society? Moreover, the situation in the film is somewhat suspect since, as one commentator points out, "Moss is told he suffers from discrimination chiefly because he is too sensitive."[3]

The role of Moss was a difficult one, and it was expertly played by James Edwards, a Knoxville College graduate and a war veteran who had gained some stage experience with West Coast theatrical companies and had played the black boxer in *The Set-Up*. Although his future seemed very promising after *Home of the Brave*, he never again had a chance at anything better than a supporting role even though he worked as an actor until his death in 1970. Ironically, in his last movie, *Patton* (Twentieth Century-Fox, 1970), he played a greying enlisted man who served as the general's valet, polishing his boots and brushing his coat.

Before 1949 had ended two of the also-rans in the contest to make the first film on the subject of relations between blacks and whites in the contemporary United States had also been distributed. Both *Lost Boundaries* and *Pinky* were concerned with "passing for white." And both were variations on the tragic mulatto theme of silent movie days, though their outcomes were somewhat happier and their prejudices less apparent. *Lost Boundaries* and *Pinky* do represent a forthright break with earlier films on the subject, but their producers were still overcautious. The poignant dilemma of the light-skinned mulatto was feelingly and sympathetically presented, but the deeper implications of the situation were avoided or shunted into the background.

Lost Boundaries is based on a ninety-one-page book by the journalist William L. White, which related the true story of Dr. Albert H. Johnston and his family. Both the doctor and his wife were very light-skinned blacks who were raised and educated in the Midwest and who had succeeded in passing for white in New England. Given the blatant discrimination that even black professional people faced in the 1920s and 1930s, Johnston and his wife had decided that their only hope for "the good life" lay in concealing their racial identity. During these years he managed to obtain a good internship in Maine, to establish a practice in a small community, to train as a radiologist at Harvard, and to become a respected doctor in Keene, New Hampshire. Wherever the family lived Mrs. Johnston was actively involved in local affairs. Their apparent success notwithstanding, Dr. and Mrs.

Johnston constantly worried about exposure and what it might do to their livelihood and to their children, who did not know they were black.

Just before Pearl Harbor Dr. Johnston volunteered for the Navy, which had already approached him twice because he was one of about 2200 trained radiologists in the country. Dr. Johnston knew there was a risk in applying for a commission because all prospective officers were investigated. But he felt that his status would be more secure if he managed to obtain it. "We won't need ever tell the children anything," he said to his wife. But the Navy turned him down when investigation showed that he "had Negro blood," though the rejection was couched in more polite terms, referring to his inability "to meet physical requirements." In the meantime, Dr. Johnston had bought a uniform and had told friends of his decision to join the Navy, so some fast explaining was called for. He decided that he had to tell his children the truth. The two younger children seem to have been able to cope with the situation, but the older boy dropped out of college and, in an attempt to come to grips with his identity, traveled to various sections of the country and looked up his family's black relatives, many of whom were reasonably well off. It took some time before he began to solve his personal problems.[4]

White's book created an enormous stir. The screen rights were sold, and the trade papers announced that Louis de Rochemont was to produce the film for MGM. The forty-nine-year-old de Rochemont had an impressive record. In 1934–35 he had been one of the originators of the *March of Time,* and he had served as executive producer of that award-winning series for several years. After World War II he applied newsreel and documentary techniques to feature films and had produced some first-rate movies dealing with topics like FBI destruction of a Nazi spy network in the United States. Budgetary considerations as well as differences over the handling of a sensitive theme led to a parting of the ways between de Rochemont and MGM. The dynamic, unorthodox producer went ahead on his own. Shooting on location and using a group of little-known actors and actresses, together with some nonprofessionals, he filmed *Lost Boundaries* in a little over two months at a cost of less than $650,000 (or about one million dollars under MGM's projected budget).

Lost Boundaries was an immediate critical hit when it was released in the summer of 1949. Even members of the black press who had criticized de Rochemont for using whites to play the family, greeted the movie enthusiastically. The *Afro-American's* assistant managing editor said that the film moved her to tears and described it as "one of the best treatments of a racial story I have ever seen out of Hollywood." Because the film dealt with a subject that long had been taboo in the industry, critics tended to overlook defects such as a slackness of structure. Certainly the film was outspoken in its attack on racial prejudice. No attempt was made, for instance, to avoid the fact that when the war began blacks could not obtain commissions in the Navy and that the service also discriminated against the race in other ways.[5]

But for all its outspokenness the screenplay skimmed over many of the issues raised in the book. Some of the changes were unimportant, such as the Johnston family being called Carter or the telescoping of the doctor's experiences into one practice in a town called Keenham. But others provide a fascinating comment on what the filmmakers believed the American movie-going public would accept. As White made clear, Dr. Johnston had decided to pass as a means of circumventing the discrimination faced by blacks. The movie blurs this decision. In an incident that has no parallel in the book he accepts an internship at a black hospital in Georgia — only to be dismissed by its black administrator for being too light-skinned. The administrator assures the doctor that "you won't have any trouble getting a job in a northern hospital." Thus, the movie's first act of discrimination is practiced by a black. Later, a white doctor, also an invention of the screenplay, urges Dr. Johnston to pass and helps him to establish a practice. In his travels the real son discovered the black middle class, but in the movie he goes to Harlem, presented as a dangerous and depraved urban jungle. This sequence, the only one involving violence in the whole film, brutally pits black against black. And it is worth noting, as one scholar points out, that "when the film moves away from the subject of 'passing' it seems only able to deal with aspects of the Negro problem in caricature or by stereotype extreme." The movie's end is also inconclusive, although the audience is assured by a narrator who speaks for the townspeople that the doctor "is still our doctor." But the romances of the children are left up in the air; the possibility of miscegenation is determinedly ignored. And in one of the final scenes, which takes place in a local church, as expressions of tolerance are heard, the daughter — who in real life married a white man — is shown running out of the building in tears.[6]

The movie speaks of tolerance, and as one black critic vigorously and correctly protested "this distorts . . . the whole point for there is nothing to be 'tolerant' of. All people should be equally treated not because it's the 'nice thing to do' but because they are equal." Moreover, the distributors were so unsure of the audience for this well-reviewed movie that they thought it necessary to play up the sensational angles of the story. Thus one advertisement showed the son looking at his hands like a veritable Lady Macbeth: "Why didn't they tell me I was Negro?" the tag line read. And until protests forced a change, the word "coon" appeared prominently on the display outside the Broadway movie house where the film premiered in New York City.[7]

The Twentieth Century-Fox movie *Pinky* was another example of what English film critic Richard Winnington has called "white conceit" among those in the industry making films dealing with "the Negro problem." The title character is a black who is light enough to pass. She has gone North to study nursing. Having become romantically involved with a white doctor who does not know her background, she flees home in confusion when he proposes marriage. The movie begins with her return to the grim but tidy cabin of her black washerwoman grandmother. Aunt Dicey with her God-fearing, passive ways is a mammy type who thinks that Pinky was wrong to have passed. At her urging Pinky agrees to nurse Miss Em, an elderly white spinster and the last survivor of a family of local aristocrats. Miss Em dies, willing her mansion and property to Pinky with the admonition that she put them to good use. Miss Em's relatives contest the will, but, aided by one of the town's eminent white lawyers, Pinky prevails. She makes a final break with the white doctor, resolving to devote her life to running a combined clinic and nurses training center for blacks in the old mansion.[8]

The movie contained some strong scenes dealing with the problems faced by blacks in the United States. While on a walk to think over her situation Pinky is accosted by two whites who tell her that they can't "let no white girl walk by herself in this nigger section." When she tells them that she lives there, they try to assault her, but she escapes. This scene was unusual in that it touched on the unhappy fact of white sexual attacks on black women. The double standard of justice many blacks faced also was sharply dramatized in the instantaneous change from servility to hostility by the local police when Pinky is involved in a brawl with a black woman and defiantly tells them she is black, too.

There is no denying the effectiveness of such scenes, but the

In *Pinky* (1949), Jeanne Crain, a white actress renowned for her all-American girl roles, was a passing sensation as a light-skinned black who renounces her deception. Here, her dark grandmother (Ethel Waters) tries unsuccessfully to interest her in some cornbread. (Courtesy Twentieth Century–Fox. © 1949 Twentieth Century–Fox Film Corporation)

rest of the movie managed to smother them. The trial scenes were pure Hollywood: besides some threatening newspaper headlines, no extra-legal pressure is brought to bear on Pinky and the justly criticized Southern judicial system bends over backward to be fair to her. The lushly inspirational ending also belies the movie's claims to honesty. Having dismissed her suitor, Pinky proceeds to bustle about her clinic and training school and then goes out onto the lawn where (in closeup) she gazes heavenward, lips parted in an expression of benign acceptance of her mission and prospective celibate existence. Even God is drawn in to prevent miscegenation. Much of the movie's potential impact was blunted, moreover, by the choice of a white actress, Jeanne Crain, then usually featured in "Miss Homespun America" parts, to play Pinky. The casting of someone like Lena Horne would obviously have elicited a different audience response, especially with the romantic attraction of Pinky and the doctor. In addition to dealing very gently with the South, the movie gave the other black characters the traditional cinematic back of the hand. For all Ethel Waters's talent (and she was nominated for an Academy Award) Aunt Dicey was just another ponderous mammy who believed that "colored folks had their place." And when Pinky brawls with a black woman the latter is shown to be toting a knife that she obviously knows how to use; her "man" is a "sport" whose shady pursuits are matched by his cowardly instincts.

The somewhat ambiguous nature of *Pinky* had caused difficulties during its production. Walter White, asked by producer Darryl Zanuck to read the script, had told him that blacks would resent the tone of much of the movie. White submitted the script to various blacks for their comment, and they were even more critical than he had been. A black technical advisor, who served only for a short period of time, submitted a number of memoranda to Zanuck suggesting various drastic changes; none were made. Director John Ford had a difference of opinion with Ethel Waters over how Aunt Dicey should be played. Zanuck recalled that "it was a professional difference of opinion. Ford's Negroes were like Aunt Jemina. Caricatures. I thought we're going to get into trouble. Jack said, I think you better put someone else on it." And Ford was replaced by Elia Kazan, who later admitted that from his point of view there were limitations to the film and that "we solve this story in personal terms."[9]

Pinky did not win the lavish critical praise that had greeted *Home of the Brave* and *Lost Boundaries*. A black reviewer called it "the poorest of the three," and he had considerable company. Yet *Pinky* did by far the best business. With a name cast that included Ethel Barrymore as well as Jeanne Crain and Ethel Waters and with the backing of a major studio sales organization, it brought in over $4 million in domestic rentals, and it was estimated to be the second-largest grossing film of 1949, after *Jolson Sings Again*. The other two black problem films also did well at the box office, so well, in fact, that *Variety* declared that "the film's leading b.o. star for 1949 wasn't a personality, but . . . a subject — racial prejudice." *Home of the Brave* grossed over $2 million in domestic rentals and was one of the best drawing United Artists releases in years. The approximately $1.8 million that *Lost Boundaries* grossed in domestic rentals was phenomenal considering that it was being distributed by a small independent company.[10]

Oddly enough, the three did exceedingly well in the South and earned a greater share of their receipts in that region than did most other films. Whites as well as blacks went to see them. In Atlanta, for instance, at the conclusion of the trial scene in *Pinky* it was not unusual for both the black and white sections of the audience to applaud. Each obviously read a different meaning into Pinky's victory. To be sure, these films faced censorship problems. Binford, to the surprise of all, passed *Home of the Brave,* but he would not allow even private showings of *Lost Boundaries*. That film also was banned in Atlanta as "likely to have an adverse effect on the peace, morality, and good order of the city." The Atlanta censor also insisted on cuts in *Home of the Brave* and *Pinky;* and a Texas exhibitor was arrested for refusing to stop showings of the latter film. These and other acts of censorship were appealed to the Supreme Court, which, however, deferred action in the area of movie censorship until February, 1952. Then in a decision involving the Italian film *The Miracle* the Court extended the Constitutional guarantees of free speech to the movies.

For all the critical and commercial success of *Home of the Brave, Lost Boundaries,* and *Pinky,* their immediate successors did not fare well at the box office. Moviegoers had begun to lose interest in films dealing with blacks and their plight. This was unfortunate because two later productions were not only better but treated the subject with more genuine sensitivity. MGM's *Intruder in the Dust* (released in the winter of 1949–50) differed so greatly in approach from its three predecessors that novelist Ralph Ellison could comment that it was the only one "that could be shown in Harlem without arousing unintended laughter."[11]

A close adaptation of William Faulkner's novel, *Intruder in the Dust* revolves around the fate of Lucas Beauchamp, a proud and intelligent old Southern black man who refuses to be a "nigger." After being accused of killing a white with whom he had quarreled, Beauchamp is jailed. Although he faces certain lynching, he remains calm and unafraid. For all his good qualities, Beauchamp is not a wholly sympathetic character. He is shown to be maddeningly self-righteous and to have more than a touch of arrogance. The film's other central character is Chick Mallison, a white teenager, who after a dunking in a creek has been offered dry clothes and food at Beauchamp's farm. The boy, raised in an environment in which no white can be beholden to a black, tries to pay Beauchamp for his hospitality but is refused. Chick is further humiliated when the black man refuses to pick up the money Chick has thrown on the floor.

But a tentative relationship grows out of this encounter. After the black's arrest, the boy, still anxious to redeem his honor, asks his lawyer uncle John Stevens to see what can be done. Steven's talk with Beauchamp proves frustratingly one-sided, for the black man says little. Beauchamp knows that an autopsy would show that death was caused by a rifle bullet rather than a bullet from his revolver. But he also knows that the authorities would never exhume a white man's body to prove the innocence of a black. Chick then decides on an unofficial exhumation. Late one night, Chick, a black teenager named Aleck with whom he has been raised, and Miss Habersham, a seventy-year-old spinster who believes in justice and who is the last of a family once prominent in the local community, go to the local graveyard. When they open the murdered man's grave, they find it empty. Ultimately the body is found: the victim has been shot by a rifle. Meanwhile the lynch mob headed by the victim's brother is held at bay by Miss Habersham, who refuses to quit the jail. The murderer turns out to be the brother of the dead man. In the final scenes Beauchamp comes to settle accounts with the lawyer. Despite

Above, Juano Hernandez, as a proud old southern black accused of murder in *Intruder in the Dust* (1949), listens skeptically to a white lawyer, David Brian. (From the MGM release "Intruder in the Dust" © 1949 Loew's Incorporated.) Opposite, Hernandez, a fine actor who never found it easy to get good roles, was a judge in the 1955 *Trial*. The scowling lawyer, foreground, is that paragon of 1950s leading men, Glenn Ford. (From the MGM release "Trial" © 1955 Loew's Incorporated)

Steven's protestations Beauchamp insists on making at least a token payment, and asks for a receipt. After Beauchamp leaves, Stevens tells Chick that the black is "proud, stubborn, insufferable," but also that he is "the keeper of my conscience."

The movie has a number of platitudinous moments, most of them stemming from the sermonizing of the paternalistically tolerant lawyer. But *Intruder in the Dust* also has some tough-minded sections. The film's treatment of the situation of blacks in the South was, for the time, extraordinarily accurate. When Beauchamp is arrested, the blacks retreat from sight and, as the movie makes clear, for good reason. A deputy tells the lawyer during his visit to the jail that the black prisoners lying quiet on their bunks are not asleep; "Not one. And I don't blame 'em when a mob o' white men are gonna bust in here with pistols and cans of gasoline . . . it won't be the first time all black cats look alike." During the nocturnal expedition of Chick, Aleck, and Miss

Habersham, their noisy passage through the black section of town arouses fearful responses from blacks who anticipate violence. One man cautiously peers out of his doorway and expresses relief when he discovers who the intruders are. The film's tone is matter-of-fact as it shows people gathering for a lynching; this is not a frenzied mob but a group of rural folk who have come by car and bus to see Beauchamp "get what's coming to him." The men lounge, the women gossip, the children play. Radios blare. People eat ice cream, play cards, and exchange news. And the crowd waits for the murdered man's kin to revenge themselves. Not only is a black man presumed guilty when charged in this environment, but it is also taken for granted that "lynch law will deny him even the most elementary forms of justice." Unlike its predecessors, this movie did not try to apologize for white actions and attitudes or to evade the issues.

Juano Hernandez's portrayal of Lucas Beauchamp was responsible for much of the impact of the film, which he dominated. Hernandez did not have an easy time during its production, for most of *Intruder in the Dust* was shot in Faulkner's home town of Oxford, Mississippi. He had to live apart with a local black businessman and found it wiser not to pick up his mail at the film company's headquarters in the town's segregated hotel. Such working conditions made Hernandez's film debut all the more remarkable. Then in his late forties, the onetime native of Puerto Rico had been active in all aspects of show business from the stage to the circus, but nothing in his career suggested how effective he would be as a film actor. He was probably best known for his work in radio, which allowed him to make good use of his rich, well-modulated voice. Hernandez's movie career seemed well launched by *Intruder in the Dust,* and three other juicy roles quickly followed. In *Young Man with a Horn,* a Hollywood version of the life of Bix Beiderbecke that Warners released in 1950, Hernandez movingly played a role that was a composite of the black musicians who had influenced Beiderbecke. Warners then cast him in *The Breaking Point,* a version of Hemingway's *To Have and Have Not,* in which he was first rate as the main character's partner and friend. And before the year 1950 was out, he played an elderly black sharecropper threatened by night riders in the post–Civil War South in MGM's *Stars in My Crown.* But after this splendid start Hernandez's movie career faltered. Some of his increasingly infrequent portrayals were outstanding (such as the judge in MGM's 1955 film *Trial*) but the last roles he played before his death in 1970 were reminiscent of the familiar movie stereotypes. For example, in the movie adaptation of Faulkner's *The Reivers* (a 1969 National General Pictures release), Hernandez played a character named Uncle Possum.

One black actor who also made his screen debut in 1950 did fare much better. In the Twentieth Century-Fox production *No Way Out*, the last in the cycle of black problem films to come from a major studio, Sidney Poitier was cast as an intern, Dr. Luther Brooks. Set in an unnamed northern American city, *No Way Out* deals with what happens when a superficially injured white patient, Johnny Biddle, being treated by Dr. Brooks dies under the eyes of his psychopathic, black-hating brother. Both Biddles have been shot in the legs by policemen while holding up a filling station. Johnny Biddle seems to be suffering from more than a leg wound. Brooks, the only black intern at the hospital, suspects a brain tumor, and while from an adjoining bed the handcuffed Ray Biddle baits him with racist remarks, the doctor performs a spinal tap. The patient dies, and Ray Biddle hysterically accuses the "nigger doctor" of murdering his brother. Brooks wants an autopsy performed so that his diagnosis and treatment may be verified. Biddle, as next-of-kin, refuses. Brooks and his white mentor, Dr. Wharton, plead their cause with Johnny's estranged wife Edie, who was once Ray's mistress. Ray convinces Edie that the doctors are lying, and she carries the news of Johnny's death and Ray's charges to the slum area where the Biddles live. Plans are made there to attack "nigger town," but the more militant blacks learn of them and attack first. In an effort to end the violence, Brooks gives himself up for murder. The ensuing autopsy vindicates his judgment. But Ray Biddle remains unconvinced and, escaping from prison, traps Brooks in Wharton's home. At the last minute, thanks to Edie, Brooks (who is shot by Ray in the process) manages to gain the upper hand. The movie ends with Brooks deciding not to shoot Ray Biddle. Instead, while the hoodlum whimpers about the pain from his leg wound, Brooks treats him, saying "Don't cry white boy, you're going to live."

Not only was *No Way Out* what one critic called "a torturous series of contrivances" but its direction was uneven and many of the characters were badly played. The movie pushed its message a little too hard for comfort. There is the predictable statement by a liberal white, in this instance Dr. Wharton, that he is not pro-black, but pro-good doctor and that a person's ability is all that counts. Once again racism is relegated to the lower classes, to the

No Way Out represented one of Hollywood's first halting attempts to portray a black middle-class family. Rising to meet some long-forgotten challenge are Poitier and, left, Ossie Davis. (National Film Archive/Courtesy Twentieth Century–Fox. © 1950 Twentieth Century–Fox Film Corporation)

Biddles and to the other slum inhabitants, one of whom spits at Brooks when he tries to treat a white injured in the race riot. She shouts at the doctor to "keep your black hands off my boy." As in the other four films the more sophisticated and insidious forms of racial discrimination practiced by the middle and upper classes are barely touched on.[12]

But *No Way Out* also had some unusual angles. As director Joseph Mankiewicz recalls, "the movie marked the first time racial violence was shown on screen . . . in modern times." Moreover, the blacks were shown as more than holding their own. Nor was blind, unreasoning racial prejudice limited to whites. Lefty, a black elevator operator in the hospital, is militantly antiwhite. He is the leader of the blacks who attack the slum whites, a scene that caused the movie censorship problems and that was shortened in Chicago and elsewhere. By contrast, an intelligent attempt was made to show the home life of the middle-class black — Brooks leads a comfortable family existence with an attractive wife, a nice mother, and pleasant relatives, all of whom are supportive of him. Indeed, the presentation of Dr. Brooks's family manages to escape the excessive melodrama that permeates the rest of the film.[13]

The most important new development in *No Way Out*, however, had to do with its treatment of the black protagonist. Lesser Samuels, who co-scripted the movie, declared that it was not meant "to apotheosize the Negro," but *No Way Out* does put Dr. Brooks on a pedestal. He is shown to be a conscientious, hardworking, attractive person who has gone through medical school with a straight-A average and who has achieved top honors in all the required examinations for the M.D. Brooks takes enormous abuse during the course of the movie without losing his composure; he eschews violence, even deciding not to shoot his chief tormentor, Ray Biddle, but rather to treat his wound. The movie underlines his difficult but praiseworthy choice by pairing the blatant white racism of the Biddles with the unthinking black militancy that Lefty personifies.[14]

Brooks was the precursor of a new stereotype: the ebony saint. Neither Uncle Tom nor militant, he remains nonviolent despite enormous provocation, and like ebony itself he remains cool. He is obviously superior in skills and ability. Nevertheless, the ebony saint recognizes that society imposes limitations on him and he implicitly accepts those that are not blatantly racist. He poses no threat to established social or sexual mores. He is such an amalgam of undemanding virtue that his detractors must be low and evil fellows indeed. For a time there seemed a chance that the ebony saint might even develop into a character that would be recognizably human — something that on-screen blacks so rarely were. But it never happened. The ebony saint continued to move in a personal vacuum: with rare exceptions, he or she never attained the dimension of humanity.

Home of the Brave, Lost Boundaries, Pinky, Intruder in the Dust, and *No Way Out* can by no stretch of the imagination be called daring — as their exhibitors liked to pretend in advertising them. However, they were unusual and important in that for the first time they presented the black as an actual protagonist in white society. While it is true that these films did raise the question of social prejudice in the United States and dealt with some formerly taboo subjects, it must also be said that they presented situations that were unusual to the point of being unrealistic. The people who made them are to be commended for their courage and their willingness to gamble on controversial material, even if they seemed more inspired by the profit motive than by idealism. It was hardly surprising that when *Intruder in the Dust* and *No Way Out* proved less successful at the box office than their predecessors the cycle came to an end.

Perhaps the most powerful on-screen evocation of the problems faced by blacks in the postwar United States came in a film that was not part of the cycle. *The Quiet One* (1948) was made independently in New York well before Hollywood's sudden and limited interest in racial problems, but did achieve some distribution because of that interest. The film was originally shot in 16mm for less than $35,000 by a talented team which included James Agee, who wrote the intelligent and sensitive narration. *The Quiet One* is not a race-problem film as such, dealing rather with a ten-year-old black boy's search for affection. His mother has no time for him; the man she is living with is indifferent to him, and the boy's grandmother (with whom he lives) has her own troubles. Donald roams the streets of Harlem, unsuccessfully looking for friends and for love. Finally in frustration and anger he breaks a glass storefront and is sent to the Wiltwyck School for Boys (which co-produced the film). There in upstate New York, in that philanthropic institution for disturbed minors, Donald begins to find his way as he makes friends with and receives direction from the staff. But the film's narration makes clear that "there is no happy ending for Donald," that the most "we can say is that the worst of his loneliness . . . is ended." *The Quiet One* is a very moving film, and one that bleakly but perceptively dissects the environment of Harlem. Much of the movie was filmed in the streets and homes of the ghetto, and this portion of *The Quiet One* is a powerfully grim depiction of black poverty.

The effect of all these movies on their audiences seems to have been negligible. Indeed, two white social scientists suggested that the Hollywood films might have had a boomerang effect, that "in order to show how wrong race hatred is" the studio film-makers had to create plots and characters that "on a less conscious level" presented the black as "a terrible burden that we must carry on our backs." But this judgment overestimates the influence of these films. It would seem that audience reactions were much more straightforward. Prejudiced whites no doubt remained prejudiced. Those blacks who took the movies at face value approved of them; those who believed that they avoided important issues disapproved. Whites and blacks who hoped that the films would have some liberalizing effect recognized that this influence was necessarily limited.[15]

Although many American movies continued to make use of subdued variations of the older stereotypes of the black, major refinements did begin to show up. Stepin Fetchit, for example, made a comeback in the early 1950s but it proved to be short-lived; that kind of bowing and scraping figure of ridicule now seemed merely embarrassing. The 1951 MGM version of *Show Boat* retained some offensive characterizations of the black, but there were significant improvements over previous screen productions of the musical. The term "darkie" was never used. The song "Ol' Man River" no longer contained the phrase "Niggers all work on the Mississippi." And the character Joe, who sang it, was made less of a caricature, as was his female counterpart, who at least was not the traditional "handkerchief head." Although *Show Boat* remained a period piece, it had "come a long way . . . from the first movie version in 1929," as *Ebony* noted.[16]

The success of the black-problem films seemed to make the industry more secure in its handling of racial themes — but the stereotypes still remained. Typical of the blend of new and old was the 1952 Twentieth Century-Fox production *Lydia Bailey*. This film treated sympathetically the revolt of the Haitian blacks against French rule as well as their fight in 1802 against Napoleon's attempts to restore white rule. The Haitian patriot Toussaint L'Ouverture is described to the white Amercan hero as being "to us what George Washington was to you." Moreover, it is made clear that Toussaint would have failed but for the assistance of King Dick, a Haitian leader who is presented as intelligent, enterprising, and courageous. True, King Dick does have eight wives, many of whom are simpering ninnies. The movie also makes use of other, older stereotypes: there are black mobs shouting "Kill, kill"; Haitians are shown as fearful and superstitious practitioners of voodoo; and a number of black characters are presented in a familiarly ludicrous way.

This ambiguous approach did result in the treatment of some formerly taboo themes, but tenuously and in a very different manner from that of the black problem films. *The President's Lady*, based on a best-selling novel, was a 1953 Twentieth Century-Fox film that told the story of Andrew Jackson and his wife Rachel. The plot has her divorcing her first husband because of his sexual involvement with a slave woman he owned. The movie makes this situation quite clear, but only through words; Rachel's husband and his mistress are never seen embracing.

The end of the black-problem film cycle and the return to good old fashioned, solid film entertainment about boy meets girl, did not mean that the black disappeared as a movie subject. In early 1950 *The Jackie Robinson Story* (an Eagle-Lion film) was released. Other blacks in organized sport also received screen treatment in the next few years: *The Harlem Globetrotters* was a 1951 Columbia release, and two years later United Artists distributed *The Joe Louis Story*. Jackie Robinson's comments about his film serve as a succinct and accurate review of the others as well: "Later I realized it had been made too quickly, that it was budgeted too low, and that . . . it could have been done much better."[17]

Nor were racial themes dropped completely. *Bright Victory* (Universal-International, 1951) dealt with the problems faced by a soldier blinded in combat in adjusting to civilian life. The film's conventional love story was played against a first-rate depiction of how blinded GI's are trained to take care of themselves. The film also made racial intolerance a minor theme. The lead character, a sergeant from a small town in the South, becomes friendly with another blinded GI at the army hospital where they are being trained. Only through some careless remarks about "niggers" does the sergeant learn that this GI is black. On leave from the hospital the Southerner has a chance to think over what has happened, and in the final scenes he seeks out the black soldier, apologizes for the remarks, and asks for his friendship again.

A more direct approach was attempted in the 1951 movie *The Well*, which was produced on a $450,000 budget by Harry Popkin, a white movie-maker whose experience included turning out all-black films for the ghetto theaters. *The Well* sternly examined the kind of racial feeling that can lead to violence. A little black girl falls down an abandoned well. She was last seen talking to a white man. Rumors spread unrest, despite the local sheriff's best efforts. Peace is restored only when the child is found and both whites and blacks cooperate to save her, the ending being an obvious artifice.

Equally artificial was the resolution of the problems raised by the 1952 Universal-International movie *Red Ball Express*, which dealt with the predominantly black troops who, after the 1944 Normandy invasion, ferried supplies by truck across France. These transport units are shown as integrated, which in fact they were not. Racial antagonisms play only a minor part in this movie and are mainly personified by a quickly settled feud between a black corporal and a Southern white private (played by Sidney Poitier and Hugh O'Brian). Those responsible for *Red Ball Express*, as one critic aptly pointed out, "have become so involved in proving that white and Negro troops just love to work and play together, that . . . the thing boils down to a mediocre war melodrama, heavily larded with love-thy-brother angles . . ."[18]

Poitier also had appeared in the 1951 movie version of Alan Paton's novel *Cry, the Beloved Country*, a book that movingly dealt with the bitter relations between the races in South Africa. Although an English movie, the production featured another black American actor, Canada Lee, as the Reverend Stephen

Kumalo, the country minister who travels to the big city of Johannesburg in search of his son. Poitier played a clergyman there who helps in the quest, which winds its way through the native slums and ends when Kumalo finds his son in prison implicated in the robbery murder of a white who was a fighter for the rights of the black. Kumalo's son is sentenced to death, and the minister returns home. There, on the day of his son's execution he comes to an understanding with the murdered man's father about the need for Christian harmony among all races. The movie carries messages of tolerance and hope, but its real impact comes from the depiction of squalor and misery that face the urbanized native. *Cry, the Beloved Country,* as one critic pointed out, "not only indicts the forces determining the life of Negoes in South Africa, but the vast proportion of what recently has been passed off as Africa on screen." For all its obvious earnestness the movie was self-consciously arty and slow.[19]

A foreign production that fell even farther off-target was the 1950 movie version of Richard Wright's powerful and controversial novel *Native Son.* It dealt with Bigger Thomas, a black youth trapped in the Chicago ghetto by racism and ultimately destroyed by it. Wright's novel, which created an enormous stir upon its publication in 1940, is a passionate but grim book. Bigger is involved in two murders and is the subject of a harrowing police chase. The movie was a reasonably faithful adaptation of the novel, mainly because of Wright's active participation in the production. He was co-author of the screenplay, and he played (rather amateurishly) the role of Bigger. The movie version of *Native Son* was backed by Argentine money, directed by a Frenchman, played by performers of various nationalities, and filmed in Buenos Aires with some exteriors shot in Chicago. Wright, who for nearly a decade had found no one in the industry interested in filming his novel, expressed hopes that the movie would be "full of meaning." But the hybrid production obviously hurt the film. *Newsweek*'s movie reviewer had considerable company when he asserted that "the net effect . . . is one of disappointment and even embarrassment."[20]

Much more effective was the British-made *Pool of London,* a 1950 Ealing Studios production that involved robbery, murder, smuggling, a police chase across London, and a budding interracial romance. This tentative relationship is a sub-plot that

Richard Wright turned actor in the 1950 movie of his novel, *Native Son*. The film was made in Argentina, which is perhaps the only thing noteworthy about it. (National Film Archive)

involves the Jamaican shipmate of the white protagonist. Johnny is befriended by an English girl after a theater doorman has insulted him because of his color. And during the course of this rather melodramatic movie, the interracial couple manage to spend some discreet time together. There is no overt preaching against racial prejudice, and at the film's end Johnny decides once more to ship out. The film dodges the implications of its sub-plot, but the relationship between the London movie cashier and the

An interracial couple (Earl Cameron and Susan Shaw) enjoy a brief encounter amid ship models in the British *Pool of London* (1950). (National Film Archive/Courtesy Rank Organization)

Jamaican steward is presented movingly, if somewhat naively.

Yet in presenting Johnny as an individual and not a symbol, *Pool of London* treated the black better than did the 1949–50 Hollywood productions. These dealt with severely limited aspects of the problems faced by blacks in the United States and cannot be judged to have done real justice to the situation. Moreover, they fallaciously presented racial prejudice as a phenomenon merely of the South and the lower classes. However well meaning individual filmmakers may have been, the black characters they had created remained stereotypes, even if (as in the case of the ebony saint) this stereotype began to take on positive qualities. And this movie stereotype still formed an important part of the process that Ralph Ellison has described as "a magic rite by which the white American seeks to resolve the dilemma arising between his democratic beliefs and certain anti-democratic practices, between his acceptance of the sacred democratic belief that all men are created equal and his treatment of every tenth man as though he were not."[21]

This was one of many segregated theaters in the country where black patrons of the 1940s watched ghetto-oriented, all-black movies.

8

A PALE BLACK
IMITATION

HOLLYWOOD HAS PRODUCED its share of stinkers over the years, but in terms of sheer dreadfulness few can match the ghetto-oriented films made by both black and white filmmakers from the late 1930s until well into the 1950s. The indigestible, though, is not necessarily the forgettable: there is something more to these films than the superficial trivia of who made them and who played in them. They are noteworthy not only because of what they have to say about blacks in the years before the civil-rights revolution — but also because of what blacks had to say about themselves and their continuing hunger after a white American dream.

Both technically and artistically these cheaply produced, quickly made all-black movies remained true to their recent silent ancestors. During that earlier period, it is true, some effort had been made in "race productions" to deal with issues such as passing for white or intermarriage and to offset demeaning racist images. But despite all the rhetoric of the sound era about "better moving pictures of the Negro" and "giving colored actors and actresses a fighting chance," most makers of films for ghetto audiences were interested only in exploiting the desire of black movie-goers to see blacks on the screen. In large part this attitude can be traced to white control of distribution and of most productions, but no matter what the race of the filmmakers was, commercial considerations always won out. The films were invariably imitations of the standard Hollywood fare. Moreover, the bias in favor of light-skinned blacks which had been so much a feature of the silent films made for ghetto audiences now found expression verbally as well as visually. The leads remained very Caucasian-looking and spoke good English; the villains and comic figures, who were more Negroid in features and darker skinned, tended to speak in dialect.

Quite often the hackneyed plots included the standard unflattering caricatures of the black. In the 1939 all-black Western *Harlem Rides the Range,* for instance, the hero's sidekick and a friend pay a visit to a deserted mine where they see what they think is a ghost. The two men respond no differently from blacks in countless industry productions. They run away, explaining later that in such an emergency they could go faster on foot than their horses could travel. This kind of humor was especially prevalent in the broad comedies, both features and shorts, which had all-black casts. Jed Buell's 1940 slapstick production *Mr. Washington Goes to Town* had such lines as "porkchops is the fondest things I is of" and included such characters as a black man in white tie and tails accompanied by a gorilla, a Lonesome Ranger astride a goat, and a magician who kept the main character popeyed by making a goldfish bowl materialize atop his head.

The most prevalent form of all-black movie was the musical. All kinds of black performers appeared either in feature-length musicals or in what *Ebony* called "long shorts." Both were designed to play with Hollywood movies in the ghetto theaters and to attract black moviegoers. Some of these featurettes, however, were nothing more than filmed vaudeville shows. For instance, *Ebony Parade,* a three-reeler released by Astor in 1947, was just a succession of performances by entertainers like Count Basie, Cab Calloway, Dorothy Dandridge, and the Mills Brothers.

It was not just independent companies which made these musical short subjects. Warners, for instance, turned out *Jammin' the Blues* in 1945, which featured the great jazz saxaphonist Lester Young and singer Marie Bryant. The band supporting them included a white guitarist but he was photographed (in *Ebony*'s words) "so that his color could not be discerned."[1]

Typical of the feature-length, all-black musicals was *The Duke Is Tops,* a 1938 Harry Popkin production. Lena Horne made her motion picture debut in a lead role. The plot was just thick enough for three *Variety* sentences: "Story of a girl-boy producer-performer team having to split up when gal gets a N. Y. break.

Boy goes down, gal goes up, and then sags. Get together for finale, when combined efforts put them into the big time." Musical numbers dominated the film. Although it ran only 72 minutes, it included two elaborate night club floorshow sequences as well as other song and dance numbers.[2]

In terms of box-office grosses one of the most successful all-black features ever made was the musical *Harlem Is Heaven,* which was produced in 1932 by a group of whites who organized themselves as Lincoln Pictures. The main attraction of this undistinguished "all talking, singing, dancing story of thrilling backstage life" was Bill Robinson, who had not yet appeared in Hollywood films. Robinson wisecracked and danced his way through the film, which included his already famous stair dance. The movie also received strong support from Eubie Blake's orchestra, performers from the revue "Hot From Harlem," and some girls from the Cotton Club chorus line.[3]

Another high-grossing film was *Harlem on the Prairie* (also known as *Bad Man from Harlem*). This 1938 Associated Features production probably was the first all-black movie patterned on the formula horse operas that flourished until the 1950s, when television did them in. Because *Harlem on the Prairie* was successful, similar features followed it down the production trail. As in studio westerns, there was generally a "hard-riding sweet-singing" group to support the hero in a song or a fight; The Four Tones first appeared in *Harlem on the Prairie.* Two other black Western musicals, *The Bronze Buckaroo* and *Harlem Rides the Range,* had the distinction of being filmed at what *Ebony* later described as "the only Negro dude ranch in the world." Located near Victorville, California, at the edge of the Mojave Desert, Murray's Overall-Wearing Dude Ranch was a one-time chicken farm.[4]

Another Hollywood staple, the gangster film, was also a favorite vehicle for the makers of these films. So thoroughly did crime themes come to dominate the ghetto market in the 1930s that one black newspaperman declared that "All-Colored Films Are Our Own Worst Enemy" and another expressed his "thanks" to a producer who said that he would not make all-black gangster films. But social commentary of a sort was one unintentional result. In their search for new material producers touched on all manner of Harlem rackets. *Moon Over Harlem,* a 1937 film made by Media Productions, dealt with criminals who offered "protection" to local merchants. The 1939 Domino Productions movie *Straight from Heaven* centered on a group of black racketeers who forced distribution of rotten canned food. *Gang War*, a 1940 Harry Popkin production, was concerned with a fight among gangsters for control of jukeboxes.[5]

A good example of the all-black gangster film is *Dark Manhattan*, a 1937 Randol-Cooper production about the numbers racket. In its publicity this 77-minute film was described as "a cross cut of life in Harlem, that great dark city within a city, from the cultured and sophisticated down to the gangster and racketeer side so well known to be prevalent there." But as might be expected, the movie failed to live up to this expansive blurb.[6]

Technically *Dark Manhattan* was good, but as *Variety* pointed

Two comic cowboys, Lucius Brooks (left) and Flourney Miller, in *Harlem on the Prairie*, a high-grossing 1939 western, give a predictably stereotyped reaction to ghosts.

out "unfortunately, scripting and acting don't par the mechanical manufacture." The ending of the movie, which saw the hero dying in his girl's arms, merely brought forth giggles from ghetto audiences. One black critic said of the lead actress that she was either "miscast — or mistreated." Burlesque artist Jackie "Moms" Mably, who was part of the stage show at Harlem's Apollo Theater when the movie played there, made her the butt of many (as it were) off-color jokes, to the great amusement of the audience. The movie was dedicated to the memories of those noted black entertainers Florence Mills, Richard Harrison, and Bert Williams — which led one black newspaperman to comment that "they were chosen, because being dead, there could be no rebuttal."[7]

The hero was played by Ralph Cooper, a good-looking, tall, ex-vaudeville performer, whose roles in such films won him billing as "the Bronze Bogart." As early as 1930 he had been featured singing and dancing in the short *Harlem Cabaret* along with other black entertainers. During the mid-1930s he became well known as master of ceremonies at the famous amateur nights held at the Apollo. His quick wit and good-natured humor as well as his easy handling of potentially difficult situations earned him a substantial following. In 1936 Cooper was brought to Hollywood by Twentieth Century-Fox to play a role in a Shirley Temple feature, but studio executives decided that he looked too sleek to play opposite her; he was shunted into other productions, such as the 1936 jungle movie *White Hunter*. Understandably Cooper was disgruntled by this turn of events. He soon decided to try to produce pictures with all-black casts and although unable to convince executives at the major studios, he did make a deal with George Randol, a black show-business veteran interested in film production, and with Ben Rinaldo, a white with some contacts in the industry. *Dark Manhattan* was their first venture, but it was made on an extremely tight budget. In fact, the partners were so strapped for finances that they had to cancel the scheduled Los Angeles premiere of the film because they were unable to talk the processing laboratory into giving them a print on credit. Within a few weeks, however, they were able to raise enough money to premiere the film at the Apollo, and it grossed enough there to get other bookings. Cooper went on to play roles in other all-black gangster films; he also played opposite Lena Horne in *The Duke*

ANOTHER 'Sock' ALL NEGRO CAST SCREEN HIT—

from the producers of 'CALDONIA' and 'BEWARE'...loaded with fun, melody and drama! Here's a feature picture that has EVERYTHING!

Astor Pictures Presents

MANTAN MORELAND

Sensational Comedy Star of Stage, Screen and Radio in the Drama Packed Musical—

TALL, TAN and TERRIFIC

with Francine EVERETT • Monte HAWLEY
Milton WOODS • 'Butterbeans' BRADFORD
Dots JOHNSON • Rody TOOMBS • Lou SWARZ
Johnny & George • Edna Mae Harris • Myra Johnson

7 Big New Song Hits

including
You're Cheatin' Yourself
Stop You're Teasing Me
It's The Sweetness of You
Stop This Tune—88 Reasons Why

★ Bevy of Sun Tan Beauties
Golden Slipper All Girl Band
SCREEN STORY BY JOHN E. GORDON
DIRECTED BY BUD POLLARD

ASTOR PICTURES CORP.
R. M. Savini, President

Like many other black gangster films, *Tall, Tan and Terrific* (1946) compensated for deficits in plot and acting by incorporating an inordinate number of song-and-dance routines. Comedian Manton Moreland was an additional attraction.

Is Tops. When ghetto interest in the gangster films began to fade Cooper tried to change his image somewhat. Toward the end of 1940 he played a doctor in the A. W. Hackel production *Am I Guilty?* but the character was still involved with gangsters.

The declining interest in gangster stories led producers of ghetto films to make more use than ever of songs and dances. Such sequences always had been an important feature of these films no matter what the subject matter. They were used, as *Ebony* later pointed out, "to make up for deficiencies [in] acting . . . and story material." *Mystery in Swing* (1941), a product of the Goldberg brothers, was typical. The plot, such as it was, revolved around the murder of a jazz musician, which afforded all kinds of opportunities for musical numbers. The 1946 Astor release *Tall, Tan and Terrific* was a corny tale about gangsters and night-club performers, and not too different from some of the movies of the 1930s. But during this movie's hour running time seven song numbers were performed. *Tall, Tan and Terrific* had an interesting plot resolution device: a cross-eyed woman photographer in a nightclub inadvertently takes a picture of a pickpocket stealing the hero's gun just before it is used in a murder — thus saving the hero from the electric chair.[8]

Many of the ghetto films were pegged to gimmicks, in an attempt to make them more attractive to black filmgoers. *The Black King*, a 1932 Southland production, was based on the activities of Marcus Garvey, the black nationalist who had built up an enormous following immediately after World War I. This movie — directed by Bud Pollard, a white who made a career of directing "all-colored pictures" — was described by the New York *Age* as "a not clever burlesque, with the central figure . . . made to appear more illiterate than the humblest of his followers." A poem by the noted black author James Weldon Johnson was the basis for *Go Down, Death!*, a 1944 Harlemwood Studios production that was a story of religion and divine retribution in a small Southern community. After a career of shameless villainy a black vice lord and murderer imagines himself in Hell and in the course of trying to flee from Satan's minions plunges to his death in a deserted canyon.[9]

As in the silent era, notable black athletes and other public personalities made movies for the ghetto market. In 1938 Joe Louis gave a wooden performance in *The Spirit of Youth*, a Globe

Pictures film whose plot paralleled the life of the heavyweight champion. Despite the participation of veterans like Clarence Muse, this movie, as *Time* magazine put it, had a "wonderful-wax-works-plus-minstrel-show quality." The next year Henry Armstrong, the only boxer ever to hold championships in three different weight divisions, starred in *Keep Punching.* Father Divine's former No. 1 angel, Faithful Mary, was cast in Merit Pictures 1938 musical western, *Two-Gun Man from Harlem.* In 1947 singer Billy Daniels, then near the peak of his fame, played the lead role in *Sepia Cinderella,* a Herald feature about a struggling songwriter.[10]

The market for these films was limited to movie houses that catered almost exclusively to black patronage — but also showed Hollywood films about eighty percent of the time. Such Jim Crow theaters were a result of legal segregation in the South and of de facto segregation elsewhere in the United States. As late as 1940, for instance, blacks were not allowed in any Indianapolis movie theater patronized by whites. Surprisingly, the number of ghetto theaters continued to grow in number well into the 1940s, even though movie houses in the South and elsewhere increasingly made segregated balconies available to nonwhites. Nor, apparently, did antidiscrimination activity check the increase of these ghetto theaters. An exact count of the movie houses that catered only to blacks and therefore were potential customers for these films is difficult to make. For instance, some Southern theaters operated on a "midnight show for Negroes" basis (at which, according to a 1946 *Ebony* report, "Jim Crow was . . . so strong that Negroes still were not allowed to sit in the orchestra at these shows"). And in many rural areas of the country theaters functioned on a split-week basis for black and white patrons. Still, industry sources estimated that there were 232 ghetto movie houses in 1937, 388 in 1939, 430 in 1942, and 684 in 1947. Television initially had a limited impact on the ghetto movie-goer. A 1954 *Variety* article estimated that "few or no Negro film theaters have been closed in recent years."[11]

The black community's support of these movie houses is understandable, even though many of them were small third-run theaters and almost all of them were white-owned. (According to one study in the 1930s there were fewer than 20 black-owned movie houses in the United States.) Most ghetto movie houses were far from luxurious, but they did provide more comfortable and less demeaning movie-going then the crowded restricted balconies. As one black employee of the white-owned Lichtman corporation proudly declared in 1936 about the ghetto film theaters that organization controlled: "where our folks used to have to go up the fire escape into the peanut galleries of the white theater . . . they can now walk without embarrassment into our theater." Another important consideration has been pointed out by black sociologist E. Franklin Frazier, who asserted in a 1940 report that "the vast majority of Negroes" preferred their own theaters to arrangements that allowed joint attendance by both races. Frazier believed that blacks felt more at home in their own movie houses because they could "then give full rein to their feelings and impulses." Moreover, the ghetto movie houses charged less for admission — a fact of particular significance, especially in the 1930s when, as *Variety* said, "many colored residents [were] financially prohibited from any ardent attendance at the movies." During that decade some ghetto theaters outside the South charged as much as forty cents per ticket, but most charged much less. And below the Mason-Dixon line (where the bulk of these theaters were located) prices for adults ranged from a dime to a quarter, with the average ticket price being fifteen cents. The cost of admission to these theaters remained low. In 1947 the *Motion Picture Herald* estimated that "admission prices at theaters catering to Negroes . . . only average from 22 to 30 cents during the week, with a five cent increase on weekends."[12]

Such low ticket prices meant that the theaters could not afford to pay much in the way of rental fees; the over-all return to the distributors and producers of all-black films was thus limited. In addition it must not be forgotten that in many neighborhoods the theaters were in competition with each other and that only one would play a particular film. By the end of the 1930s the most successful ghetto theaters in the South would pay about $500 for an ordinary week's run while a Harlem theater such as the Apollo might pay as much as $1,000 for a first showing of a film. However, after the movie had been in distribution for a while the rental rate might fall to $6 or $7 a day. During the war years producers and distributors of all-black films did quite well in that market; the economy boomed and even in the ghetto there was

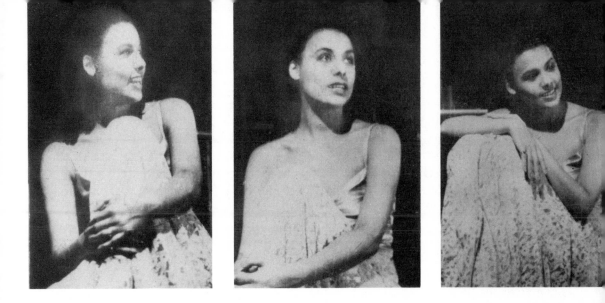

money to spend. By 1946 rental fees for the newer ghetto films had shot up, sometimes to more than $400 a booking. Many times a film played a theater for a percentage of the earnings, with the guarantee being several hundred dollars. But the older ghetto films continued to command a low price. In the postwar years black moviegoers became more choosey, and the ghetto film began to fall on hard times. By the mid-1950s, even though the theaters continued to draw well, the quickie "all-colored" movies no longer held much interest for black audiences. Operators of ghetto film theaters reported to *Variety* in 1953 that "the general run of Hollywood product covers the demand . . . of the colored patron."[13]

Because producers of the ghetto film recognized the limitations of its market in the United States and overseas, they budgeted their filmmaking accordingly. Many of the early 1930s movies were made for less than $5,000, the average cost being about

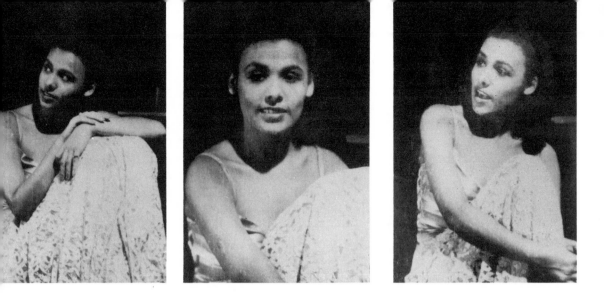

$6,000. Costs rose during the decade but *Harlem on the Prairie,* as one trade critic put it, "was made with plenty change coming out of a $20,000 bill." The producer of the Henry Armstrong vehicle, *Keep Punching,* was considered extravagant for spending over $28,000. Rarely did shooting schedules extend more than two weeks. *The Duke Is Tops* was filmed in ten days, and *Mr. Washington Goes to Town* was shot in six days. But *Mr. Washington* cost over $15,000, and by the time of its production in 1940 the average cost of a ghetto film had jumped to about $17,000. Much of this rise in costs came because the white technicians who worked on these pictures now had to be paid union scale. In the postwar era the average cost per movie jumped to about $20,000 and the shooting schedule occasionally stretched over a month. Economy still dictated the pace at which a movie was shot, however, and retakes remained rare. Unlike many Hollywood movies, even shorts, for which the ratio of footage shot to that used often was five to one or more, *Ebony Parade* had a shooting ratio of less than three to one.[14]

By budgeting so carefully and economizing wherever possible the producers of these films made a good return on their investments. And sometimes a movie did extremely well at the box office. *Harlem Is Heaven* grossed $4000 in a single week. *Harlem*

Lena Horne began her acting career in all-black films. These rare early photos were intended as publicity shots for *The Duke Is Tops* (1938). (National Film Archive) *on the Prairie* grossed over $50,000 during its first year of distribution. A *Variety* reporter estimated in 1940 that the producer's share of the gross on the ghetto-oriented films that had been produced during the preceding decade ran from $12,000 to $60,000, which meant that relatively few of these films had failed to make a profit. In 1942 Jack Goldberg judged the gross on the ghetto films that he and his brother had turned out to be about twice the cost of production, certainly no mean ratio. *Ebony* declared in 1946 that during the war years "the moviemen in the Negro market . . . waxed fat," and the magazine asserted that they averaged profits of up to 200 percent.[15]

Much of that profit was made at the expense of the performers, who often were the only blacks connected with the making of the film. The Goldbergs in 1942 said that they paid principals in their productions about $100 a week and that supporting players averaged around $60 a week. These figures seem to have been standard during the 1940s; the 1950s brought little improvement. During the 1930s the wages paid performers often were less, and some producers apparently paid no salaries at all. Lena Horne remembered that the producer of *The Duke Is Tops* had trouble with his financing and that he and his partners were "paying off in promises." The practice was all too common. The New York *Age* co-sponsored with the white-owned Action Pictures Company an all-black movie, *Harlem Aristocrat* (later released under the title *Sugar Hill Baby*). The paper urged its readers to apply for roles, promising that here was not only "a bona fide chance" to appear in the movies, but also a "chance to continue to work in future . . . productions at good salaries." Since *Harlem Aristocrat* was "a test production," however, the newspaper announced that "no salaries will be paid to those who are selected for this first production." Apparently, enough black actors and actresses had trouble getting paid during the 1930s for observers to notice the problem: in 1939 one black newspaperman in commenting on the future of all-black films declared as "most important" in this area that "performers must get their money and not excuses . . ." But rhetoric alone has rarely produced change. In 1947 some black veterans formed Pioneer Films to make an all-black movie dealing with "a handsome young buck who fell in love with and took away his father's second wife." The performers received what one black magazine called "the fanciest contracts the motion picture

Francine Everett, the female lead in *Tall, Tan and Terrific*, was an actress whose fortunes rose and fell with the ghetto film.

industry has seen in many a paper moon," but the sums involved were to come from a sliding scale of the grosses it was hoped the film would earn. Needless to say, the actors received little or nothing.[16]

A number of the black actors and actresses who played in these ghetto films appeared over and over again. Monte Hawley's career spanned the heyday of the all-black quickie, but like his Hollywood counterpart — the journeyman actor who labored in relative obscurity — it was unlikely that he was well known even to ghetto moviegoers. Hawley, who, like many of the people cast in these films, had gained acting experience with the Lafayette Players in Harlem, played a wide range of secondary parts, such as that of a racketeer in *Gang War;* occasionally he played a romantic lead such as Handsome Harry in *Tall, Tan and Terrific*. The female star of this movie was one of the few black actresses to appear in lead roles in more than a couple of ghetto films during the 1930s and 1940s. Francine Everett had become a chorus girl at sixteen in 1936, the year of her marriage. After being widowed at seventeen, when her husband was killed in an accident, she had become part of a nightclub act, The Black Kat Four, and she later became part of a WPA Federal Theatre Project group. In 1938 she appeared in an important part in *Keep Punching* and thereafter continued to play lead roles in all-black films even though she certainly was no more talented as an actress or singer than other women in the profession. In 1946 she was cast as the female lead in *Tall, Tan and Terrific*, and that same year she played *Dirty Gerty From Harlem, U.S.A.*, a Sack release that was an uncredited reworking of Maugham's *Rain* with a *Carmen Jones* ending in which Gerty is knifed by her jealous former lover. Everett's career faded along with the ghetto film.

Blacks who had made a reputation in Hollywood also starred occasionally in these ghetto films, and their names had real marquee value. In an obvious reference to *Imitation of Life,* Louise Beavers appeared in 1937 in an all-black film called *Life Goes On.* Nina Mae McKinney, when she could find no work in the industry in the late 1930s, appeared in ghetto quickies like *Straight to Heaven* and *Daughters of Jamaica.* In 1934, while still in England, she had appeared in a Gaumont-British film, *Kentucky Minstrels,* which had a partly black cast. It related the fall and rise of a team who starred in English blackface shows. In the United States this film, which had been directed by the British quickie specialist John Baxter, was called *Life Is Real,* another obvious attempt to cash in on *Imitation of Life.*

Perhaps the most successful commuter between the ghetto film and the Hollywood feature was Mantan Moreland. Born in Louisiana in 1902, he ran away from home while still in his early teens, to go into show business. After various stints with a traveling circus, on the black vaudeville circuit, and in several New York all-black shows, he wound up stranded in Hollywood in the mid-1930s. He soon found work in the movies and made over seventy-five films. For a while in the early 1940s he shared a series with Frankie Darro, a perennial juvenile tough guy. When Darro was drafted, Monogram Pictures, the studio that turned out that series, cast Moreland as Charlie Chan's chauffeur in another series that it had just taken over. Between 1944 and 1949 Moreland appeared in 15 Chan films. In them the black actor was, as Peter Noble aptly points out, "a stooge in true tradition."

No black actor "has ever rolled his eyes with such abandon . . . has ever tried so hard to revert to the Stepin Fetchit sub-human characterization." Curiously, he played the same in his many ghetto films. His success in both ghetto films and in Hollywood led white producer Ted Toddy to star him in such movies as *Mantan Messes Up* (1948), which drew well in black neighborhoods for years. Among Moreland's most demeaning as well as his funniest ghetto films are those he made with Flourney Miller. One of the co-authors of *Shuffle Along*, the 1921 smash all-Negro hit that launched the 1920s vogue for black singing and dancing, Miller was also an accomplished comedian. However, except for a bit in *Stormy Weather*, his movie work seems to have been limited to all-black films, of which he made many. Among the films Moreland and Miller worked in together were *Harlem on the Prairie* and *Mr. Washington Goes to Town*. In the 1950s a changing attitude toward this kind of comedy as well as serious illness brought Moreland's career to an almost complete halt. But in time he began to work again, his appearances including a part in an all-black theater production of *Waiting for Godot* and small parts in two movies at the end of the 1960s.[17]

Direction of these performers was usually in the hands of whites. Oscar Micheaux continued to direct his own films, but there were very few other blacks who got the chance to do so. One was Spencer Williams, who directed *Go Down, Death!* Williams, who had a long career in ghetto films in various capacities, including acting, had also been in charge of the production of *The Blood of Jesus*, another religiously oriented feature that had been released by Sack in 1942. Generally speaking, the white directors of all-black films, like most of the technicians involved, were men with experience in the industry but with little stature in it. Edgar Ulmer, the director of *Moon Over Harlem*, has recently become a darling of the auteur critics because of his Hollywood films; movie historian and critic Andrew Sarris called him "one of the minor glories of the cinema." But most of the more than one hundred films he directed were trashy productions like *Girls in Chains* and *The Pirates of Capri*. The director of *Harlem on the Prairie* was Sam Newfield, who was also involved in a variety of cheaply made Hollywood movies including the Lone Rider series. Jed Buell, the producer of *Harlem on the Prairie* and the director of *Mr. Washington Goes to Town*, was described by *Time* as "a man who has made a specialty of shoe-string productions." Arthur Leonard, who was responsible for such ghetto films as *Straight to Heaven,* was a one-time assistant director for Warner Brothers; he became involved in making all-black movies when the company closed its New York City production facilities. In his words: "I figured there wasn't a chance in the Hollywood market and . . . the best thing I could do was to enter some freak field."[18]

Production and distribution were also almost exclusively controlled by whites. And concerned as they were with making a profit, they gave little thought to changing the movie image of the black or of furthering his knowledge of film production. These whites probably were not consciously racist, but their attitudes and efforts were a further manifestation of American society's "put down" of the black community.

Jack and Bert Goldberg were among the more important producers and distributors of ghetto films. They had other show business interests as well, but they concentrated on all-black films, operating under a succession of corporate identities, among which were International Roadshows, Hollywood Productions, and Herald Pictures. The tall, swarthy, somewhat older Jack was the more important of the two brothers. In 1912, while still in his mid-teens, he became involved in the movie business, working for Marcus Loew. In the early 1920s he and his brother began producing all-black films on a limited basis. The late 1930s was the period of their greatest activity. Jack Goldberg, according to one white newspaperman, was called "the 'Abraham Lincoln of Harlem' among show folks above 125th St." And he did offer hard pressed black performers considerable if low-paid employment as well as some chance to demonstrate their talents. But his general attitude was a sure indication of why white control of all-black films was so unfortunate. Jack Goldberg said that he and his brother were "crazy about our colored associates. We find them willing, eager, accomplished, and always gay. There's never a downcast moment when a Negro film is in production." This view of the black also extended to Goldberg's concept of what the "wonderful" ghetto audiences wanted to see. He said there was "nothing sophisticated" about them, "all they know is that they want plenty of singing and dancing or drama depicting Negro life in a Negro spirit."[19]

This attitude also seemed to dominate the management of Sack Amusement Enterprises, described by the trade press as "the largest distributor" of black films in the United States. Most of this company's energies were concentrated on the distribution of these films to the ghetto. Alfred Sack was a tough-minded Southerner who knew how to move with the times. (After World War II he opened one of the first foreign film theaters in Texas.) Under his direction the company was very promotion-minded; in distributing all-black films it played up any angle that seemed likely to increase a film's business. Unfortunately, the usual advertising and publicity were of the kind that emphasized the outlandish, the lurid, the caricatured images with which the black community had been stereotyped. Thus the pressbook of *Go Down, Death!* proposed as one catch phrase for advertising the film: "That Old Time Religion Lives Again In All Its Glory." Moreover, Sack seemingly was unwilling to gamble on all-black films that deviated from the caricatures or to provide a more realistic approach to black problems and life in the United States.[20]

Astor Films was a latecomer to the field. Robert Savini, the genial head of the company, had started working in the industry in 1904 with Dixie Film Corporation and had built up experience in various aspects of the business. In 1946 the sixty-year-old Savini decided that all-black films could be a profitable venture. *Tall, Tan and Terrific* was Astor's first all-black feature: it was quickly followed by Louis Jordan in *Beware*. Savini correctly anticipated "much success," but as the ghetto market faded, Astor under his successors moved on to foreign-film distribution — its most notable presentation being *La Dolce Vita*.[21]

Blacks interested in producing films for the ghetto market rarely worked without white associates, and those who did go it alone had great difficulty. In 1929 William Foster in a renewed burst of enthusiasm tried to organize another Foster Photoplay Company to produce all-black films. Foster and his partners did manage to convince the California authorities that the company should be allowed to sell stock. The prospectus ringingly declared that "white companies defiantly say 'if you want better pictures of your race, make them yourself,' and the reply of the Foster Photoplay Company is 'we will.'" But for all this brave talk, Foster's plans came to naught. In 1930 some blacks organized the Biltmore Corporation to make "creditable talking pictures of Negroes that will show them on the screen doing more than acting a monkey or coward," but again nothing came of their efforts.[22]

Oscar Micheaux, after declaring bankruptcy in 1928, had become increasingly dependent on white financing. And at the beginning of 1931 the New York *Age,* commenting on the activities of the Micheaux Film Corporation, reported that "while Mr. Micheaux remains the titular head of the motion picture company, the control has passed into the hands of the lessees of the Lafayette and other theaters in Harlem." These men were white. The *Age* also reported that the first film to be produced under this new arrangement would be *The Exile.* This film, which premiered during the spring of 1931, was very similar in spirit and content to many of Micheaux's earlier productions. *The Exile* told of a young black whose fiancée comes into ownership of a mansion in Chicago that serves as a combination cabaret and brothel. The young man, appalled, leaves the city for the plains of South Dakota. There he meets a pure and virtuous young girl whom he assumes is white. He becomes her friend and protector, but the race barrier stands between them until it is revealed that (as one black critic put it) "she has the one tenth of one per cent Negro blood in her veins which makes her a Negro." There are also a number of complex sub-plots, including one about an Ethiopian student who falls into the clutches of the mansion's owner and who kills her when she tries to throw him over.[23]

The Exile had some interesting and imaginative touches. One was the unauthorized filming of the outside of steel magnate Charles Schwab's New York City mansion to represent the Chicago bawdy house. Another was the sensuous exhibition of "muscle dancing" by Louise "Jota" Cook, a Harlem nightclub favorite. But on the whole the movie was crude, old fashioned, and not very interesting. According to one report, "the Harlem audiences giggled in the wrong places at the absurd plot." Nevertheless, Micheaux (still thought of as the "daddy of Negro moving pictures") and *The Exile* were spared harsh criticism in the black press. This may explain why the New York *Age* critic, while indicating that the film had "many obvious faults," could still assert that it was "genuinely entertaining."[24]

As the years passed the black community's response to Micheaux's films became more critical. Between 1931 and 1940 he turned out over ten movies, but all were old fashioned in content and inferior in style and technique even to the quickies made for the ghetto market. In 1939 he circulated statements asserting that *Lying Lips,* his latest film, as well as his other productions, was "being nixed by Harlem theaters in favor of pictures made by white concerns." But Micheaux's lack of bookings can also be explained by the poor quality of his films, which made them commercially nonviable as he came under increasing criticism from other blacks. In 1933 the Baltimore *Afro-American* carried an "Open Letter to Oscar Micheaux" expressing admiration for his efforts, sincerity, and tenacity, but strongly criticizing his "jumbly-fumbly manner of directing" as well as urging him to "give the public less smut" and to "forget for a while that colored gentlemen go West, or North . . . and become millionaires . . . and come back to Chicago and Harlem to spend their cash and kick up hell." Two years later a New York *Age* columnist in commenting on Micheaux's latest features said that the producer might be a pioneer in making black films but that "when he does so by holding . . . the rest of us to . . . ridicule, we can well do without him — and gladly."[25]

The tempo of criticism increased so much that in 1938 Micheaux's latest effort was greeted with a picket line when it premiered at an RKO theater in Harlem. *God's Step Children* was a crude film but not much different from many of Micheaux's earlier works. It was about a selfish, light-skinned mulatto who, although raised by a black foster mother and married to a black man by whom she has a son, continually "disdains the race" before she comes to a well-deserved end. The demonstrations against the movie were tied to the Communist party's intense interest in enlisting black support, and the demonstrators were led by members of various party groups and front organizations. The afternoon of the first day of picketing, a spokesman for the demonstrators declared that "we asked that the picture be withdrawn immediately because it slandered Negroes . . . , presenting the false picture that all light Negroes hate their darker brethren. We also protested against speeches made by characters in the picture implying that Negroes fell for any kind of gambling game and that only 'one Negro in a million tries to think.' The theater manager refused to heed the protest and infuriated a delegation sent to see him when he asserted 'sorry, but that was

The later films of Oscar Micheaux drew severe criticism from blacks for exploiting his race. *God's Step Children*, about a mulatto woman who spurns her black origins, was picketed at its premiere in 1938 and soon withdrawn from distribution.

Negro life.'" By mid-evening Micheaux had agreed to delete some of the scenes that aroused objection, but this concession satisfied no one. The next day brought another large picket line as well as meetings between Micheaux, RKO personnel, and spokesmen for the protesters. The outcome of these talks was an end to the showing of the movie, an announcement by RKO that no theater in its chain would book *God's Step Children,* and expressions of regret by Micheaux, who said that he "realized now that there were objectionable features to the picture" and that he "intended to remedy the siuation."[26]

Micheaux, however, went on as before. During the war years he turned once more to the novel and had some limited success in publishing his books. His last major film effort was released by Astor in 1948. *The Betrayal* was a static, uneven, and fuzzy reworking of this first movie, *The Homesteader,* and had a three-hour running time. But Micheaux still retained some of his finesse as a promoter. He premiered this dud in New York City at the mid-town theater where the play *The Green Pastures* had run for a number of seasons. Three years later, on April 1, 1951, Micheaux died in Charlotte, North Carolina, while on a tour of the South to promote his books and films. His passing caused little stir, for the times had passed him by, and he had long outlived the adulation he had once received. Micheaux is important because he was one of the first black filmmakers to make an energetic attempt to break through the barriers erected by white society. But it was a failed attempt and one that ultimately resulted in a parroting of the industry's demeaning image of the black.

The quickies that had superseded Micheaux's productions did not long outlive him as a genre. The all-black film rapidly faded away as blacks began to get better roles in major studio films and as integration became a major concern in American life. Still, the ghetto films had given black performers a chance to exhibit their considerable talents, and not always within the accepted stereotyped molds. True enough, they frequently played stooges and buffoons in these films, but they also played heroes and heroines; occasionally these movies could buoy the spirits of their audiences. Certainly ghetto kids could look up to Herb Jeffries, the lead in *The Bronze Buckaroo,* just as their white counterparts admired Gene Autry. Beyond all this, however, the value of these

Herb Jeffries (center) was the Gene Autry of black
westerns. Here he has just punched out the villain
in *The Bronze Buckaroo* (1939).

films to the black community was, as a 1939 *Sight and Sound*
article judged, "dubious." If the all-black film offered its performers a wider range of roles, it did so in anything but a realistic
milieu, the setting inevitably being an artificial and essentially
degrading one created by the dominant white culture. This
aspect of these films is particularly poignant. Movies were the
most immediate expression of the American dream in which
everybody could make good, in which the humble triumphed
over wicked adversaries, in which the deserving weak outwitted

the unjust powerful, in which there was the promise of economic well-being, freedom, and happiness for all. The all-black films, whether made by blacks or whites, tapped the mythic base of the United States, drew on the mainstream of American popular culture, and gave blacks a place within it. And yet, these movies were designed to be shown in separate and inferior theaters, a reality that irrevocably darkened the bright illusion on the screen.[27]

9

TOWARD
A NEW IMAGE

FROM THE EVIDENCE presented on the screen, it would have been hard to tell that the 1950s and 1960s were a period of some of the greatest social, economic, and demographic upheavals in the history of the United States, especially for the black. In 1954 the Supreme Court made Jim Crow public schools illegal. Nonviolent sit-ins and demonstrations to integrate Southern public facilities began, bringing to the fore the Reverend Martin Luther King, Jr., and his brand of passive resistance. Congress passed civil-rights legislation dealing with voting and public accommodations. As the historian Otis Graham, Jr., sardonically pointed out, "now that the laws of the nation required equal treatment for all regardless of color, blacks could presumably begin to vote and go to school and eat and get haircuts along with everyone else and live happily ever after."[1]

Black militancy increased, however, as it became clear that a more vicious kind of economic discrimination persisted, condemning most American nonwhites (as well as many whites) to second-class citizenship. President Lyndon Johnson initiated a "War on Poverty," but funding fell increasingly short as the war in Vietnam escalated. As large segments of the black population

Two escaped convicts, Sidney Poitier and Tony Curtis, make their improbably symbolic way through a southern slough of despond in Stanley Kramer's 1958 *The Defiant Ones*. (National Film Archive/ Courtesy United Artists)

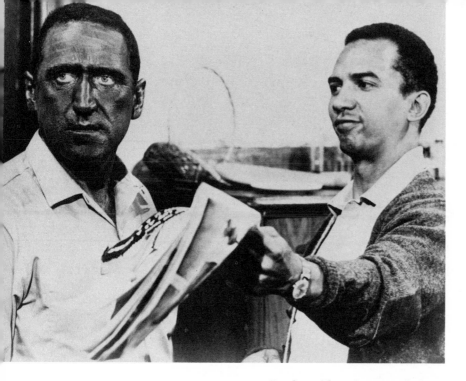

Looking like a burnt-cork impersonator out of D. W. Griffith, James Whitmore, left, acted a white writer who changed color to see how it felt in *Black Like Me* (1964). Al Freeman, Jr., is the real black. (Courtesy Walter Reade-Sterling)

grew ever more angry about rotten housing, poor jobs, and inferior standards of living, "Black Power" and militant confrontation replaced Dr. King's ideal of nonviolence. There was widespread rioting in the urban ghettos — the most violent and serious outbreaks taking place in the summer of 1967. If violence has lessened since then, the posture of the black community remains a militant one.

Meanwhile, only a handful of films touched on these themes. There was, for instance, *Take a Giant Step*, a 1958 Hecht-Hill-Lancaster production for United Artists release, which dealt with a black adolescent's increasing awareness of what it means to be black in a white world even when shielded by middle-class comforts in a friendly white neighborhood. Resistance to school desegregation was the subject of *The Intruder*, which was produced and directed by Roger Corman — a prolific filmmaker much better known for his many horror films. This 1961 movie shows how an agitator comes to a small town and stirs up the populace against integration. The result is Ku Klux Klan torch-light parades, the terrorization of a black family, the bombing of a black church and death of its minister, the savage beating of a white editor whose respect for the law is stronger than his distaste for integration, and the attempted lynching of a black student leader because of false charges of rape that had been arranged by the agitator. In its final moments the movie deteriorates into corny melodrama, but *The Intruder* is a movie that deserves to be remembered. The same cannot be said of *Black Like Me*. This 1964 Walter Reade-Sterling release rings false even though it was based on the adventures of a real white person, the author John Howard Griffin, who in the late 1950s had darkened his skin and had traveled through the South, posing as a black. In the movie the hero runs a predictable gamut of humiliation, discrimination, segregation, and hostility. The gimmick was interesting, but events were moving so fast that such experiences already seemed hopelessly dated: *Black Like Me* has value only as a curiosity piece. A much tougher film, made the same year, was *The Cool World*. Produced by Frederick Wiseman and directed by Shirley Clarke, it used both professionals and amateurs in its cast, and was among the first movies to depict the urban black culture. In its treatment of teenagers in Harlem the film graphically portrayed the bleakness and shoddiness of ghetto life.

That year also saw what must be one of the most vital portraits of black people ever made — Michael Roemer and Robert Young's independent production, *Nothing But A Man*, a movie that has continued to live up to its makers' claim "to present . . . Negro characters as human beings." *Nothing But A Man* is about Duff Anderson, a worker on a railroad section gang that comes to a small Alabama town. There he meets and marries the schoolteacher daughter of a preacher. But he runs into trouble and, unable to cope with his difficulties or with his wife's pregnancy, runs away. After a visit with his dying alcoholic father, Duff decides to return to his wife and try to come to terms with the world in which he lives. The movie ended free of cliché and with neither a contrived resolution or portentous promises. The couple was beautifully acted by Ivan Dixon and Abbey Lincoln, who were almost universally praised, as was the movie. *Nothing*

In the 1953 *Androcles and the Lion* Woody Strode was highly visible — as the lion. (National Film Archive)

But A Man did shrink from showing the bias and hatred in that world, but it sensitively explored the meaning of love and honor. The participants in a 1969 multi-racial conference on "The Negro Film Image" declared that this film "could well serve as a model for filmmakers and producers."[2]

These movies, and a few others like them, were out of the mainstream of distribution and were not widely seen at that time. For the most part, blacks continued to be relegated to secondary roles — when they were visible at all. A few producers did attempt to exploit the changed situation. Otto Preminger, for

But as late as 1961, Strode was still playing benighted savage roles, as in *The Sins of Rachel Cade*. (Warner Brothers)

instance, while filming his 1962 adaptation of the novel *Advise and Consent,* garnered an unusual amount of publicity by announcing that Dr. King would play a bit part as a U.S. Senator from Georgia. He never did, as it turned out, but Preminger got a lot of free advertising.

If, as Thomas Carlyle once postulated, "history is the essence of innumerable biographies," then much of the history of the black in the movies of this time must be told in terms of the careers of stars like Dorothy Dandridge, Harry Belafonte, and Sidney Poitier. It was around them — whether willingly or not — that the old movie fantasies were revised and new ones were introduced.*

Consider the bittersweet progress of Dorothy Dandridge, the first black woman to be nominated for an Oscar as best actress. She earned it for her interpretation of a fiery, lustful, amoral slut — the title character in the 1954 Otto Preminger production of the Broadway hit *Carmen Jones*. Although thirty-two years old at the time the film was made, Dandridge had spent more than two decades in show business: her career both before and after the nomination typifies the problems black actresses encountered even as the traditional movie stereotypes of the black woman began to change.

As a child Dorothy Dandridge had appeared in bit parts or as an extra in movies such as the Marx Brothers comedy *A Day at the Races* (MGM, 1937). In her late teens and early twenties she played maids and native girls or appeared as a singer in the musical sequences of various features. During the late 1940s and early 1950s she became a highly successful nightclub singer. But this did not lead immediately to better movie roles. In her two 1951 releases, which marked her return to film, she played a jungle queen in a Tarzan movie and the girlfriend of a Harlem Globetrotter basketball star. The next year, in an unusual example of off-beat casting, she acted a warmhearted, sensitive, quiet, small-town grade-school teacher in the MGM production *Bright Road*, which was released in 1953.

Made with an all-black cast (except for a single white actor who played a doctor), *Bright Road* was an adaptation of a short story written by a young black teacher from Alabama, Mary Elizabeth Vroman. The movie, set in a segregated Southern school, recounts the problems of a new third-grade teacher and her relationship with a "backward" eleven-year-old boy. Confused but stubborn, antagonistic but proud, he has spent two years in each grade and is considered a potential delinquent. The teacher finds a way to reach him and through her loving patience

---

*First-rate black actors and actresses like Godfrey Cambridge, Ossie Davis, Ruby Dee, Gloria Foster, Al Freeman, Jr., Bernie Hamilton, Brock Peters, and Beah Richards appeared in the movies during these years. But neither they nor the films they appeared in were seminal to the changing treatment of the black on screen. For all the enjoyment derived from Ossie Davis's performance in the 1963 film version of his hit play *Purlie Victorious*, this comedy's satiric utilization of the traditional caricatures had almost no impact as a film and was not widely seen.

his transformation begins. The movie treated both adults and children without parody or condescension but otherwise cannot be said to have done much for the black image. The only direct reference to discrimination occurs when the boy is told that all men on earth are brothers and he asks "if white people and black people are brothers how come they don't act like brothers?" Nor did the movie give any indication of the social changes then underway. Harry Belafonte, who in his first screen appearance appeared in a small role as the school's principal, some years later characterized the movie as "a nice, bland Lassie-like thing." In any event, MGM allowed the movie to languish in distribution. Certainly the studio, which in its inappropriate publicity described Dandridge as a "sexy, satiny nightclub singer," had relatively little at stake. *Bright Road* was made on a shoestring with a low-paid cast and a two-and-a-half week shooting schedule. As the producer commented, "the Negro audience will just about pay for the cost of this picture."[3]

Carmen Jones was released in the fall of 1954, nearly eleven years after the successful all-black reworking of Bizet's opera by Oscar Hammerstein II had opened on Broadway. In both, a flamboyant, passionate siren seduces a man from his duty and, after getting him into serious trouble, goes away with another lover. In the end, the first man kills her. The opera's French version of early nineteenth-century Spain had been transformed and updated to the southern United States and Chicago during World War II. Instead of being a worker in a Spanish cigarette factory Carmen Jones is an employee in a war plant that turns out parachutes. The man she seduces had become Joe, a black MP from a nearby army camp. And when she goes away it is not to Seville with a toreador but to Chicago with a champion prizefighter. The movie closely followed Hammerstein's adaptation.

James Baldwin commented that the movie depended "very heavily on a certain quaintness, a certain lack of inhibition taken to be typical of Negroes . . ." Certainly the central characters carry the exaggerated taint of earlier caricatures. The picture drawn of black women is an unpleasant one. As Baldwin pointed out (and he was echoed by others) "the implicit parallel between an amoral Gipsy and an amoral Negro woman is the entire root idea" of Carmen Jones. She is a direct descendent of Chick, the vamp in Vidor's *Hallelujah*, although, given circumstances in the

Dorothy Dandridge was one of the most beautiful and talented black actresses, but her road to stardom was hard, lonesome, and ultimately tragic. Here she plays a ladies maid in *Lady from New Orleans* (1942), a native princess in *Tarzan's Peril* (1952) (National Film Archive), the temptress (vamping a willing Harry Belafonte) in *Carmen Jones* (1954) (Courtesy Twentieth Century–Fox. 1954 Twentieth Century–Fox Film Corporation), and a West Indian shop girl who falls in love with a white civil servant (John Justin) in *Island in the Sun* (1957). (Courtesy Twentieth Century–Fox. © 1957 Twentieth Century–Fox Film Corporation)

1950s, she is less crude. But Carmen's irresponsible views on life and love are made clear in the first number. Wearing as suggestive an outfit as the Code would allow in 1954, she sings:

> Love ain't nobody's angel-child,
> And he won't pay any mind to you . . .
> You go for me, and I'm taboo,
> But if you're hard to get, I go for you.
> And if I do, then you are through . . .

Her friends are equally unprincipled and wild. At a black roadhouse, the dancers move with frenzied abandon while a character (played by Pearl Bailey) sings lines such as:

> Beat out that rhythm on a drum,
> And I don't need no tune at all . . .
> I feel it beatin' in my bones.
> It feels like twenty million tom-toms.

Although the leads had achieved fame as vocalists, their voices were dubbed in the musical numbers because of the operatic quality of the score; Marilyn Horne sang for Dorothy Dandridge.[4]

The black actress won critical acclaim and a contract with Twentieth Century-Fox for her performance. But although she was now considered a star and was able to command over four times the $18,000 paid her for *Carmen Jones,* she was disappointed in the roles offered her. She did not want to be cast as a wanton but as "a woman seeking love and a husband, the same as other women." These roles were denied her because, as her manager later explained, "the public wasn't ready for this yet . . . a Dorothy Dandridge had to sizzle on-screen." She now faced the same difficulty that had stymied black actresses in the past and would continue to do so into the 1960s. Except for roles as teachers or social workers, they could still expect to be restricted to playing menials or exotics of one sort of another. Miss Dandridge was not the only one who found herself in this bind. For instance, among Pearl Bailey's few film roles at the time were a wise-cracking housekeeper in Paramount's *That Certain Feeling* (1956) and a drunken blues singer in MGM's *All the Fine Young Cannibals* (1960). Thirty years after Louise Beavers' screen debut, she made her last film appearance as a maid in the 1961 United Artists release *The Facts of Life*. Eartha Kitt, who had been a smash in the Broadway review *New Faces of 1952* and in the 1954 screen version of the show, thereafter played mainly roles of women with a scarlet past. As for Dandridge, the one film she made after *Carmen Jones* in which she did not portray a sexy native girl was another all-black musical, *Porgy and Bess*, in a role similar to that of Carmen.[5]

The character of Bess is (in the words of playwright Lorraine Hansberry) that of "a slit-skirted wench . . . who sniffs 'happy dust' and drinks liquor from a bottle at the rim of an alley crap game." She is ignorant, superstitious, and wayward — a throwback to an older caricature, as were most of the other leading characters in this 1959 Goldwyn production. The movie was set in a pre-World War I ghetto area of Charleston, South Carolina, known as Catfish Row. Whites are seen briefly and then only as figures of authority such as policemen. Porgy, a good-natured cripple who gets around in a goat-drawn cart, is also an inveterate craps player. After Bess's lover Crown savagely kills a man during a dice game and flees to avoid the police, Porgy offers her shelter. Later, in a scene reminiscent of the demeaning pre-World War I "nigger subjects," Bess is persuaded that a document Porgy buys from a lawyer for $1.50 gives her the legal right to live with him, even though they are not married. After an outing on a nearby island during which a rakish dope peddler, Sportin' Life, pokes fun at Biblical teachings, Bess is caught by Crown. Despite her protests that she is now Porgy's woman, Crown forces her to stay with him. After a few days Bess is able to return to Porgy. Crown follows — and is killed by the cripple. Porgy is arrested. Sportin' Life successfully tempts Bess into going to New York City with him. Porgy returns to Catfish Row a few days later, finds Bess gone, decides to find her, and leaves for the North in his goat-drawn cart.[6]

This movie had its origins in a 1920s novel by a white Southerner, DuBose Heyward, who with his wife turned it into a successful 1927 theater production. In the early 1930s a number of people including Al Jolson (who envisioned himself as Porgy) were interested in adapting the work as a musical. Heyward chose to collaborate with George Gershwin, who used the dramatization as the basis for what he called a "folk opera." *Porgy and*

Bess, which premiered in 1935, contains some of Gershwin's most lyrical and haunting music. But the concept of a folk opera resulted in mixed critical reactions, and the production was not a financial success. When it was revived in 1942 the musical recitatives were changed to spoken dialogue and other operatic elements were pruned. These revisions and an increased awareness by the critics contributed to the revival's enormous success, and it had a long run. In the early 1950s the work was successfully revived once more, having by this time attained the stature of an "American classic." It became a staple of the U.S. government's cultural exchange program. Various productions toured the world for a number of years. Each successive production of the Gershwin work in the United States had been revised somewhat in language and style to offset protests against its well-meaning but unfortunate depiction of black life.

In the past black performers, whatever their personal feelings about *Porgy and Bess*, had appreciated the opportunity for work. But when Samuel Goldwyn announced his intention to film it in 1957, there were not only strong objections voiced by such groups as the NAACP but also a boycott of the proposed film by black performers. Sidney Poitier, who at first agreed to play Porgy, balked and withdrew from the project. After this withdrawal Goldwyn seems to have had trouble casting black actors and actresses. But the situation changed suddenly in December, 1957, when Poitier again agreed to play Porgy. He told the press then that he was "confident that Mr. Goldwyn with his characteristic good taste and integrity will present the property in a sensitive manner." Some years later Poitier indicated that other factors may have influenced his decision: "I hated doing *Porgy and Bess* but pressure was brought to bear from a number of quarters and there was a threat of my career stopping dead still." After Poitier's change of mind, a company was put together quickly. But problems continued to plague the production. In 1958, after rehearsals had started and just before shooting began a mysterious fire destroyed the Catfish Row set and the costumes. Meanwhile, Rouben Mamoulian, who had staged the original Gershwin work, was fired as director and replaced by Otto Preminger — whose interpretation only provoked further disputes.[7]

If the finished movie was a flop, changing times played a large part in its failure. By 1959 the civil-rights revolution was well under way. The movie received much more criticism from the black community than had earlier films like *Carmen Jones*. The performers' boycott had been one manifestation of this feeling. To be sure, the black press was not uniformly hostile; one columnist even declared that the NAACP should award Goldwyn a medal. But much of the comment was similar to the remarks made by A. S. "Doc" Young in the Los Angeles *Sentinel*, who attacked the movie because it was simply another showcase for the old caricatures. "The big evil it does can be charged to this: Hollywood will not, Goldwyn will not, produce an antidote. If he will spend $7 million to make the story of Dr. Martin Luther King . . . and distribute . . . this saga around the world, then I'll say, let him have *Porgy and Bess*." The industry might change its way of interpreting black life in the years to come; but Hollywood would not really improve its vision of it.[8]

But more than just a veteran producer's failure to understand a changing American society doomed *Porgy and Bess*. It was a bad film. As in *Carmen Jones*, there was dubbing of the voices of the leads in the musical numbers; critics commented on the inappropriateness of the voices and the imperfect synchronization. The production was static, flawed, and curiously lackluster despite the millions spent on it. Neither of the two leads received good notices, and even those critics who liked the movie were not kind to Dandridge, who was miscast as Bess. It was her last American film, and a few years later she was dead. A disastrous marriage, career disappointments, an inability to cope with a racist society, and ultimately, too much alcohol and too many pills, killed her at the age of 42.[9]

But the sad story of Dorothy Dandridge cannot end without mention of one other film in which she starred. The 1957 Darryl F. Zanuck production, *Island in the Sun*, is noteworthy not for its inherent merit — it had little — but because it sympathetically treated miscegenation. By the time that *Island in The Sun* was filmed, the Code had been revised to allow this formerly taboo subject in industry films. As a black newspaperman sarcastically put it, "colored and white could get together . . . as long as it is all in good taste." The decision to end this ban of some twenty-five years' standing was the result of many factors, not the least of which was a sharply declining box office. As one black magazine pointed out, "U.S. studio bosses . . . have watched foreign films profit from interracial romance themes." In Zanuck's words, "controversial pictures . . . can be pretty good box office." *Island in the Sun* was certainly that. The film, which cost about $2,500,000 and grossed over $8,000,000, was among the most profitable films Zanuck made as an independent producer.[10]

Island in the Sun gave movie goers not just one but *two* mixed romances, with a tragic mulatto theme thrown in for good measure. The eldest son of an aristocratic family on the British West

Harry Belafonte and Joan Fontaine made more contact in this publicity still for *Island in the Sun* than they ever did in the actual movie. (National Film Archive/Courtesy Twentieth Century–Fox. © 1957 Twentieth Century–Fox Film Corporation)

Indian island of Santa Marta finds out that he has "a strain of colored blood." When his family's racial ancestry becomes public knowledge he attempts to make use of it in a losing electoral fight with a young native labor leader. But the revelation also drives him to gloom, drink, wife abuse, and murder. At the movie's beginning the labor leader (played by Harry Belafonte) and a native shop girl (Dorothy Dandridge) are lovers, but they both take up with whites — he with a rich and attractive woman (Joan Fontaine) and she with one of the governor's English aides.

But for all this interracial gadding about, the film treated the physical aspects of these relationships gingerly. The shop girl and the aide do embrace. But it is made clear that they must leave Santa Marta to find happiness, and so they cheerfully trot off to England and Happily-Ever-After. The relationship between the Belafonte and Fontaine characters was treated even more circumspectly. There were no love scenes between them, only, as one critic put it, "glances of admiration and dialogue of almost Firbankian simplicity." A scene in which he lifts her down from a carriage seemed erotic simply because there was virtually no other physical contact between them in the film. Zanuck denied that fear of censorship influenced his handling of the relationship: "there is no scene that calls for kissing. There was no conscious effort to avoid it." But an angry Belafonte thought otherwise. He asserted that "where the normal sequence of events would have led to romantic situations between myself and Joan Fontaine they were played down." Later he recalled somewhat whimsically that he and Fontaine were permitted a scene drinking from the same cocoanut, "but the day we filmed that I caught cold. I guess that's what happens in these interracial situations." Ultimately the two characters go their separate ways after he rejects her, arguing that for a white woman to marry a black "would mean only snubs and misery for the girl." And he adds that someday the girl "would forget herself and call me a nigger."[11]

The box-office success of *Island in the Sun* led other film producers to climb on the miscegenation bandwagon, and to imitate the treatment of interracial couples in the Zanuck production. There was an obvious double standard that governed the intimate relationships of blacks and whites of the opposite sex. Insofar as the Code then allowed, white men and black women were physically shown as lovers. But there was no on-screen sexual contact between black men and white women; that sort of physical relationship would remain forbidden well into the 1960s.

Moreover, when a white man got involved in an interracial pairing, the girl was often a mulatto character — who was portrayed by a white actress. (Neither setting nor period seemed to affect such casting.) Yvonne De Carlo, for instance, played a mulatto in the 1957 Warner Brothers production *Band of Angels*, which was set in the antebellum and Civil War South. Based on a powerful Robert Penn Warren novel, which had an entirely different emphasis, the movie was slack and silly in its portrayal of a mulatto girl who was raised as white by her Kentucky planter father. On his death she discovers the truth about her ancestry, and is sold downriver as a slave. In New Orleans she is bought by an ex-slave trader turned planter (Clark Gable). His major-domo (Sidney Poitier) flees North and becomes a Union soldier. In due course the Gable and DeCarlo characters fall in love. The Civil War interrupts this romance, but thanks to the major-domo, whose earlier hatred for his master has abated, the lovers are enabled to face the future together. Miscegenation was not the movie's only selling point; as *Ebony* put it, "the film's most startling scenes are provided by crackerjack Negro actor Poitier . . . who, during a climactic argument with DeCarlo, slaps her across the room."

More such films soon followed. *Kings Go Forth*, a perfectly dreadful 1958 United Artists release, was set in southern France during the latter part of World War II. Natalie Wood played a mulatto woman who becomes involved with two American soldiers who are on leave. At the end of the movie, one of them is dead; the other, who has lost an arm in battle, returns to the woman, and it is implied that they will marry (would it have been permissible if he had retained all his limbs?). According to producer Frank Ross, an admitted opponent of miscegenation, pressure was brought to bear on him to have a nonwhite actress play the girl. He "resisted that idea because I felt that the picture would lose its dramatic kick if the girl were Negro."[12]

In the 1959 remake of *Imitation of Life* produced by Ross Hunter for Universal-International, the plot was essentially the same as in the 1934 version. But this time the light-skinned daughter who wanted to pass was played by white actress Susan

Kohner, who won an Oscar nomination for her portrayal. This character was now known as Sarah Jane, and her mother was called Annie Johnson. As in the earlier version the Johnsons live with a white widow, but the widow no longer runs a pancake business. Instead she is an actress who has sacrificed everything to further her career. The loyal Annie (played by Juanita Moore, who also won an Oscar nomination) serves as her housekeeper and confidante. The director, Douglas Sirk, assumed responsibility for the demise of the pancake business. "Nowadays," he said, "a Negro woman who got rich *could* buy a house, and wouldn't be dependent to such a degree on the white woman . . . So I had to change the axis of the film and make the Negro woman just the typical Negro, a servant, without much she could call her own but the friendship, love, and charity of a white mistress." Most of the other twists on the plot involved Sarah Jane. When she runs away, it is to become a chorus girl. And she acquires a white boyfriend who, after discovering that her mother is black, beats her up to the accompaniment of screaming jazz music.[13]

Such sensationalist scenes were also found in other movies, for as time went on, an interracial relationship between a white man and a black woman was in itself neither startling nor profitable. The 1959 Albert Zugsmith production *The Night of the Quarter Moon* describes the consequences of a rich, eligible white bachelor's decision to marry a woman (played by Julie London) who is one-quarter Portuguese Angolan. Because he is still suffering the aftereffects of brainwashing attempts in a North Korean POW camp, he breaks down in the face of opposition to his marriage from his mother and from neighbors who harass him. (Why did white men who fell in love with black women always seem to have domineering mothers?) The mother tries to annul the marriage, but the wife fights back, hiring a black attorney. Finally in a courtroom scene that had to be seen to be disbelieved, the attorney tears the clothes off her back to shock her husband out of his mental blackout. The trick works, and the couple are reunited. Even more trashy was the 1960 Allied Artists release *I Passed for White*, which relates what happens when a light-skinned woman decides to do just that. Publicized by advertisements such as "I look white, I married white, now I must live with a secret that can destroy us both," this movie was a poor attempt to exploit the theme of miscegenation.[14]

A black lawyer (James Edwards) rips the dress from Julie London's back in *The Night of the Quarter Moon* (1959), a tepid shocker about interracial love. (From the MGM release "Night of the Quarter Moon" © 1959 Loew's Incorporated and Albert Zugsmith Productions, Inc.)

The most intelligent use of the subject was made in non-Hollywood movies. Two movies made by New York filmmakers did at least attempt to treat relationships between white men and black women with some honesty. *Shadows*, directed by John Cassavetes and released commercially in 1960, grew out of improvisations by the performers at an acting school where Cassavetes held classes. This movie is not quite "the best American film about race relations yet made," as one black critic claimed in 1960, for in retrospect much of it seems a little too arty and mannered to be true. But this story of two black brothers (one dark-skinned and one "a Negro white man") and their light-skinned sister provided an intense, thoughtful, and provocative glimpse of black-white relations in a "bohemian" urban environment. There is a chilling moment when the white seducer of the sister learns she is part black and awkwardly attempts to mask his feelings. Much more tough-minded in its approach to the black-white relationships is *An Affair of the Skin,* a 1963 film written, directed, and co-produced by Ben Maddow. Despite its title, the film is not concerned with racial relationships as such, but with the love affairs of a world-weary quartet of white New Yorkers. The most memorable role in this somewhat pretentious movie was that of a black commercial photographer (Diana Sands) who becomes involved in the lives of some of the four. She personifies what one critic called "the hip, sagacious Negro woman who is already disappointed in her experiences with men, white or Negro . . ."[15]

In the English film *Sapphire* an interracial relationship served

Dancer's image: the title character, right, of the British thriller *Sapphire* (1959) was the tragic mulatto updated. She is murdered by the sister of her white fiancé. (Courtesy Janus Films)

as the touchstone for an engrossing murder mystery. This 1959 Michael Ralph-Basil Dearden production details the hunt for the brutal murderer of the title character, a beautiful young woman who was passing for white. Made after a series of violent outbursts in some English cities directed against the growing black immigrant population from the West Indies, this film examined black-white relationships in London. Racial prejudice in one form or another is encountered throughout the police investigation; "the mystery of who done it being the mystery of human responses," as one critic put it. These responses include the resentment of whites against the newly arrived blacks and the antipathy of some blacks to women like Sapphire. The murderer is revealed to be the unbalanced older sister of Sapphire's white fiancé. *Sapphire* is not without its flaws; somehow most of the blacks in it contrive to spend their time drinking, dancing, and gambling. Indeed, the black manager of one dive tells the police that "no matter what the color of their skin, you can always tell them when the bongo drums start beating." Moreover, the film is glib, self-satisfied, and somewhat preachy.[16]

Movies depicting intimate relationships between black men and white women were much rarer, and again, the best were made outside of Hollywood. In 1961 Claude Bernard Aubert, a socially conscious French filmmaker, wrote, directed, and produced *Les Lâches Vivant d'Espoir* about a love affair between a French girl and an African student in Paris. They are well-matched, but their romance nearly founders under the pressure of race hatred. This film, called *The Colour of Love* in England, is symbol-ridden and marred by some *nouvelle vague* techniques, but there is great visual impact in the opening few minutes, during which the girl is rushed to a hospital, to give birth to a black baby. This scene obviously accounts for the title of the atrociously dubbed American version, *My Baby is Black,* which was exploited on the worst possible level.

Though social mores have changed since 1964, when the independent production *One Potato, Two Potato* was released, it remains among the most sensitive handlings of an emotional relationship between a black man and a white woman. Unlike most recent movies that treat such relationships mostly in terms of sex, this production dealt with love and companionship. Set in an Ohio town, the movie starred Bernie Hamilton and Barbara Barrie

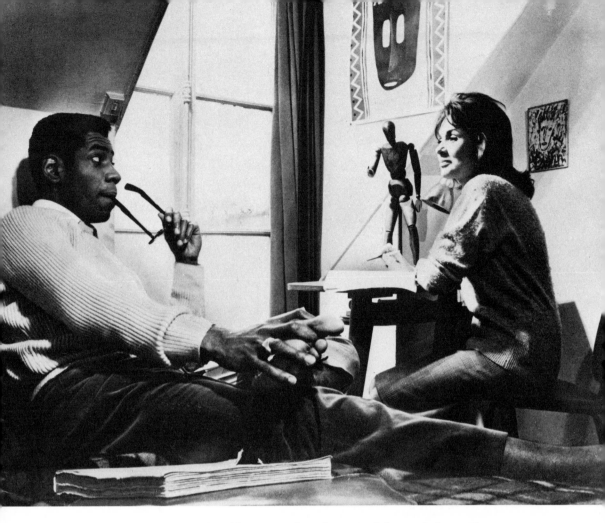

An African student loves and has a baby with a white French girl in the 1961 *Les Laches Vivant d'Espoir* — which appeared in America as *My Baby Is Black*. (National Film Archive)

as Frank and Julie, a couple who court and marry despite their awareness of the obvious problems inherent in their relationship, including the barely veiled hostility of his parents. They are co-workers at a factory, he in a more responsible position. She is a divorcee with a young daughter. Their life together works out well and they have a baby, which reconciles Frank's proud parents to his white wife. But then Julie's first husband, who had deserted her, returns and sues for custody of her daughter. The court rules for the real father despite the girl's desire to stay with Frank and Julie.

Barbara Barrie and Bernie Hamilton (center) are the happily married mixed couple in *One Potato, Two Potato* (1964). But in the end, the court takes her white daughter from her. (Courtesy Cinema V)

The court's decision seems more a dramatic contrivance than an accurate reflection of what might have happened in life. But if the film falters on that point, it is elsewhere a touching portrait of an interracial romance and a toughminded demonstration of social oppression. To the first husband the idea of a serious emotional relationship between his ex-wife and a black man is incomprehensible, and he tries to seduce Julie. Given the child-custody suit, Frank is constrained from doing anything to the man who molests his wife, but he recognizes that the situation would be the same even if the suit were not pending. In an emotional moment he cries out "they won't let me be a man." Earlier in the film a policeman who sees Julie with Frank assumes that she is a prostitute simply because she is consorting with a black man. *One Potato, Two Potato,* was acclaimed by the critics but it did not reach as wide an audience as did the typical industry fare, partly because of its independent origin and partly because of its subject. But it is a noteworthy movie, not least because of its characterization of Frank, who is presented as a complex man, full of dignity and charm.

Roles such as that of Frank had eluded Harry Belafonte, even though his career outside of the movies had been enormously successful. After his discharge from the Navy in 1946 and some brief stints at various dramatic workshops in New York City, he had won almost instant stardom in nightclubs and records through his skillful rendering of ballads and folksongs, particularly calypso numbers. A strikingly handsome man who once was dubbed "the nation's first Negro matinee idol," Belafonte had made his film debut in *Bright Road* while still in his mid-twenties. He later recognized that he had been too young-looking to play the part of a high-school principal. His next film, *Carmen Jones,* he dismissed as "bootleg Bizet." And *Island in the Sun,* his third experience before the movie cameras, he described after its release as "stinking." Like many another successful black entertainer of the past he found almost no movie roles of consequence being offered him; he decided to produce his own films, and in 1957 formed Harbel Productions.[17]

Harbel's first film was *The World, The Flesh, and The Devil,* a joint venture for MGM with veteran producer Sol Siegel; it was released in 1959. This interesting but weak film marched, in the words of one commentator, "steadfastly from a promising idea through the syrupy marshes of cliché." Belafonte played Ralph Burton, a miner who survives an atomic disaster because he has been trapped underground by a mine-shaft cave-in. Finally working his way to daylight, he finds what appears to be a deserted world and heads for New York City, where he appears to be the only survivor. In a twist on previous movie characterizations of the black he demonstrates intelligence, resourcefulness, and bravery as he establishes his solitary presence in the city.

However, when a second survivor finally turns up, he becomes irresolute. Sarah Crandall is a lovely but fearful white woman, who at first screams at him, "Don't touch me!" But in time she falls in love with Burton. Despite similar feelings for her, he refrains from any kind of intimate contact; race, he feels, is an insurmountable barrier to romance, even in an empty world. Soon a third survivor appears, inevitably a white man. He quickly becomes hostile to Burton, not because of his race but because Sarah prefers the miner. The hostility between the two men ignites into violence in an eerie and inconclusive shootout among the deserted skyscrapers of Wall Street, but in the end the three walk off together hand in hand. Belafonte recognized the inconsistencies of the movie, but he apparently lacked control over the production. He publicly agreed with the criticism that the movie shied away from "the more delicate aspects of racial relations."[18]

Moreover, the movie hardly fulfilled Belafonte's avowed aim of showing "Negroes as we are, as people with the same hopes and loves, weaknesses and problems as other people." Burton was just another ebony saint. Nor was Harbel's next production much of an improvement, even though *Odds Against Tomorrow* was produced by Belafonte alone in order to avoid compromises. Released in 1959 by United Artists, the film managed to put across the message that racial prejudice is destructive, but in other respects it was merely dreadful. It did have the unusual distinction for that time of showing a normal middle-class black home, which gives it at least curiosity value. Belafonte played John Ingram, a night-club entertainer who has lost $7500 betting on the horses and whose ex-wife and daughter are threatened because he has not paid this debt. Like Burton, Ingram is more than just an object, and, in addition, he is hostile to whites. His racial feelings, however, are not nearly so intense as those of Slater, an embittered and frustrated white southerner down on his luck. Ingram and Slater, an odd couple who could only exist on celluloid, agree to participate in a robbery. But Slater's antagonism to the black fouls up their getaway. The two end by shooting it out in a gas tank storage area, causing an explosion that so burns their bodies that, like a pair of tar babies, their blackened remains cannot be told apart. The symbolism of *Odds Against Tomorrow* was crushing. The film also did badly at the box office, and a disappointed Belafonte avoided movies for the next ten years.[19]

The roles that Belafonte played when he finally returned to filmmaking reflected the striking change in the presentation of the on-screen black that took place at the end of the 1960s. In the 1970 United Artists release *The Angel Levine*, another Belafonte production, he played an angel sent in response to an appeal to Heaven from an elderly Jewish tailor. This atypical angel comes in the guise of a militant black street hustler whose speech is laced with obscenities. At the core of this confused and dreary movie lay a variation on the theme of the old Harbel productions — although this time the problem was posed as a question of faith. The old Jew cannot believe in a black angel who tells him to forget that "wing shit." The angel must temper his character and get along with the tailor, for he has only a limited time in which to prove that he is Heaven-sent. When belief finally comes, it is too late for all concerned. The Bernard Malamud story on which the movie was based ends happily and characterizes the angel differently; but Belafonte found it necessary "to get some black reality in there." Whatever satisfaction Belafonte derived from *The Angel Levine* had to come not from the box office but from giving some young blacks a chance to learn about filmmaking and from his feeling that this production was "the first picture I have even been involved in where . . . I could really do my black thing." He did his "black thing" again in *Buck and the Preacher*, a 1972 Columbia release that he co-produced with Sidney Poitier. It dealt with attempts by whites in the post–Civil War South to prevent freed blacks from fleeing peonage by going west. The usual cliché situations were reversed, and at the end the Indians joined with the blacks to defeat the villainous whites. Belafonte — hiding his good looks if not his charm behind stained teeth, a mustache, and a scraggly beard — played a fradulent preacher who was handy with a gun, a bottle, and a woman and who helped the blacks to emerge victorious.[20]

Belafonte was involved in the production of both movies, but neither of them added much to his stature as a performer. His problems in finding decent roles also plagued other blacks who had achieved show business success outside the movies in the fifties and sixties. Performers such as Diahann Carroll, Ella Fitzgerald, Nat "King" Cole, Louis Armstrong, and Sammy Davis, Jr., found only certain limited kinds of movie roles being offered to them.

Take the example of Sammy Davis, Jr. Though a preeminent entertainer, his movie career has been erratic. His first film, *Anna Lucasta,* represents one of the last manifestations of the old-style, all-black films made for general distribution. A 1958 United Artists release, this tale of a prostitute who becomes respectable and of her ambivalent relationship with her family originated in the 1930s as a downbeat play by Philip Yordan about Polish immigrants; it remained unproduced until 1944 when the American Negro Theatre expressed an interest in it. Yordan obligingly revised the play, adding more comedy and an upbeat ending. The revised drama, presented by the ANT with an all-black cast in the basement of a Harlem library, was successful enough to move to Broadway, where it had a long run. In 1949 Columbia, to the outrage of many blacks, filmed the play with a white cast headed by Paulette Goddard. However, by the time the all-black movie was made the story had become stale and "playing white folks in blackface," as one commentator put it, was no longer a novelty. Davis took a critical drubbing: *Time*'s movie reviewer called him a "blackface Bugs Bunny."[21]

Since then the versatile Davis has essayed a variety of roles, in addition to cameo appearances doing song-and-dance numbers. Unfortunately they too often seem to recall the black roles of an earlier era. As Sportin' Life in *Porgy and Bess* Davis was little more than an energetic caricature. A better case in point is *Sergeants Three,* one of the films he made with Frank Sinatra and Dean Martin early in the 1960s. In this 1962 United Artists release, a farcical reworking of Rudyard Kipling's *Gunga Din* and of the 1939 movie based on it, the setting was moved from India to the 1870s American West, and the lowly native water carrier became a none-too-bright ex-slave who attached himself to the three sergeants and served them. As interpreted by Davis this character was played for laughs, and even though the part had moments of heroism it also had Uncle Tom overtones.

In 1966 Davis appeared with Peter Lawford in a very different kind of movie. *A Man Called Adam* dealt with the emotional turmoil suffered by a black trumpet player who cannot come to terms with himself. In the context of the story, the Embassy Pictures release touched on racism and the civil rights movement.

The emphasis was on nonviolence, on sitting in, on ending segregation in the South. At one point, while playing in a segregated Southern theater, the black musician and his white protégé direct their trumpets toward a cheering black audience in the balcony. The trumpet player also has an ill-fated romantic fling with a black woman who is active in the civil-rights movement. The woman was played by Cicely Tyson, who, in the words of one writer, "displayed a truly Afro-American type of beauty, quite different from the Caucasian standard common to other black actresses . . . who achieved leading role status in American films." (Tyson would break away from the white woman mold for black actresses even more dramatically a few years later in *Sounder*.) Davis, who played Adam, also was involved in the production of the film, which, for all its good intentions, proved stilted and overwrought. Still, whatever the films's artistic drawbacks or sociological limitations, it is a significant example of the changing movie treatment of black people.[22]

The best index to this change, however, is the career of Sidney Poitier, who came to personify the Black Man on Screen. Indeed, a standard joke in Hollywood during the 1960s was "if you can't get Sidney Poitier, rewrite the part for a white man." Among the blacks who had achieved prominence in the movies, Poitier was unique, for, as an *Ebony* article made clear in 1959, "unlike other Negro stars . . . [he] did not carry to Hollywood a name as an entertainer. He does not sing or dance. His calling card reads Actor." Poitier was the first black actor to achieve and maintain true star status within the industry. And he was the first black superstar. It was not just that he was a good actor: no one had ever played the ebony saint quite so well. A handsome, intelligent man, there was nothing about his image on screen or off that could be construed as "sexually aggressive" (to use one critic's 1969 estimate). Nor was there anything about him "that might invite the jealous resentment of white male filmgoers or . . . feed the old but still potent racial fear of the over-endowed negro."[23]

Poitier's climb was not made on a golden ladder. Born in the United States in 1927, he had been raised by his parents in their native Bahamas. While still in his early teens he had endured segregation in Florida and poverty in New York City. He had slept wrapped in newspapers on rooftops. After being thrown out of an American Negro Theatre audition because of his West Indian accent, Poitier bought a radio for fourteen dollars and tried to dissolve his accent by imitating the voices on the air. After a second audition he was hired. He toured with the ANT production of *Anna Lucasta* and got his first movie roles. But prestigious films like *No Way Out* and programmers like *Red Ball Express* brought him little money or opportunity. In 1954 at the age of twenty-seven he seemed to have reached a dead end.

The turning point came when he was cast in *The Blackboard Jungle,* which MGM released the following year. In this indictment of urban public education, Poitier played Gregory Miller, a black high-school student with natural leadership abilities and with the potential to better himself. But seeing only a second-class status for himself upon graduation, he has remained uninterested in learning. He joins in the harassment of the teachers, although he does not participate in the more violent actions such as attempted rape, beatings, and the driving of the pregnant wife of one teacher to a miscarriage. Sensationalistic but corroborated by events, *The Blackboard Jungle* also had its brighter side. In a confrontation with the brutal ringleader of the troublemakers, the teacher who is the hero of the movie receives help from Miller and other students. The ending holds out more than just hope for Miller and ghetto students like him. It was a strong movie, and much of its force was generated by Poitier's portrayal. The critical acclaim he received for his interpretation of Miller did not mean that he had an easy time of it for the next year and a half. He appeared in only one film during that time, a 1956 Warners release, *Goodbye My Lady,* in which he played a hired hand in a Southern rural area. Poitier had other offers but turned them down because, as he told an agent, "I won't use my talent to retrogress." And his stand was justified, for during 1957–58 he played important parts in six films — the most important of them being *Edge of the City* and *The Defiant Ones.* His roles in these two productions defined both his screen persona for the next decade and that of the black male leading man in general — a morally and intellectually superior figure who is limited only by the prejudice of society.[24]

Edge of the City was very much a New York movie, both in outlook and style. This David Susskind production (released by MGM in 1957) was based on an award-winning TV play called *A*

Man Is Ten Feet Tall. In both versions Poitier superbly played
Tommy, an articulate, generous, happy-go-lucky stevedore gang
boss. Tommy befriends a confused white misfit, Alex, and is
destroyed in the process. The black tells the younger white that
if a man believes in himself and stands up to life he can be ten
feet tall. In practicing what he preaches Tommy is killed trying
to protect Alex from a brutal and bigoted foreman. Once again
the white man runs away from life, but he finally stands up to the
killer and avenges Tommy's death. This movie was unusual not
only in its depiction of the black as a superior person but also in
its characterization of his comfortable home and gracious, stead-
fast wife. Moreover, the movie shows Tommy and his wife introducing Alex to a white girl they know well, and the two couples
spending time together. For all the movie's optimism, however,
Tommy appears to be the only black working at the freight
terminal, and it is clear that it it were not for society's racial
barriers a man with his capacities would have fared much better.

The Defiant Ones makes much more use of symbolism, and the
Poitier character is even more noble, more Christlike. The 1958
United Artists release, produced and directed by Stanley Kramer,
was the story of two convicts, a toughminded black (Poitier's
extraordinary portrayal earned him an Oscar nomination) and a
blustering white (Tony Curtis). They are chained together
because, as one character cynically asserts, "if they escape we
don't worry about catching them. They'll kill each other before
they can get fifty miles." But escape they do when the truck they
are riding skids over an embankment. They argue and fight as
they scramble across the Southern countryside, ultimately finding
refuge at the farm of a young white widow. There they free
themselves of their chains. The woman deliberately misdirects
the black into a swamp and certain death, but he is warned in
time by the white man — who is then shot by the woman's son.
The two men reach a rail line, the black hops a train, but the
wounded white is too weak to make it. The black jumps off to
stay with him. The last scene shows the sheriff finding them —
the wounded white cradled in the arms of the black, who is
singing "Long Gone."

The movie was nominated for an Academy Award — and yet
even in 1958 there were critics who found the freakish symbolism
and the mawkish ending "a blank failure of vision." Certainly

since then the black convict's throwing away of his chance for freedom has become unacceptable as a dramatic resolution and tends to cause snickers or anger among many blacks. One teacher reported in 1971 that after assigning his classes to view the film on television he found that "the kids simply could not swallow that ending."[25]

Poitier became a screen hero but not one in the traditional sense, and the oddity of his position was a sharp comment on American racial mores. His movie roles varied enormously, but what most of them had in common until the late 1960s was that his dealings with whites were, as one commentator said, "in areas of conscience, not sex." Only once in the thirteen movies he made between 1958 and 1966 was he cast in a role that allowed him a movie star's usual on-screen romantic involvements, and that was as the expatriate jazz musician who woos Diahann Carroll in *Paris Blues*.[26]

But in most of his roles the human dimension remained absent. He starred in the 1963 Ralph Nelson production *Lilies of the Field* and won an Oscar playing an unwilling good samaritan to an impoverished group of nuns who have escaped from Eastern Europe to settle in Arizona. Three years later in another Nelson production, the western *Duel at Diablo*, he played a tough army veteran turned bronco buster. He also appeared as a psychiatrist treating a young American Nazi tough (in the 1962 Stanley Kramer production *Pressure Point*), as a magazine correspondent in an ill-fated U.S. Navy ship playing cat and mouse with a Russian submarine (in the 1965 Columbia release *The Bedford Incident*), and as a hard-boiled marine sergeant in *All the Young Men*, a 1960 Hall Bartlett production about the Korean war. The latter casting reflected the movies's changed depiction of the U.S. armed forces. Hollywood now invariably portrayed them as being integrated even when history had to be distorted — as in Kramer's *Judgment at Nuremberg* (1961) in which black military policemen worked side by side with white ones at a 1948 war crimes trial. President Harry Truman's order desegregating the armed forces had yet to go into effect.

At this stage in Poitier's career the role that gave him most satisfaction was that of Walter Lee Younger in *A Raisin in the Sun*, which he played both on stage and screen. The Lorraine Hansberry play concerned a working-class black family in Chicago and what they hope to do with a $10,000 insurance benefit being paid out after the death of the father. His widow wants to move the family out of its cramped ghetto apartment and into a house in a middle-class neighborhood; the daughter wants financial help to study medicine; the married son Walter, whose wife is pregnant and who feels hemmed in by his chauffeur's job, wants to open a liquor store with some friends. The mother, after placing a deposit on a house and setting aside some money for her daughter's education, gives the bulk of the money to her son, but he is cheated out of the cash. Another chance for the family to make some money occurs when a white man, representing the neighborhood where the mother has selected a house, offers to buy it at a profit. At first Walter agrees, but ultimately he saves his self-respect and agrees with his mother to spurn the offer. At the end the family goes off to live in the new house and face an uncertain future. The 1961 David Susskind-Philip Rose production for Columbia came just about two years after the play had opened its successful run. The movie was almost a literal transcription of the stage production and was mostly performed on one set. Poitier's portrayal on stage and in the film was vivid, forceful, and moving. In an electric performance he captured Walter's frustration, agony, and desire.

Poitier had a right to be proud of his performance, as did other members of the cast — notably Claudia McNeil, who played the mother. But *A Raisin in the Sun,* though a milestone in the characterization of black people, was naively well-intentioned. Hansberry did not consider her work "a Negro play," but one that was "about honest-to-God, believable, many-sided people who happened to be Negroes . . ." This was true only to a point; for although Miss Hansberry's characters are not stereotypes, they are very much stage creations.

The human dimension continued to elude Poitier even in his most successful films. In 1967, the year in which he reached the peak of his popularity, he starred in *To Sir with Love, In the Heat of the Night,* and *Guess Who's Coming to Dinner.* Each one rather aptly illustrates the problem he faced. In the English-made *To Sir with Love* (a Columbia release) he played a black teacher at a high school in a London slum district. His students, in their final term before graduating, are tough and insubordinate — though not nearly so savage as the students of *Blackboard*

Uncertain progress: a grateful Poitier and an adoring
Katherine Houghton receive Spencer Tracy's paternal
blessing in *Guess Who's Coming to Dinner* (1967).
(Courtesy Stanley Kramer/Columbia Pictures). But as
the gambler and bon vivant in *For Love of Ivy*, released
the next year, Poitier was clearly trying to break away
from his Ebony Saint image. (Palomar Pictures International). The break was complete, but not very successful, in *The Lost Man* (1969), which saw him portraying
a black militant leader. (Courtesy of Universal Pictures)

Jungle. Within a short time Poitier has them in hand and has
tamed even the most unruly among them. His method is to
abandon the usual course of instruction. The movie makes little
of Poitier's race. In the book on which the movie was based, a
white teacher becomes romantically involved with the hero; the
movie turns her into a platonic friend. As one critic remarked
about Poitier, "it's another of his sweet, saintly, sexless performances."[27]

That criticism did not hold for *In the Heat of the Night*
(United Artists). Poitier played a character named Virgil Tibbs,

who is picked up in Sparta, Mississippi, as a murder suspect; he turns out to be a Philadelphia police detective who has come South to visit his mother. Circumstances force Tibbs and the bigoted local police chief to cooperate in solving the murder. But the movie is not so much about the solution of a crime as the relationship between Tibbs and the chief, which progresses from strong antipathy to respect and rapport. This development may be corny and unreal, but the movie does have the grace not to take itself seriously and to treat the obvious superiority of the urbane black as a source of gentle humor. Although Tibbs stoically endures abuse, he also fights back. It was a step forward, and yet critic Andrew Sarris was right when he asserted that Poitier was still "a civil rights commercial."[28]

If Poitier hoped that *Guess Who's Coming to Dinner* would modify such judgments, he was again mistaken. He chafed at the fact that in the bulk of his films he "had never worked in a man-woman relationship that was not symbolic." But unhappily *Guess Who's Coming to Dinner,* another Stanley Kramer production, was not much of an improvement — though he did get to kiss and keep the white heroine. Poitier played John Prentice, a world-famous thirty-seven-year-old doctor who falls in love with the twenty-three-year-old daughter of a crusading newspaper publisher. The movie centers around the couple's meeting their respective parents at the publisher's home. It does speak out against prejudice, but given his status and her wealth, their liaison is obviously hardly a typical interracial marriage. Kramer has asserted that the black is drawn as he was because neither the girl nor her parents (Katherine Hepburn and Spencer Tracy) would have been interested in a garage attendant. The movie is pleasant enough and did well at the box office, but it took a deserved critical beating: *The Reporter* critic described it as "Abie's Irish Rose in blackface" and one angry black writer called it "warmed-over white shit."[29]

This last comment is indicative of the changing nature of the black revolution in America. Poitier's screen persona, which for nearly a decade had been the dominant image of the black on-screen, was no longer considered pertinent. No longer did the black press refer to Poitier's career as a "Hollywood Milestone." Unfortunately, his attempts to adjust have not proved wholly successful.

Even in the days of his greatest acclaim Poitier had been attacked by both black and white critics for appearing in "one-dimensional" movies and playing "simplistic" parts. Poitier was aware of these criticisms. But as he told one interviewer at the height of his success: "if the fabric of the society were different I would scream to high heaven . . . to deal with different images of Negro life that would be more dimensional. But I'll be damned if I do that at this stage of the game. Not when there is only one Negro actor working in films with any degree of consistency, where there are thousands of actors in films . . ." However, criticism of Poitier increased, and it took various forms. In a newspaper article black playwright Clifford Mason posed the question "Why Does White America Love Sidney Poitier So?" and in answering it asserted that the actor was "a showcase nigger, who is given a clean suit and a complete purity of motivation so that, like a mistreated puppy, he has all the sympathy on his side . . ." During the introductory program of the 1968 CBS television series *On Black America* Poitier was described as "always helping little old ladies across the street . . . whether they want to go or not." In 1970 New York *Times* movie critic Vincent Canby in commenting on Poitier's latest films said that "his blackness is now invisible." Understandably Poitier resented such criticism. "I used to think that my success . . . was essential to the success of . . . maybe even all black people," he has said. "But I'm not going to be put in that bag anymore . . . and that goes for anybody who thinks I'm the carrier of his dreams. Screw him. Let him carry his own dreams."[30]

As Harry Belafonte has pointed out, "it is perfectly clear that Poitier has been treated unfairly by the press . . . treated qualitatively different from the way white superstars . . . are treated." Poitier should not be faulted for the shortcomings of the industry in which he worked. It is all very well to reprove him for not participating in more meaningful movies earlier in his career; but such films simply were not being made. The image of the ebony saint had been forced on him. Considering the changes in the presentation of the black presence from the beginning of his career to the mid-1960s, one must agree with James Baldwin's assessment that "the *presence* of Sidney, the precedent set, is of tremendous importance . . ."[31] The ebony saint's problem was that a whole iconology was forced upon him.

Jim Brown, the onetime football great, grapples with a pair of Mexican soldiers in the 1969 *100 Rifles*. In the era of the Blaxploitation film, whites began to get the short end of the cinematic stick for a change. (National Film Archive/Courtesy Twentieth Century–Fox. © 1968 Twentieth Century–Fox Film Corporation)

10

BLACK IS
BOXOFFICE

PERIODICALLY during the late 1950s and early 1960s *Variety* and other trade journals took note of the "growing Negro audience," which was "now a sizable segment of film patronage as a whole." But this fact seemed to make little difference at the time. In 1963, however, after the NAACP abandoned persuasion and threatened to take legal and economic action against the industry, blacks began to play policemen, civil servants, students, and workers both in features and in movies and shows filmed and taped for television. The studios increased their hiring of blacks as extras so much that the payroll cost for them in one month showed an increase of 700 percent over the same period a year earlier. More blacks were also cast in minor parts.

By the mid-1970s blacks were seen on screen with a frequency that could almost be called reasonable. Black actors and actresses appeared in everything from crowd scenes to leading roles — and not just in ghetto-oriented films. If black actresses suffered from the paucity of decent female roles available, so did their white counterparts. But black actors did quite well. For instance, in an acclaimed film, *The Last Detail* (a 1974 Warners release), Otis Young played the subordinate but important role of one of the two veteran navy men escorting a young sailor to prison. Though Young did not garner as much publicity as leading man Jack Nicholson, he received considerable praise for his portrayal. Moreover, black actors were well represented in the law-and-order movies that flourished in 1973 and 1974, and not just as criminals. Unfortunately, this realistic screen image of the

black was almost completely overshadowed by a new caricature — Superspade. Although he was as defamatory and inhu-
man as Sambo had been, Superspade was at least emotionally
more satisfying to most black moviegoers. An NAACP official
might condemn the transformation "to super-nigger as just another form of cultural genocide," but black moviegoers turned out
in droves and (in the words of NEWSWEEK) "produced the first
gold mine in years for the struggling industry" and the phenomenon of the "blaxploitation" film.[1]

It was Poitier's success that had brought home to filmmakers
just how significant a percentage of the moviegoing public was
black: in 1967, he was one of the top five box-office draws in the
United States. According to a 1967 estimate, although blacks
represented only about 15 percent of the American population,
they accounted for roughly 30 percent of the moviegoing audience in the nation's cities, where the biggest movie theaters were
located. As one industry executive summed up the situation: "the
black population of this country comprises a much larger proportion of the motion picture audience than its proportion of our
total population would indicate." Once the industry grasped this
fact, filmmakers began to reappraise and revise their product.[2]

The new "hip" image of the aggressive urban black that they
created soon found its first star, in the person of Jim Brown, whose
movie career began while he was still an All-Pro fullback with the
Cleveland Browns. In the 1964 Twentieth Century-Fox feature
Rio Conchos, he was cast as a cavalry sergeant; obviously the
studio hoped that his name would be a marquee attraction. His
role was not far different in style from the kind of parts Poitier
was playing. In this post–Civil War saga about gun-running to
the Apaches, the sergeant refuses to repay Indian brutality in
kind, with the terse comment that "doing like they do, don't make
it right." Brown did not make another movie for two years.
Then, in the summer of 1967, while working on the MGM release, *The Dirty Dozen,* he found his film commitment overlap-
ping the football season. He was forced to make a choice and his
choice was acting.

Brown proceeded to make eleven films in three years, developing an on-screen image far different from Poitier's. A Brown
character might still perform what one critic dubbed "the Noble

Negro Act," as in the 1968 *Dark of the Sun.* In this violent MGM release about mercenaries fighting in central Africa, the high-minded black (Brown) tells his larcenous white friend and commander, "to you this is a job; to me this is our Bunker Hill." Because of such sentiments the black is killed by another mercenary, an ex-Nazi. But Brown more often played strong-willed men of action — aggressive, sure of themselves, self-disciplined, and in most situations superior to whites. The 1968 MGM release *The Split* has him humiliate a group of white criminals, in order to convince them to accept his leadership in planning and executing a daring robbery. Ultimately he is the only one who escapes with a share of the loot. (Interestingly enough, this role originally had been written for a white actor, Lee Marvin.) When, in the 1970 National General film *The Grasshopper,* his lovely white wife is assaulted by a Mafia-type boss, the Brown character exacts a savage revenge with his fists even though the action later costs him his life.

In many of these films Brown was paired with white actresses, though they were frequently presented as being of mixed blood. Raquel Welch, who starred with him in *100 Rifles* (Twentieth Century-Fox, 1969) played a half-caste Mexican; however, advertising for the production treated her as white. The 1970 National General western *El Condor* made it clear that a white woman's sexual lust for the Brown character led her to betray her white lover, a general, and his fortress command. Many of Brown's romantic scenes with these actresses were unusually explicit, if rarely poignant — a quality he only approached in some scenes with black actresses.[3]

It cannot be said that Brown has been a critical success. Pauline Kael epitomized many opinions when she declared that "Jim Brown is handsome and stiff — the essence of straight. He looks like an Indian, and he acts like a wooden one . . ."; but his films did make money. Nevertheless, in 1970 Brown's new career came to a halt. Some run-ins with the law, none of which resulted in a conviction, and, more important, an industry judgment that he had become "difficult" seem to have been the reason. According to Brown, "these film people were used to dealing with cats that let them get away with anything. But they don't mean a damn to me. I let 'em know right off that I didn't come into the movies with my hat in my hand asking somebody to do me a favor."

We've come a long way, baby: Today, Hollywood thinks nothing of allowing a black to pistol-whip a white, as Calvin Lockhart does in *Melinda*. (From the MGM release "Melinda" © 1972 Metro-Goldwyn-Mayer Inc.) Nor of showing torrid sex between races as in *100 Rifles*. Here, Jim Brown's willing consort is Raquel Welch. (National Film Archive/Courtesy Twentieth Century–Fox. © 1968 Twentieth Century–Fox Film Corporation)

Brown's movie career only picked up again after the boom in black-oriented films began late in 1971.[4]

Brown was not the only black performer to benefit from the industry's changing attitude. Ossie Davis appeared in a number of films, including the 1968 United Artists release *The Scalp-hunters*, in which he and Burt Lancaster had a slam-bang but inconclusive fight, one of the first such physical confrontations between black and white on screen to end without a white winner. Calvin Lockhart, a Bahamian who was touted for a time as "the next Sidney Poitier," made an auspicious debut in his first major role as the boyfriend of the white title character in *Joanna*, a 1968 Twentieth Century-Fox release made in England. Roscoe Lee Browne appeared in a number of films at this time, his best performance being in the 1969 Columbia release *The Liberation of L. B. Jones* in which he played a successful but doomed Tennessee undertaker. This man's love for his errant wife, who is carrying on an affair with a brutal white policeman, serves as the catalyst for a grim display of racial bigotry, including a vicious beating of the wife by her lover and the murder and castration of the undertaker by white policemen. Mercifully less violent was the part that Diana Sands played in the 1970 United Artists release *The Landlord*. In this tasteless farce about an empty-headed liberal who buys an old brownstone in a Brooklyn ghetto, she is the tenant who has a baby with him while her husband is in jail.[5]

Next to Jim Brown, however, the most successful black performer to emerge in the late 1960s was Raymond St. Jacques. Imposing of feature, stirring of voice, this physically striking actor had been known as Chubby when he was a boy in New Haven. He began his acting career in New York in the 1950s while still in his twenties. Like so many of his black contemporaries, he made his mark early in the 1960s in Jean Genet's prize-winning off-Broadway play *The Blacks*. Bit parts in movies came his way. Then, in 1964, as a result of the NAACP pressure on the studios, he was cast as a cowboy in the television series *Rawhide*. His first movie role of distinction was that of Concasseur, a brutal police captain, in the 1967 film *The Comedians*, based on a novel by Graham Greene. In this uneven attempt to expose the grim police state that Haiti had become, St. Jacques had a small but powerful part that, among other unpleasant things, called for him to push Lillian Gish in the face and shove her to the ground.

Soon after, St. Jacques appeared in a group of films that considerably advanced his career — and that were also important in terms of the black presence on screen. The first was *Up Tight*, a 1968 movie produced and directed by Jules Dassin, an unsuccessful attempt to encompass contemporary changes in black political life and its social ethos. This production was an attempt to reinterpret and update a 1930s classic, *The Informer*, in a black setting. It is the story of Tank, a former union stalwart who has become so much of a drunk that he is unable to help a group of militants rob an armory of rifles. During the course of the robbery his friend Johnny fatally wounds a guard. Later Tank is ostracized from the movement by B.G., the leader, played by St. Jacques. Tank betrays Johnny to the police for money. His reckless spending arouses the suspicion of Johnny's friends. He flees from them, but they finally corner him.

But the major interest of the film lies not with the fate of Tank but with his surroundings. Much of the movie was shot in Hough, Cleveland's ghetto area, and these scenes provide an unusually authentic view of urban slums. The filmmakers were unusually frank in showing such aspects of ghetto life as the numbers racket, prostitution, welfare, sidewalk evangelism, and hostility to the police. *Up Tight* began with documentary footage of the black community's response to the murder of Dr. King in April, 1968, and a discussion of what the response to his assassination should be launches the action. White liberals are henceforth to be excluded from black activity. B.G. carries the day, declaring: "Selma, lunch counters, Birmingham — yesterday: A phase we went through together. Now we don't walk together anymore. Now no whites. It's policy."

Up Tight was unlikely to convince anyone but the committed. But it was unique in being a propagandistic statement that was financed and released by a major studio. It seems likely that much of the responsibility for the film's handling of black life and politics belongs not to Dassin but to the director's co-scriptwriters — Ruby Dee, who played Tank's girlfriend, and Julian Mayfield, a black writer who played Tank.

St. Jacques also played the lead in two potboilers made at this time. Although neither film was received with anything but contempt by the critics, he received good notices. Still the movies are interesting because they represent notable changes in the image of the screen black. The transition from ebony saint to Superspade can be seen in the character St. Jacques acts in *If He Hollers Let Him Go*. This 1968 release told of a gifted, intelligent black who is falsely convicted of raping and murdering a white woman. He breaks out of jail only to find himself involved in a white man's plot to murder his wife. The black saves the woman. Like many of the Jim Brown films, *If He Hollers Let Him Go* relied little on logic or dramatic development and much on violence and seminude love scenes. St. Jacques later declared that "artistically it was a fake, but the 'brothers' loved it because I kicked hell out of a white man." *Change of Mind*, which was released the next year, was equally bad but had the additional fault of being pretentious. The brain of a white liberal Southern district attorney, a terminal cancer patient, is transplanted into the body of a black man, with predictable results: the D.A.'s white wife retreats from his touch, and the black wife finds him inadequate; his first case after the transplant is a murder, which splits the black and white citizens in the community. *Change of Mind* was, in one critic's words, "a progressively glib and at times offensive series of heavily underlined messages about racial harmony."[6]

There was no such message in the 1970 United Artists release *Cotton Comes to Harlem*, which co-starred St. Jacques and the comedian Godfrey Cambridge. They played Grave Digger Jones and Coffin Ed Johnson, the black police detectives who are the main characters in a series of novels by the black writer Chester Hines. In this film the white characters are seen mainly as thugs, junk dealers, gangsters, and morons. Indeed a sexy black woman makes such a fool of one white policeman that he winds up in the corridor of an apartment with his gun in his hand but wearing nothing but a paper bag over his head. The white authorities have been taken in by a Back-to-Africa swindle perpetrated by the Rev. Deke O'Malley, cleverly played by Calvin Lockhart. It is the theft of $87,000 paid by poor people in Harlem for passage to Africa, which results in a series of confused but highly entertaining adventures as the two black detectives try to recover the money. They quell a possible race riot in front of the precinct station by promising that the money will be returned to those who contributed, and they expose O'Malley for the fraud he is.

Playing two detectives in *Cotton Comes to Harlem* (1970), Raymond St. Jacques, left, and Godfrey Cambridge run into a truckful of watermelons. For obvious reasons, the sight gag delighted black audiences. (National Film Archive/Courtesy United Artists)

Although they never do recover the money (which has been hidden in a bale of cotton and found by an old black junkman who uses it to establish himself in Africa), the detectives do restore an equal amount of money to the swindled victims. They accomplish this by forcing a white Harlem Mafia boss to put up the cash under threat of a black takeover of his numbers racket.

Coffin Ed and Grave Digger are tough, aggressive, concerned, sharp nongrafters who in their own way are quite moral. They are angry at O'Malley not because he is a swindler but because he has defrauded his own people. They are proud, effective, and black — until this time an unusual combination in American movies. But they are also the only admirable black characters in the movie. The rest are not much better than the whites, even if they are slyer and more attractive. The black female characters are shown to be beautiful (albeit by white standards) but also to be oversexed, lustful, and amoral — a depiction that would unfortunately become a pattern in later black-oriented films.

Cotton Comes to Harlem freely satirized ghetto inhabitants and mores but did so in a good-natured way. Racial antagonisms were touched on but only as existing facts of life. Although there was plenty of action, there was none of the savage violence or gory mayhem that has marked other black-oriented films. Good use was made of unfamiliar Harlem locations and numbers of ghetto residents got a chance to work as extras. A reporter present at the shooting of one street-corner scene remembered that "the excitement was like August lightning as extras recruited from the neighborhood swarmed around . . . and waited for shooting to begin." Everyone was having such a good time that the director had difficulty getting the proper reactions from the crowd.[7]

Much of this enthusiasm was generated by director Ossie Davis, who also co-authored the script. As Davis said, he "was offered the job as an actor first and ultimately wound up being offered the job as director." He had hoped to stress the black experience even more but the producer had been worried about too strong an emphasis. Davis recalled that "the fear was that if you didn't make a film that white folks would see and appreciate, since they constituted in Hollywood's mind the audience to whom you appeal, that you were, you know, that you were cutting your own throat." Davis was not satisfied with the film, and he later commented that "using a maximum 100, I give myself a score of fifty or sixty on a sliding scale, in terms of artistic accomplishment." He did predict, however, that it would be a commercial success, and it was — thanks to black moviegoers who turned out in unprecedented numbers to see it. The movie cost about $1.2 million to make, but it grossed over $5.5 million in domestic rentals. In the big cities where most of this gross was earned, it was estimated that the audience for the film was over 80 percent black.[8]

That audience did not turn out in such large numbers for the 1972 sequel, *Come Back, Charleston Blue,* in which St. Jacques and Cambridge once again played Coffin Ed and Grave Digger. Davis did not direct the sequel, for he "had strong reservations" about how the subject matter was to be treated. He was replaced by Mark Warren, a black television director best known for his work on *Laugh In.* It was his first experience directing a feature film, and the finished movie, with its profusion of vaudeville touches, reflected his television background. The technique often seemed at odds with the story: a sharp black fashion photographer tries to murder his way into control of the Harlem heroin traffic. Coffin Ed and Grave Digger know what is going on, but because the photographer is thought by ghetto residents to be a crusader working to rid the area of drugs, it takes the detectives time to set matters straight.[9]

This film was financed and released by Warner Brothers. United Artists had decided not to undertake another Coffin Ed-Grave Digger film because *Cotton Comes to Harlem,* despite its good grosses, had not broken into the white market. In retrospect Warners' decision was correct, although the disappointing grosses of *Come Back, Charleston Blue* had little to do with the reaction of white audiences. But the movie failed to draw black customers, despite an extensive publicity campaign that included a radio commercial that featured a fast-talking black hustler conning a young-sounding white liberal type into paying more than the regular box-office price for a pair of tickets. *Come Back, Charleston Blue* lacked the excessive gore and sex that had come to characterize black-oriented films in the months after the release of *Cotton Comes to Harlem.* Nor did the movie have as its central figure the Superspade character who now attracted the mass of black moviegoers.

This extremely rapid change in film content and in black moviegoing tastes can be traced to two 1971 films: *Sweet Sweetback's Baadasssss Song* and *Shaft.* Both of these films were directed by black men. Indeed, *Sweet Sweetback's Baadasssss Song* was almost entirely the creation of one black man — Melvin Van Peebles — who produced, directed, and wrote this movie as well as playing the lead role. The multitalented Van Peebles was the first American black to direct a feature film, albeit a French one, commercially released in the United States. Born in Chicago in 1932, raised in Harvey, Illinois, he majored in English literature at Ohio Wesleyan University. An Air Force veteran, he worked for a time as a San Francisco cable-car gripman; his first book was a romantic picture story about the cable cars. A first novel, he remembers, was rejected by American publishers, who told him "that I didn't write enough like a Negro." He also had some bitter experiences in Hollywood when he went there at the end of the 1950s to sell some short films he had made. Van Peebles recalls being told by an agent that "if you can tap dance, I might find you some work. But that's about all." Shortly after he went to Europe, where he earned his keep in a variety of ways, among them editing cartoon sequences for the French edition of *Mad* and acting with the Dutch National Theatre. Van Peebles explained the steps leading up to directing his first film in the following way: "When I learned that French law allowed writers to direct their own movies . . . I went to work as a journalist. Journalism enabled me to get a book publisher . . . My screen treatment of the book earned a director's permit for me from the French Film Center."[10]

This first film, based on his novel *The Pass* (the movie was in French and English), dealt with the experiences of Turner, a black G.I. stationed in France. He earns a three-day pass by Uncle Tomming his prejudiced captain. On leave in Paris, Turner is at first frustrated in his attempts to get to know women, but then he meets Miriam, a French shopgirl who likes to spend time with men she does not know well. They drive to the Normandy coast and spend two happy nights together, making mutual declarations of love. But their brief holiday has been marred by a meeting with some white G.I.'s from Turner's base — who tell the captain about the affair. When Turner returns he is confined to quarters. The intervention of a delegation of black clubwomen who are touring the area secures his release. When he phones Miriam's shop in Paris, he is told that she is away "ill" — the same excuse she used to go away with him.

This simple, bittersweet tale touched on themes that would become much more pronounced in Van Peebles' later films. The white figure of authority, in this instance, the captain, is both bigot and boob. Turner has a hip alter ego who appears on screen and who is very different from the idealistic and good-natured G.I.: this character gives vent to some very strong racial feelings.

Role reversal: Godfrey Cambridge, in whiteface, is the cocksure insurance salesman who wakes up one morning, black. Opposite, his wife tries to comfort him

Miriam, despite her sexual intimacy with Turner, has fears about blacks and in a nightmarish sequence she fantasizes that she is being chased through the jungle by spear-wielding natives who threaten to rape her.

In France this film, which was released in 1967, was called *La Permission.* Its production costs were partly underwritten by a grant from the French Cinema Center, an official organization that helps to finance films that are "artistically valuable but not necessarily commercially viable." The film achieved American

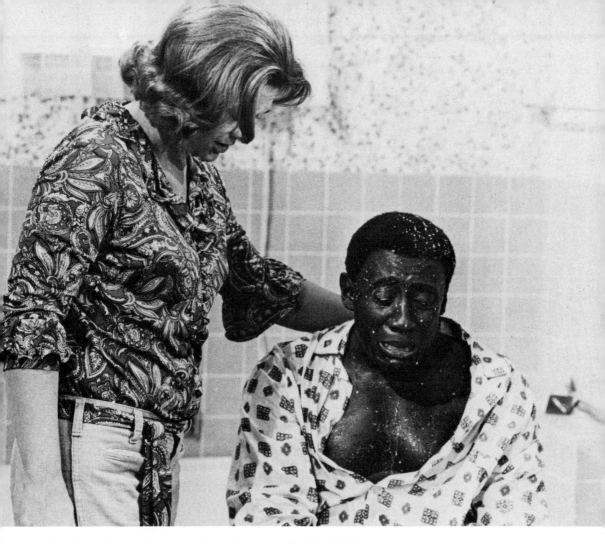

when he finds that his new color will not wash off. (Both: National Film Archive/Courtesy Columbia)

distribution in 1968 as *The Story of a Three-Day Pass* after it was shown at the San Francisco Film Festival that year. The festival exposure and the good notices the film received, as well as Van Peebles' achievement in completing it in six weeks on a budget of only $100,000, brought him to the attention of the industry. Van Peebles signed a contract with Columbia.

His first directorial assignment was *The Watermelon Man*, a comedy which attempts, with varying success, to make some smarting comments about what it means to be black in the United

States. The film centered on Jeff Gerber, an obnoxious, wise-cracking suburban insurance salesman who wakes up in the middle of the night to find that he has become a black man. Despite lengthy baths in quarts of milk, lavish use of Blond Soul and Beautiful Bleach obtained in a ghetto drugstore, and other equally inane treatments, his new pigmentation will not wash off. His doctor can find no logical explanation for the transformation but does tell Gerber that his records have been transferred to a young black doctor. Instead of being called Mr. Gerber he now is called Jeff by the black counterman at the drugstore where he normally gulps his breakfast. And when he somewhat hysterically talks about his transformation, the counterman (a splendid cameo by Mantan Moreland) tells Gerber to cool it. The reaction of Gerber's office manager is one of delight, for now the company can exploit the black market. And the blonde office sexpot, who had ignored Gerber until now, goes to bed with him when his ostentatiously liberal wife is suddenly no longer interested in physical contact. His family receives obscene phone calls and his neighbors proceed to buy him out, paying many times more than his property is worth. Ultimately Gerber loses his family, abandons the white world, and becomes part of the urban black culture. At the end of the movie he has become a ghetto businessman, has joined a black power group, and is shown drilling with a group preparing for the coming revolution.

The Watermelon Man was a gimmicky movie. Godfrey Cambridge played Gerber before and after the transformation, and the effect of the early sequences is somewhat destroyed by the appearance of a black in whiteface; audiences tended to be overly fascinated by technicalities. Moreover, for all its biting humor the movie was uneven and ambiguous in its implications. The transformation destroys Gerber's life, yet it is clear that being black is better for him. He enjoys a solidarity with blacks that never existed for him with whites; he appears happily rid of his well-meaning but nagging wife and two bratty kids; he changes from a conservative dresser into a "cool cat"; and he loses his overbearing obnoxiousness as he begins to shake off many of the conventions that had previously governed his life. Moreover, the implication is that the urban ghetto for all of its drawbacks is a better place to live than white suburbia.

Van Peebles was not happy with his situation at Columbia, and he later recalled that "eighty percent of the creative energy that I put into *Watermelon Man* went into the corridors of power wrestling for freedom to direct the film as I saw fit." He was to enjoy that freedom with his next film, *Sweet Sweetback's Baadasssss Song*, which was released in 1971. He not only directed this film but also produced, wrote, and edited it, as well as composing the music and playing the lead role. He chose the distributor (Cinemation, a firm known for handling exploitation films) and helped to merchandise his production into one of the top-grossing films of all time. He had shot his film in less than three weeks for roughly $500,000. This cost represented about $100,000 of his own capital (nearly everything he owned), funds he promoted and fees he managed to defer, plus considerable help from friends like Bill Cosby, who came up with $50,000 when money was vitally needed to continue production. Moreover, Van Peebles managed to get away with using nonunion personnel (many of them black) by pretending that he was making a pornographic film.[11]

The hero of Van Peebles' movie is a professional stud. "Oh, God, Oh, son," moans the whore who breaks him in sexually while he is still a youngster. "Oh, . . . you got a sweet sweetback." As an adult Sweetback performs in sex shows for an interracial audience at a whorehouse in the Los Angeles ghetto. One night two white policemen come to find a black man, any black man, who can be exhibited as a suspect for one or two days to still public clamor for action in a murder case. The whorehouse operator tells Sweetback to go with the police, and he does. Enroute to the station the police stop to arrest a young black militant called Moo-moo, and beat him. Sweetback at first ignores what is happening but then suddenly bashes in the cops' heads with his handcuffs. The police department undertakes a ruthless and savage manhunt. Sweetback evades them, helped by pimps, gamblers, whores, and other ghetto low life. He is recaptured once but escapes when some black children set fire to the patrol car he is riding in. Another time he spears a policeman with a pool cue. Finally Sweetback flees to the desert and strikes for the Mexican border. He runs much of the way: eating a live lizard for sustenance, swabbing his sore flesh in urine soaked sand, and killing several dogs used by white trackers. Meanwhile he has made good use of his sexual prowess: once to persuade a black woman to free him from his handcuffs; another time in a sex duel with Big Sadie, a white woman who is the best a white Hells Angels-type gang can offer; and finally when he rapes a black woman at knife-point in the bushes at a rock festival so that when the police close in, "all they see is a black guy and a girl making love . . . they laugh . . . and walk off." Ultimately Sweetback gets away and just before the movie ends a message flashes across the screen in giant letters: "A BAADASSSSS NIGGER IS COMING BACK TO COLLECT SOME DUES."[12]

As might be expected, this movie generated enormous controversy. Van Peebles' movie was directed, as he later explained, "toward the decolonization of black minds, [to] reclaim the black spirit from the centuries of manipulation by the power structure." It has been suggested by one black commentator that Van Peebles may have "started out to make a fun thing, a satire probably, and somewhere along the way the game became serious . . ." This is an interesting hypothesis, but there is no evidence to support it. In any event, Van Peebles' public statements as well as the advertising gave no hint that it was anything but a serious film. The claim was that "this is the first black film that tells it like it is."[13]

The film was condemned by most white reviewers except for an occasional one like Stuart Applebaum, who admired "the filmmaker's skill at stating his case in such devastatingly effective terms . . ." Most black commentators found more to praise than did their white colleagues. For instance, Sam Washington, writing in the Chicago *Sun-Times*, found fault with various aspects of the production but concluded that over-all it was "a grotesque, violent, and beautifully honest film that takes no crap from Whitey" and that "for the first time in cinematic history in America, a movie speaks out of an undeniable black consciousness." Not all black critics agreed. Lerone Bennett, Jr., granted that cinematically the film was interesting and that "after it we can never again see black people in films (noble, suffering, losing) in the same way." But Bennett also maintained that *Sweet Sweetback's Baadasssss Song* was "trivial and tasteless, neither revolutionary nor black" as its supporters contended, and a revival of "antiquated white stereotypes." As he pointed out, "nobody ever f***ed his way to freedom. And it is mischievous and reactionary . . . for anyone to suggest to black people in

1971 that they are going to be able to sc*** their way across the Red Sea . . . If f***ing freed, black people would have celebrated the millennium 400 years ago."[14]

Such adverse criticism had no effect on the extraordinary drawing power of *Sweet Sweetback's Baadasssss Song*. Black moviegoers, who comprised the vast majority of its audience, seemed less concerned with verisimilitude than with the opportunity to see Sweetback strike back at those whites who called him "nigger" or "boy." As one black Chicago woman said after seeing the film: "how many blacks would *not* like to work over a few racist cops or outwit scores of white pursuers." One newspaperman commented on "the euphoric black audiences" who responded with "wholehearted emotion and enthusiasm" to the beating of the two white policemen, and the killing of two others. Opening in a few theaters early in 1971, the movie quickly proved itself an excellent moneymaker. During its first year of distribution it grossed around $10 million. Nothing illustrates the amazing grosses of this film better than the balance sheet of the distributor. Cinemation Industries lost five cents a share in the quarter April–June, 1970; a year later when handling Van Peebles' film the company claimed earnings of fifty-six cents a share. Van Peebles had chosen this company to distribute his film over more important and prestigious distributors because he thought that the latters' terms were bad. In his words, "Fuck that . . . I wanted bread and control. In the end I LEASED the film to . . . Cinemation." A fascinating footnote to this arrangement is that Van Peebles later found it necessary to sue for an accounting.[15]

That the fantastic box-office response of blacks to Van Peebles' film was not just an isolated phenomenon, that there existed a large black audience hungry for its own kind of heroes was vividly demonstrated once more by the spectacular grosses earned by *Shaft*, which was released just a few months after *Sweet Sweetback's Baadasssss Song*. As nothing else could have done, *Shaft* confirmed that black moviegoers would turn out in great numbers to see one of their own win. Within less than a year after *Shaft* first began playing movie theaters, it had earned MGM over nine times the film's $1.2 million production cost. Less coarse and antiwhite than Van Peebles' film, *Shaft* also attracted white moviegoers. In the main, though, blacks were responsible for the film's success. They were obviously attracted

Richard Roundtree, as the suave private detective hero of *Shaft* (1971), epitomized the new screen image of the black. (From the MGM release "Shaft" © 1971 Metro-Goldwyn-Mayer Inc.)

by the title character — who in his own way was able to cope with white society in a manner that Sweetback could not.

John Shaft is a private detective. As portrayed by Richard Roundtree, he is bold, resourceful, intelligent, and brave. He works out of an office in Times Square but keeps in close touch with events in Harlem. Black underworld boss Bumpy Jonas sends two black thugs to bring Shaft to him. One thug is knocked out; the other dies in a three-story fall. The police warn Shaft that his private detective's license will be suspended unless he helps the department find out why Bumpy has suddenly begun to stir things up. Meanwhile the racketeer, seemingly unfazed by the fate of his gunmen, asks Shaft to find his daughter, Marcy. She supposedly has been kidnapped by a band of black militants, headed by Ben Buford — an old friend of Shaft's. Bumpy agrees to pay the detective his usual $50-per-hour fee. It turns out that Marcy's kidnappers are Mafia mobsters who are out to take over Bumpy's operations in Harlem. Marcy and her captors are traced to an uptown hotel, where she is rescued by Shaft and Ben and his militants.

Surely a super black hero called for a super-hackneyed plot. John Shaft, whom MGM publicists billed as "a new James Bond," is physically fearless and superbly resilient. After being machine-gunned by a white mobster, he is out of action for just a few minutes. When called a nigger by a Mafia gangster Shaft calls him a wop and later breaks a bottle across the white man's face. Shaft walks across Times Square against the traffic lights, and when an angry white motorist blows his car horn, Shaft gives him the finger. When asked by a young policeman where he is going, Shaft replies "I'm going to get laid. Where are you going?" He has an attractive black girlfriend but is not above picking up white women, and in one scene he is shown showering with one such pickup and making love to her. Shaft lives in an expensive and well-furnished Greenwich Village brownstone apartment but seems to be at home everywhere with his beige cashmere turtleneck and black leather trench coat. Moreover, the advertising and publicity campaigns played up John Shaft, carefully punning on the name. In the words of the president of the black advertising agency that created the copy to promote the film in the black community, John Shaft was presented as "a lone, black Superspade — a man of flair and flamboyance who has fun at the expense of the white establishment." And MGM's advertising slogans also touted this aspect of the character. One tagline was "Shaft's his name, shaft's his game." Another was "The mob wanted Harlem back. They got Shaft . . . up to here."[16]

Shaft not only did splendid business at the box office but also received many favorable reviews as a film that was "highly work-manlike and enjoyable," to quote one white critic. There were also those reviewers, both black and white, who asserted that the film was mediocre, a "B-grade gutpuncher . . . seat pounding trash," to use another white critic's words. One of the film's most critical black reviewers was Clayton Riley, who damned it in a New York *Times* article. Riley called *Shaft* a "disaster" artistically and technically, a "film that lacks both style and substance." And he charged that the basic premise of the movie was "an extended lie." Riley maintained that the private-detective film had collapsed as a movie genre by the beginning of the 1960s, and that *Shaft* represented "a handsome and intelligent Black man picking up the leavings, the broken down legacy of some distant fantasy figures like . . . Mr. Kean, Tracer of Lost Persons." John Shaft, asserted Riley, was nothing but "a xerox copy of all the fraudulence America can construct in its mania for hero worship or white anti-hero worship." But most black commentators concurred with the judgment of its black director, Gordon Parks, who described the film as "a Saturday night fun picture which people go to see because they want to see the black guy winning."[17]

Parks is an accomplished man who has made a name for himself in various fields. He has written well-received fiction and a moving personal memoir and has composed both popular and serious music. He is one of the foremost practitioners of realistic photo-journalism. Born in 1912, he was one of 15 children. He spent his boyhood in Fort Scott, a small Kansas town where he experienced both a warm family life and the many humiliations that came from segregation and bigotry. This period of his life has been sensitively recaptured in his autobiographical novel *The Learning Tree*, which was published in 1963. By the end of the 1930s, he had become a successful fashion and society photographer. He also worked as a photographer for the Office of War Information during World War II and then for Standard Oil of New Jersey. In 1948 he became *Life*'s first black staff photographer. He stayed with the magazine for twenty years and won dozens of awards. During that time he became interested in film and made a number of short fiction movies as well as some documentaries. In 1968 he was signed by Warner Brothers to direct the screen version of *The Learning Tree* and with this film Parks became the first American black man to direct a feature at a major studio in the United States.

In addition to directing the 1969 release Parks produced it, wrote the screen play, and composed the musical score. The movie, like the novel, is a nostalgic look at two black teenagers, their families, and their surroundings in a small Kansas town during the early 1920s. One of them, Newt, has a happy home and an affectionate and understanding mother. The other, Marcus, has neither, and his father is an embittered man. Parks lovingly depicts the blacks' way of life in that time and place — ranging from open-air barbecues to services at the black church. But then a white farmer is murdered. Newt in his testimony at the trial of the white drunkard charged with the murder implicates Marcus's father, who kills himself. The strain proves too much for Newt's mother, who dies of a heart attack. Marcus seeks to revenge himself but is shot in the back by the local peace officer. However, as one critic aptly phrased it, "the movie makes no glib equation, it knows that on balance insults are less deadly than bullets." Newt, who had been told by his mother to use life's incidents as a "learning tree," faces life with new understanding. *The Learning Tree*, though a bit old fashioned and slow in spots, is a marvelously evocative film.[18]

Movies like *The Learning Tree*, however, were anything but moneymakers. The industry recognized that what the mass of black moviegoers wanted was not just black participation in films. Nor did they want weighty films like *The Great White Hope* (Twentieth Century-Fox, 1970), a flawed version of the play based on the career of heavyweight boxing champion Jack Johnson. As *Variety* informed its readers, black moviegoers "don't cotton to such pix, as . . . they feature . . . blacks in a losing light . . ." What these moviegoers wanted to see was what John Shaft and Sweetback had offered them. Initially exhibitors had no more films like these to present and had to rely on little beside showmen's ingenuity. One Chicago theater chain added a large picture of Roscoe Lee Browne to an advertisement for the 1971

Warner Brothers release, *The Cowboys*. Previously only John Wayne had been shown, but the ad copy was revised to read "also starring Roscoe Lee Browne as Big Duke's valiant sidekick on the cattle drive." Browne's role was that of a cook.[19]

Soon after, however, a veritable avalanche of black superheroes descended on the nation's screens. Thanks to the demise of the Code in the 1960s, its replacement by a weak industry-administered rating system, and a series of Supreme Court decisions relaxing the definition of obscenity, these films were filled with sadistic brutality, sleazy sex, venomous racial slurs, and the argot of the streets. Social commentary of any sort was kept to a minimum. Superspade was a violent man who lived a violent life in pursuit of black women, white sex, quick money, easy success, cheap "pot," and other pleasures. In these films white was synonymous with every conceivable kind of evil and villainy. Whites were moral lepers, most of whom were psychotically antiblack and whose vocabulary was laced with the rhetoric of bigotry. Writing about the portrayal of whites in these movies, Pauline Kael charged that "except when we were at war, there has never been such racism in American films." She is right to a point. These films are a mirror image of the way the black was for years treated on screen. It is only in our permissive society that the industry in its search for a black audience can carry the reversal much farther than the original.[20]

A sampling of the black-oriented films released since 1971 strikingly illustrates the industry's changed treatment of the black. In both of Jim Brown's 1972 films his primary white antagonists, who are vicious racists, are burned to death — thanks to his good offices. *Melinda*, a 1972 MGM release featuring Calvin Lockhart as a flashy disc jockey, begins with the Lockhart character preening before a mirror and asserting "God, but I'm a lovely motherfucker" and ends with him hitting the white villain again and again and again. In *Black Caesar*, a 1973 Peter Sabiston production, another former football player, Fred Williamson, played a black gangster who fails in a savage attempt to win a share of the graft squeezed from the ghetto by the Mafia. *The Spook Who Sat by the Door* (a 1973 United Artists release) was described by *Variety* as an "atypical blaxploitationer" because it had "little gore but lotsa racist and revolutionary blather" in developing a plot whose theme was that "anything violent goes — including mass-murder — providing the victims are white." The 1974 Warner release *Black Belt Jones* blended the black power theme with the kung fu craze, pitting a group of young blacks headed by martial arts champion Jim Kelly against some stock white gangsters. Among the most fanciful of these movies was *Three the Hard Way* (a 1974 Allied Artists release) starring Brown, Kelly, and Williamson, who defeat an all-white fascist group planning to exterminate blacks in Detroit, Los Angeles, and Washington. This is to be accomplished by dropping what looks like sparkling burgundy into the reservoirs of these cities: it would affect blacks only — "something like sickle-cell anemia" explains a scientist.[21]

Among the most controversial of these films (as well as one of the largest grossers) was *Superfly,* a 1972 Warner Brothers release, directed by Gordon Parks, Jr. It earned over $5 million in one year on an investment of less than a million. The title refers to the ghetto name for cocaine and the film is about Youngblood Priest, a black dealer who is looking to make one last big sale and retire. He succeeds despite the attempts to relieve him of his loot and his life by high-ranking white police officials, one of whom is described as New York City's biggest cocaine supplier. At the film's end the cocaine-sniffing Priest drives off in his magnificent Rolls Royce, a rich and happy man. In the process of achieving his goal, moreover, he has not only beaten up black thugs and white policemen but has enjoyed his loyal black mistress and an eager white girl.

A fascinating intermingling of the Superspade image and the old black-as-threat-to-white-society image was achieved in the 1973 James Bond thriller, *Live and Let Die* (United Artists). This screen adaptation of Ian Fleming's novel seemed to be designed to appeal not to a universal movie-going audience but to a specifically white audience and a specifically black audience. For the white audience, a threatening combination of efficient black gangsterism and eerie voodoo finally is defeated by Superwasp James Bond. And the black audience is given a glimpse of a brilliantly efficient operation manned by blacks as well as a repeated emphasis on how close white society is to falling to black power. In this connection, perhaps the most powerful image in the movie is the final one, that of actor-dancer Geoffrey Holder, the supposedly dead voodoo prince, perched on the cowcatcher of a train carrying Bond and laughing eerily as though to say that the battle of black versus white has not ended.

There can be no question about the black superhero's capabilities, but his humanity is another matter. For Superspade was no less a caricature than the earlier ones that so grossly insulted black people. And this was even more true of the typical black woman who was presented in these films. Take the nightclub singer in the 1972 Twentieth Century-Fox release *Trouble Man*, about a fancy black detective known as Mr. T. The movie makes it seem as though she spends all of her time waiting for "Mr. T." to call: she even refuses a chance to perform out-of-town lest she be absent when he needs her. As one critic said, "no matter that her hair is cut Afro, nor the objets d'art surrounding her are African, she's still a house slave." At a time when women's lib had become increasingly militant, these films served as splendid examples of male chauvinism.[22]

Lynn Hamilton, a black actress with good television credentials, recounted her experience when auditioned by a producer to play what was described as "a strong Angela Davis type." Almost immediately she was asked if she would play nude scenes. She could barely hide her anger: "Here is this woman who holds all kinds of academic degrees and has a high position opening the door totally nude to admit her boyfriend, a policeman. The first thing he says is 'Fix me some breakfast.' She starts to fry bacon. It was completely unrealistic. Any woman knows that bacon spatters grease, and she certainly would not cook it without clothes on. While all this is going on, the boyfriend is patting her butt and feeling her breasts . . ."[23]

There were a few exceptions to this piggish rule. Two disparate examples are *Lady Sings the Blues* (a 1972 Paramount production) and *Foxy Brown* (a 1974 American International release). The first is the story of the singer Billie Holiday. A moving, well-made film, which benefits greatly from a first-rate performance by Diana Ross, *Lady Sings the Blues* took various liberties in recounting Holiday's life. This is not unusual for purportedly biographical films; in this case the facts were distorted to emphasize white venality and hostility. *Foxy Brown* belongs to that recent group of films in which the main character is a female superspade. *Variety's* summation of the movie, which featured Pam Grier, Peter Brown, and Kathryn Loder, leaves

Ain't Ms.-behaving: Pamala Grier aims a sawed-off shot-
gun at an unseen malefactor in the 1973 *Coffy*. (National Film Archive/Courtesy American International)

little unsaid: "Before femme might makes right, Grier and callgirl Juanita Brown have a brawl in a lesbian bar . . . , doxy Sally Ann Stroud has her throat slashed, two degenerate white thugs who've raped Grier are burned to death, and white thug Brown is castrated. Tasteful finale has Grier delivering Brown's private parts in a pickle jar to white vice ring leader Loder, before driving off with neighborhood vigilante leader . . ."[24]

It is hardly surprising that black community leaders and critics blasted these films. In addition to condemning the industry for showing black women as persons of loose morals, they charged that these movies glorified drugs, imitated successful white stereotypes, set forth impossible and ultimately debilitating fantasies, developed a negative image of the American black man and woman, and took no real cognizance of black oppression in the United States. This criticism carried across political lines. Junius Griffin of the NAACP called these movies "a rip-off" and "blaxploitation" by white producers. Roy Innes, national director of CORE, stated that "the present Black movie phenomenon . . . in its ultimate destruction of the minds of Black youth, is potentially far more dangerous than 'step-n-fetch-it' and his lot." Imamu Amiri Baraka, poet and radical political leader, described the movies as mere "diversion," declaring that "black films haven't been made." Ossie Davis said that blacks should shun movies like *Superfly* since "we're paying for images of our degradation." Dr. Alvin Poussaint, an eminent black psychiatrist and author, argued that the emphasis of these movies on the degrading aspects of the ghetto culture has resulted in the "leadership capabilities" of "many black youths" being "misdirected and wasted."[25]

There is no denying, however, the reaction of black audiences. Critic Joy Gould Boyum reported that a predominantly black audience watching one of these movies in mid-1974 cheered and applauded every assault on whites and "apparently loved the film because it seemed to speak for [the blacks'] own bitterness and hostility." Black people continued to attend these movies in vast numbers and ultimately it is this voting with the feet and the pocketbook that determines the industry product. Peter Bailey of *Ebony* summed up the problem when he declared that "as long as blacks in large numbers continue to patronize pix considered . . . racially unflattering, they will get much more of the same shoddy product."[26]

Admittedly these movies did give blacks a chance to work behind as well as in front of the cameras. Gordon Parks was understandably proud that *Shaft* "opened up a lot of doors for black people" — including the gaffer, the wardrobe mistress, and the film editor. Isaac Hayes got his first chance to write a musical score for a film. A number of other black-oriented films were also directed by blacks. But for the most part it was not blacks who profited. Whites packaged, financed, and sold these films, and they received the bulk of the big money. This held true even for *Superfly*, a project conceived by blacks. Its backers received a percentage of the receipts after Warner Brothers bought the distribution rights to the film, but the studio made the sequel without Phillip Fenty (the black screenwriter for *Superfly*), Gordon Parks, Jr., and the various black people who financed it. Actor-writer Max Julien told one interviewer that when production of the black-oriented films was first announced, "you felt you had your foot in the door, but then you found out they were just using it for a doorstop." His wife, actress Vonetta McGee, whose credits include *Melinda* and *Blacula,* said that "If you didn't laugh at it, this place [Hollywood] could get your head fucked up." Richard Roundtree got only $12,500 for playing John Shaft and would have received no more than $25,000 in the glossy 1972 sequel, *Shaft's Big Score* (MGM), had Parks not intervened. And despite the exertions of black directors as well as the pressure brought by black groups and the government, the technical unions have largely kept blacks out of their ranks, for all their brave talk of minority hiring programs.[27]

But not all black-oriented films made money. Some sincere efforts that eschewed the imagery of the Superspade films fared badly. Among such lost films were *Man and Boy,* a low-key 1971 western produced by and starring Bill Cosby in a somewhat creaky tale about black homesteaders in the post–Civil War West. Another was *Black Girl,* directed by Ossie Davis, which dealt movingly with contemporary (1972) black family life and a girl's attempt to escape from the ghetto. A little over a year before, Davis had shot *Kongi's Harvest* in Nigeria, but this feature about African life found no distributor. Also faced with problems of distribution was *The Bus Is Coming*, a film directed by Wendell Franklin, who was the first black man admitted to the Screen Director's Guild. Produced in the Watts ghetto area of

Los Angeles with the cooperation of the city government, this film utilized many blacks in cast and crew. Its story of a young black veteran who chooses nonviolence over militancy is somewhat naively presented but there is no gainsaying Franklin's statement at the 1971 San Francisco film festival that "every black story I see is a bring down, I want to bring people up."[28]

One notable exception to that rule was the 1972 Radnitz-Mattel production *Sounder.* This film was the moving story of the Morgans, a black family in Louisiana during the Depression. The father, a sharecropper, steals some food to feed his wife and three children, is caught, and is sent to a prison camp. The mother (in a top-notch performance by Cicely Tyson for which she received an Oscar nomination) carries on. She is a strong and sympathetic woman, and it is her love and strength that hold the family together. Because of a leg injury the father is released, and at the end of the film persuades his oldest son to go away to school. The beauty of the film lies not in the plot, which is on the tepid side, but in the characters and in the film's general ambience. There are many scenes showing the Morgans' richness of life in the midst of poverty. Among the most pleasant interludes is the family's joy at the father's pitching triumph in a baseball game; and his homecoming is a genuine tear-jerker. The Morgans are neither symbols nor objects but believable human beings.

Unlike the Superspade movies *Sounder* had no gratuitous sex or violence. It tried to deal with the dignity of the human spirit. The movie was warmly embraced by leaders of the black community because of what they considered to be its positive approach. And *Sounder* did make money. Within nine months of its first commercial showing the film had earned over five times its production costs. Black moviegoers were a significant portion of the paying customers but nothing like the percentage that

In a still too rare portrayal of blacks, Paul Winfield, left, and Kevin Hooks, the father and son of *Sounder* (1972), share a moment that is neither violent nor sexual. (Reproduced by permission of Radnitz/Mattel Productions, Inc., from *Sounder,* a Robert B. Radnitz/Martin Ritt film released by Twentieth Century–Fox)

turned out for a film like *Shaft*. Moreover, even though *Sounder* was well received, there were many blacks who criticized it as irrelevant, as "a white man's movie," and as an attempt to emasculate the newly emerged image of the powerful black man.

It seemed clear by 1974, however, that the "blaxploitation" film had just about run its course. During 1973, *Shaft in Africa* (MGM), *Superfly T. N. T.* (Warners), and *The Soul of Nigger Charley* (a Larry Spangler production) all failed to live up to expectations at the box office. It was not merely that black audiences were proving more discriminating, but that most of the ghetto-oriented films failed to attract white patrons. As *Variety* reported, "the typical black melodrama . . . appeals to a predominantly black audience. The most successful of them start out like a house afire . . . however, the fire suddenly burns out as . . . such films simply run out of patrons." Producers began to recognize that those films that maintained their popularity, such as *Sounder* or *Lady Sings the Blues,* had to have at least some appeal for white audiences. This aspect of a film's box-office potential was especially true in the European markets (so important these days to an American film's commercial success), where blaxploitation "drew big yawns and little boxoffice," to use *Variety's* phrase.[29]

But even with the decline of blaxploitation films, a reasonably true-to-life alternative — a type of movie that (in the words of black critic Ellen Holly) shows "the full spectrum of black life in all its remarkable variety" — has not taken their place. *Claudine* was touted as such a film. This 1974 Twentieth Century-Fox release is ostensibly a comedy about a black welfare mother of six, her troubles with her brood, and her courtship by Roop, an extroverted garbage man. A product of Third World Cinema (a bi-racial group), this film, amidst some very funny sequences, made some telling comments about the bureaucratic miasma facing welfare recipients and about the pressures of ghetto life on the young. But in a significant sense *Claudine* fails, and not just because Diahann Carroll and James Earl Jones fail to convince as the title character and the garbage man. Richard Schickel pinpoints one of the film's major drawbacks in saying that *Claudine* is a "blend of obnoxious stereotypes . . ., the libidinous black woman who cannot stop having children despite her poverty [and] . . . the stern, loving matriarch urging the middle-class ethic on her children." And Roop, as this critic puts it, "is merely single-line stereotype, the stud who has fled his obligations to one family and is now doing his best to love and leave Claudine."[30]

Except for a few notable exceptions like *Sounder, The Learning Tree,* and *Nothing But A Man,* the film image of the black is as condescending and defamatory as it has ever been. Movies are entertainment, but they are also symbols, and behind every shadow on the big screen is the struggle to impose definitions upon what is and what should be. The power of any single movie to influence a viewer permanently is limited, although repetition obviously has its effect. Constant repetition that emphasizes certain stereotypes — as is the case with the black presence on screen — is overpowering. And this reinforcement has residual effects even when the stereotypes have begun to change. Whether as Sambo or as Superspade the humanity of black people is still being denied in the movies. One can only hope that cultural changes in other areas (which can result in TV productions such as the moving and vital *Autobiography of Miss Jane Pittman*) will continue to make themselves felt in theatrical films, and that what were notable exceptions soon will become the rule.

Notes

KEY TO NOTE ABBREVIATIONS

Sources that have been assigned abbreviations in the notes to the text are listed below in alphabetical order.

Afro-American	Baltimore *Afro-American*
Age	New York *Age*
Courier	Pittsburgh *Courier*
Defender	Chicago *Defender*
GJOH	George Johnson Oral History, Bancroft Library, University of California, Los Angeles
JC	George Johnson Negro Film Collection, Bancroft Library, University of California, Los Angeles
MPH	*Motion Picture Herald*
MPW	*Motion Picture World*
News	New York *Amsterdam News*
NYPL-SC	Schomburg Collection, New York Public Library, New York City
NYPL-TC	Theatre Collection, Research Library for the Performing Arts, New York Public Library
NYT	The New York *Times*
WNET transcript	Transcript of WNET-TV show *Free Time,* November 9, 1971

NOTES

INTRODUCTION: THE LACK OF HUMANITY

1. Stanley Elkins, *Slavery*, 2nd ed. (Chicago: University of Chicago Press 1968), p. 82
2. MPW, May 7, 1910, p. 240.
3. Quoted in Ernest Lindgren, *The Art of the Film*, 2nd ed. (London: George Allen and Unwin, 1963), p. 172.
4. *Age*, May 23, 1914, p. 6.
5. *News*, January 6, 1940, p. 16; L.D. Reddick, "Educational Programs for the Improvement of Race Relations," *Journal of Negro Education*, 13 (Summer 1944): 367, 369.

1. THE GAMUT FROM A TO B

1. Mayor Phelan quoted in Roger Daniels, *The Politics of Prejudice* (New York: Atheneum, 1968), p. 21; Burton Hendrick, "The Great Jewish Invasion," *McClure's Magazine*, 28 (January, 1907): 307; MPW, October 19, 1907, p. 505, November 16, 1907, p. 599.
2. C. Vann Woodward, *Origins of the New South* (Baton Rouge: Louisiana University Press, 1951), p. 352; MPW, November 18, 1911, p. 553; Rayford Logan, *The Betrayal of the Negro* (New York: Collier Books, 1965), pp. 371–72; Abel Green and Joe Laurie, Jr., *Show Biz* (New York: Holt, Rinehart and Winston, 1951), p. 8; quoted in Loften Mitchell, *Black Drama* (New York: Hawthorn, 1967), pp. 31–32.
3. Langston Hughes, "The Negro and American Entertainment," in *The American Negro Reference Book*, ed. John Davis (Englewood Cliffs, N.J.: Prentice-Hall, 1966), p. 381.
4. Mordecai Gorelik, *New Theatres for Old* (New York: Samuel French, 1940), p. 161; Farrin Belcher, "The Place of the Negro in the Evolution of the American Theatre" (Ph.D. thesis, Yale University, 1945), pp. 1–2.
5. Eugene Walter, *The Easiest Way*, in *Chief Contemporary Dramatists*, ed. Thomas Dickinson (Boston: Houghton Mifflin, 1921), p. 174.
6. MPW, January 11, 1913, p. 139, April 5, 1913, p. 53.

7. Mabel Rowland, ed., *Bert Williams: Son of Laughter* (New York: English Crafters, 1923), p. 150.
8. *Age*, March 5, 1914, p. 6; *Defender*, July 7, 1916, p. 6; *Age*, April 16, 1914, p. 6; MPW, August 22, 1914, p. 1077, February 21, 1914, p. 1012.
9. Edison catalogue reprinted in Terry Ramsaye, *A Million and One Nights* (New York: Simon & Schuster, 1964), pp. 609–10; *Show World*, October 12, 1907, p. 16.
10. *Biograph Bulletins, 1896–1908*, compiled by Kemp Niver, ed. Bebe Bergstern (Los Angeles: Locare Research Group, 1971), p. 207.
11. MPW, July 2, 1910, p. 45.
12. Ibid., January 18, 1913, p. 263; *Bulletin* quoted in Robert Henderson, *D.W. Griffith: The Years at Biograph* (New York: Farrar, Straus & Giroux, 1970), pp. 109–10.
13. MPW, July 19, 1913, p. 338.
14. Ibid., April 11, 1908, p. 325
15. Ibid., January 23, 1909, p. 93, January 11, 1913, p. 166.
16. Peter Noble, *The Negro in Film* (London: Skelton Robinson, c. 1947), p. 29; MPW, December 16, 1911, p. 905. Noble's work is among the first book-length treatments of the black in film, but it is marred by error and unevenness.
17. MPW, June 19, 1915, p. 1965.
18. Ibid., August 26, 1911, p. 55, July 15, 1911, p. 64.
19. Quoted in Neville Hunnings, *Film Censors and the Law* (London: George Allen and Unwin, 1967), p. 50.
20. Joseph Boskin, "Sambo: The National Jester in the Popular Culture," in *The Great Fear*, ed. Gary Nash and Richard Weiss (New York: Holt, Rinehart and Winston, 1970), p. 166.
21. Thomas Cripps, "The Myth of the Southern Box Office," in *The Black Experience in America*, ed. James Curtis and Lewis Gould (Austin: University of Texas Press, 1970), p. 118, fn. 2.
22. Russell Merritt, "The Impact of D.W. Griffith's Motion Pictures from 1908 to 1914 on Contemporary American Culture" (Ph.D. thesis, Harvard University, 1970), p. 182.
23. John O. Killens, "Hollywood in Black and White," in *White Racism*, ed. Barry Schwartz and Robert Disch (New York: Dell, 1970), p. 401.

2 THE BIRTH OF A NATION

1. MPW, April 24, 1915, p. 602.
2. Ibid.
3. Ibid., "Fighting Race Calumny," *The Crisis*, 10 (June, 1915): 87.
4. James Agee, *Agee on Film: Reviews and Comments* (Boston: Beacon Press, 1958), p. 314.
5. *The Theatre*, January, 1906, p. 21; New York *Globe*, January 9, 1906, p. 7.
6. Vachel Lindsay, *The Art of the Moving Picture* (New York: Liveright, 1970), p. 75; Dixon quoted in Ramsaye, p. 641; Francis Hackett, "Brotherly Love," *New Republic*, 7 (March 20, 1915): 185.
7. Lillian Gish, with Anne Pinchot, *The Movies, Mr. Griffith, and Me* (Englewood Cliffs, N.J.: Prentice-Hall, 1969), p. 162; James Hart (ed.) *The Man Who Invented Hollywood: The Autobiography of D.W. Grif-*

fith (Louisville, Ky.: Touchstone Publishing Company, 1972), p. 30.

8. *New York Dramatic Mirror,* September 2, 1914, p. 14.

9. Quoted in Henry S. Gordon, "The Story of David Wark Griffith," *Photoplay,* 10 (October, 1916): 92; Seymour Stern, "Griffith's 'The Birth of a Nation,' " *Film Culture,* Spring-Summer, 1965: 14.

10. C. Vann Woodward, *The Strange Career of Jim Crow* (New York: Oxford University Press, 1966), p. 69; Ray S. Baker, *Woodrow Wilson: Life and Letters* (Garden City, N.Y.: Doubleday, Doran, 1931), Vol. 4, p. 222; James F. Rhodes, *History of the United States from the Compromise of 1850* (New York: Scribner's, 1906), Vol. 6, p. 39; William Dunning, *Reconstruction: Political and Economic 1865–1877* (New York: Harper and Brothers, 1907), p. 1.

11. Quoted in Gordon, p. 92.

12. Boston *American,* May 2, 1915, Boston *Globe,* April 7, 1915, clippings in D.W. Griffith scrapbooks (microfilm), Roll 1, Book 5, Museum of Modern Art, Library, New York City; Rev. Dr. Charles Parkhurst quoted in *Focus on The Birth of a Nation,* ed. Fred Silva (Englewood Cliffs, N.J.: Prentice-Hall, 1971), pp. 102–103.

13. Wilson quoted in Raymond Cook, "The Man Behind *The Birth of a Nation,*" *North Carolina Historical Review,* 38 (October, 1962): 530; Dixon quoted in Lawrence Freedman, *The White Savage* (Englewood Cliffs, N.J.: Prentice-Hall, 1970), p. 171; Wilson quoted in Arthur Link, *The New Freedom* (Princeton: Princeton University Press, 1956), p. 254.

14. Addams quoted in Thomas Cripps, "The Reaction of the Negro to the Motion Picture *The Birth of a Nation,*" in *The Making of Black America,* ed. August Meier and Elliott Rudwick (New York: Atheneum, 1969), Vol. 2, p. 155.

15. *Age,* May 14, 1921, p. 4; George Tindall, *The Emergence of The New South 1913–1945* (Baton Rouge: Louisiana State University Press, 1969), pp. 186–87; Ruth Preston and L.L. Thurstone, *Motion Pictures and the Social Attitudes of Children* (New York: Macmillan, 1933), pp. 35–38.

16. *The Village Voice,* July 24, 1969, p. 37.

3. The Freezing of an Image

1. Benjamin Hampton, *History of the American Film Industry* (New York: Dover, 1970), p. 313.

2. Marshall Neilan quoted in *Courier,* September 4, 1926, p. 10; Cripps, "Myth," pp. 121, 125, 128.

3. MPW, January 27, 1923, p. 198, April 10, 1920, p. 202; Natalie Barkas, *Behind the Camera* (London: Geoffrey Blas, 1934), p. 77.

4. MPW, April 15, 1916, p. 516.

5. Ibid., June 7, 1924, p. 354, April 8, 1922, p. 525.

6. Reddick, p. 372; *Vitagraph Bulletin,* August, 1915, p. 13.

7. *Age,* August 17, 1918, p. 6, October 17, 1918, p. 6.

8. Terry Ramsaye, "The Rise and Place of the Motion Picture," *Annals of the American Academy of Political and Social Science,* 224 (November, 1947); 7–8; *Age,* September 3, 1921, p. 1; *Courier,* July 9, 1927, Sec. 2, p. 1.

9. Quoted in Ruth Inglis, *Freedom of the Movies* (Chicago: University of Chicago Press, 1947), pp. 114–15.
10. Press book for *Ham and Eggs at the Front*, NYPL–TC; Woollcott quoted in *Age*, May 6, 1922, p. 4.
11. MPW, July 26, 1924, p. 302; *Afro-American*, May 1, 1926, p. 10.
12. MPW, August 13, 1927, p. 480; Stephen Zito "The Black Film Experience," in *The American Film Heritage*, ed. Tom Shales *et al.* (Washington, D.C.: Acropolis Books, 1972), p. 65.
13. MPW, April 15, 1922, p. 761.
14. *Courier*, December 25, 1927, Sec. 2, p. 1; *Age*, March 6, 1926, p. 6.
15. *Courier*, October 18, 1924, p. 6.
16. MPW, June 12, 1920, p. 879; *Age*, January 15, 1921, p. 6; *Courier*, July 17, 1926, p. 10.
17. Quoted in Herbert Blumer, *Movies and Conduct*, p. 257.

4. "All-Colored" — But Not Very Different

1. *Defender*, October 9, 1915, p. 6, August 9, 1913, p. 5, October 18, 1913, p. 8, November 22, 1913, p. 6.
2. Ibid., September 27, 1915, p. 5.
3. Ibid., May 22, 1915, p. 2.
4. Thomas R. Cripps, "Movies in the Ghetto, B.P. (Before Poitier)," *Negro Digest*, 18 (February, 1969): 23.
5. *Variety*, December 6, 1918, p. 38.
6. MPW, February 23, 1918, p. 1105; JC; copy of George Johnson article sent to "all Negro newspapers" in 1918.
7. *Billboard*, March 23, 1918, pp. 35, 153; *Variety*, December 6, 1918, p. 38.
8. Chicago *Tribune*, December 8, 1918, p. 19; *Billboard*, December 14, 1918, p. 48; *Variety*, December 6, 1918, p. 38; *Defender*, September 6, 1919, p. 8.
9. Synopsis in *Defender*, September 20, 1919, p. 9; *Billboard*, December 14, 1918, p. 48.
10. Quoted in James Alabrook, "Historic Color Bias in Print," *Journalism Quarterly*, 48 (Spring, 1971): 481.
11. Plot synopsis in JC; *Defender*, April 7, 1917; GJOH, *passim*.
12. GJOH, *passim; Age*, April 10, 1920, p. 6.
13. JC: Clipping.
14. Plot synopsis in JC; GJOH, *passim*.
15. *Defender*, January 12, 1918, p. 4
16. JC: Clippings.
17. *Age*, July 20, 1916, p. 6, May 17, 1917, p. 6, August 9, 1917, p. 6.
18. W.E.B. DuBois, "The Talented Tenth," *The Negro Problem*, ed. Booker T. Washington *et al.* (New York: James Pott & Co., 1903), p. 33; plot synopsis in *Age*, July 20, 1916, p. 6.
19. *Age*, May 17, 1917, p. 6, August 9, 1917, p. 6, March 6, 1920, p. 6.
20. *Afro-American*, February 17, 1922, p. 6; *Defender*, August 20, 1921, p. 7; *Age*, August 6, 1921, p. 6.
21. Wesley Curtwright, "Motion Pictures of Negroes," typescript, c. 1939, NYPL-SC; *Defender*, July 30, 1921, p. 6.
22. *Courier*, February 27, 1926; Margaret Just Butcher, *The Negro in*

American Culture, rev. and updated (New York: New American Library, 1971), p. 153.

23. Norman Kagan, "Black American Cinema," *Cinema,* 6 (No. 2): 3; it should be mentioned that Kagan draws very, very heavily on the Cripps *Negro Digest* article.

24. Dust-jacket blurbs on Oscar Micheaux, *The Forged Note* (Lincoln, Neb.: Western Book Supply Co., 1916) and *The Case of Mrs. Wingate* (New York: Book Supply Co., 1945); GJOH, *passim.*

25. Plot synopsis in *Defender,* February 22, 1919, p. 11.

26. JC: clippings; *Courier,* June 11, 1927, sec. 2, p. 1, April 11, 1927, sec. 2, p. 1.

27. *Defender,* July 8, 1922, p. 6.

28. *Afro-American,* January 29, 1927, p. 6; *Age,* March 31, 1923, p. 6.

29. *Variety,* November 26, 1924, p. 1, Thomas R. Cripps, "Paul Robeson and Black Identity in American Movies," *Massachusetts Review,* 11 (Summer, 1970): 471; Eslanda Goode Robeson, *Paul Robeson: Negro* (London: Victor Gollancz, 1930); Marie Seton, *Paul Robeson* (London: Dennis Dobson, 1958); Anatol Schlosser, "Paul Robeson" (Ph. D. thesis, New York University, 1970).

30. *Age,* September 18, 1920, p. 6; *Courier,* December 19, 1925, p. 9.

31. *Age,* June 14, 1917, p. 6, March 6, 1920, p. 6; *Afro-American,* July 31, 1926, p. 9.

32. Carlton Moss, "The Negro In American Film," *Harlem USA,* ed. John Clarke, rev. ed. (New York: Collier Books, 1971), p. 183.

5. Shufflin' into Sound

1. Robert Kimball and William Bolcom, *Reminiscing with Sissle and Blake* (New York: Viking, 1973), p. 138.

2. Quoted in Martin Quigley, Jr., and Richard Gertner, *Films in America 1929–1969* (New York: Golden Press, 1970), p. 12.

3. Geraldyn Dismond, "The Negro Actor and the American Movies," *Close Up,* 5 (August, 1929): 95–96; Elmer A. Carter, "Of Negro Motion Pictures," ibid., 119.

4. JC: Clippings.

5. "A Letter from Walter White," *Close Up,* 5 (August, 1929): 105.

6. Los Angeles *Examiner,* March 8, 1929, p. 15; Chicago *Whip,* May 18, 1929, p. 10.

7. Robert Stebbins quoted in Otto Lindenmayer, *Black History: Lost, Stolen, or Strayed* (New York: Discus Books, 1970), p. 184.

8. "Stepin Fetchit Comes Back," *Ebony,* 7 (February, 1952): 64; *Afro-American,* July 6, 1929, p. 8; NYT, February 24, 1935, IV, p. 3; "Whatever Happened To Stepin Fetchit," JC: clipping; *Ebony,* 27 (November, 1971): 202.

9. King Vidor, *A Tree Is a Tree* (New York: Harcourt Brace, 1953), p. 175.

10. *Afro-American,* June 8, 1929, p. 9; *Age,* October 20, 1928, p. 6.

11. Vidor, p. 175; Forsyth Hardy, ed., *Grierson on Documentary* (Los Angeles: University of California Press, 1966), p. 83

12. *Courier,* February 8, 1930, p. 16, letter quoted in Reddick, p. 373; *Hallelujah* scrapbook, NYPL-TC, Robeson quoted in Noble, p. 54;

Chicago *Whip*, February 15, 1930, p. 12; W.E.B. DuBois, "Dramatis Personae — Hallelujah," *The Crisis*, 36 (October, 1929): 355.

13. E. Franklin Frazier, "Recreation and Amusement among American Negroes," typescript, 1940, NYPL-SC, pp. 75, 80, 91.
14. *Age*, October 28, 1929, p. 1.
15. *Courier*, April 12, 1930, Sec. 2, p. 6; Charles Higham and Joel Greenberg, *The Celluloid Muse* (London: Angus & Robertson, 1969), p. 232; *Billboard* article reproduced in *Afro-American*, April 6, 1929, p. 8.
16. *Afro-American*, April 27, 1930, p. 8, May 17, 1930, p. 8.
17. *Courier*, March 8, 1930, p. 10; *Defender*, March 13, 1930, p. 9; *News*, June 6, 1936, p. 16.
18. JC: Clippings.
19. Green and Laurie, p. 357; *Life*, 3 (August 9, 1937): 32.
20. Arthur Draper in *New Theatre*, 3 (January, 1936): 30.
21. *News*, January 6, 1940, p. 16.
22. *Courier*, January 6, 1940, p. 4.
23. Higham and Greenberg, p. 106.
24. Natalie Barkas, *30,000 Miles for the Films* (London: Blackie & Son, 1937), p. 160.
25. *Age*, March 27, 1937; *Documentary News Letter*, 1 (June, 1940): 8.
26. *Afro-American*, August 13, 1962, p. 6.
27. Ibid., October 8, 1932, p. 6; Langston Hughes, *I Wonder as I Wander* (New York: Rinehart, 1956), p. 75.
28. Bobby Short, *Black and White Baby* (New York: Dodd, Mead, 1971), p. 110, *Age*, February 9, 1935, p. 4; *Opportunity*, 13 (April, 1935): 121–22, 13 (May, 1935); 154, 13 (March, 1935): 87.
29. *News*, September 21, 1935, p. 10.
30. Curtwright, p. 5.
31. Garvey quoted in Schlosser, p. 408.
32. *Courier*, September 30, 1933, p. 18.
33. Cunard quoted in Schlosser, p. 232; *Sunday Worker*, May 10, 1936, p. 12; *Rotha on Film* (Fairlawn, N.J.: Essential Books, 1958), p. 159.
34. JC: Clippings.
35. Harry Watt quoted in Seton, p. 100.
36. Quoted in Seton, p. 121.
37. MPH, July 21, 1940, p. 40.
38. Mantle quoted in *Courier*, June 6, 1931, p. 6.
39. *Afro-American*, September 28, 1929, p. 10.
40. *Age*, February 23, 1935, p. 6.

6. A Limited Response

1. Bureau of Motion Pictures, Office of War Information, *The Government Manual for Motion Pictures*, quoted in Richard Lingeman, *Don't You Know There's a War On?* (New York: Putnam, 1970), p. 184.
2. *Afro-American*, March 25, 1944, p. 6; *Agee on Film*, p. 108.
3. Dalton Trumbo, "Minorities and the Screen," *Proceedings of the Writers Congress* (Berkeley: University of California Press, 1944), p. 497.
4. Albert Johnson, "The Films of Minelli," *Film Quarterly*, 12 (Winter, 1958): 24; *Afro-American*, April 3, 1943, p. 5.

5. Lena Horne and Richard Schickel, *Lena* (Garden City, NY: Doubleday, 1965), pp. 136, 134.
6. *PM*, July 8, 1943, p. 10.
7. *Afro-American*, February 13, 1943, p. 8; William G. Still, "The Negro and His Music in Films," *Proceedings of the Writers Congress*, pp. 278–79.
8. *Afro-American*, June 6, 1942, p. 13.
9. William L. Burke, "The Presentation of the American Negro in Hollywood Films, 1946–1961" (Ph.D. thesis, Northwestern University, 1965), p. 136.
10. Frank Capra, *The Name Above the Title* (New York: Macmillan, 1971), p. 358.
11. *Agee on Film*, p. 80.
12. National Association for the Advancement of Colored People, *Annual Report for 1942*, p. 32; Walter White, *A Man Called White* (New York: Viking, 1948), p. 201.
13. *Afro-American*, August 29, 1942, p. 10.
14. *Ibid*, April 4, 1942, p. 13; Michael Curtiz quoted in George Murphy with Victor Lasky, *Say . . . Didn't You Used To Be George Murphy?* (n.p.: Bartholomew House, 1970), p. 257; Los Angeles *Tribune*, February 20, 1944, p. 8).
15. *Afro-American*, January 9, 1943, p. 11.
16. Ibid.
17. Horne and Schickel, p. 135.
18. *Variety*, November 27, 1946, p. 1.
19. *Afro-American*, February 16, 1946, p. 10; *Courier*, November 15, 1947, p. 16; Charles R. Metzger, "Pressure Groups and the Motion Picture Industry," *Annals of the American Academy of Political Science*, 254 (November, 1947): 113, 114; *Courier*, March 2, 1946.
20. *Afro-American*, January 23, 1943, p. 8.
21. Lester Velie, "You Can't See That Movie," *Collier's*, 125 (May 6, 1950): 11–12; Theodore Kupferman and Philip J. O'Brien, "Motion Picture Censorship — The Memphis Blues," *Cornell Law Quarterly*, 36 (Spring, 1951): 276.
22. JC: Clipping.
23. NYT, October 26, 1947, II, p. 4.
24. "Needed: A Negro Legion of Decency," *Ebony*, 2 (February 1947): 36.
25. "Skirts Ahoy," *Ebony*, 7 (April, 1952): 44.
26. NYT, November 10, 1947, p. 21.
27. *Afro-American*, December 14, 1946, p. 10; *Variety*, December 4, 1946, p. 1.
28. *Variety*, April 2, 1952, p. 2.

7. GLIMMERS OF CHANGE

1. *Variety*, February 23, 1949, p. 3, March 2, 1948, p. 3.
2. "Home of the Brave," *Ebony*, 4 (June, 1940): 60–61.
3. Richard Winnington, "Critics Forum," *Sight and Sound*, 18 (January, 1950): 27; Lindsay Anderson, "Lost Boundaries, Pinky, Home of the Brave," *Sequence*, January, 1950, p. 182; "Home of the Brave," *Newsweek*, 33 (May 16, 1949): 86; *Negative Space: Manny Farber On the Movies* (New York: Praeger, 1971), p. 69.

4. William L. White, *Lost Boundaries* (New York: Harcourt Brace, 1948).
5. *Afro-American,* August 13, 1949, p. 8.
6. Samuel Bloom, "A Social Psychological Study of Motion Picture Audience Behavior: A Case Study of the Negro Image in Mass Communication" (Ph.D. thesis, University of Wisconsin, 1956), Appendix, p. 90, n. 10.
7. *Afro-American,* December 31, 1949, p. 9.
8. Winnington, p. 28.
9. Mel Gussow, *Don't Say Yes Until I Finish Talking* (Garden City, N.Y.: Doubleday, 1972), p. 151; "Pinky," *Ebony,* 5 (October, 1949): 25.
10. *Afro-American,* December 31, 1949, p. 9; *Variety,* November 30, 1949, p. 1.
11. Ralph Ellison, *Shadow and Act* (New York: Random House, 1964), p. 281.
12. *Monthly Film Bulletin,* August, 1950, p. 115.
13. Mankiewicz quoted in Gussow, p. 158.
14. NYT, July 30, 1950, II, p. 5.
15. Martha Wolfenstein and Nathan Leites, "Two Social Scientists View No Way Out," *Commentary,* (October, 1950): 391.
16. "Showboat," *Ebony,* 6 (July, 1951): 71.
17. Jackie Robinson as told to Alfred Duckett, *I Never Had It Made* (New York: Putnam, 1972), p. 101.
18. Fred D. Moon of the Atlantic Journal quoted in Gerald Weales, "Pro-Negro Films in Atlanta," *Films in Review,* 2 (November, 1952): 459.
19. Martin Dworkin, "The New Negro on Screen," *The Progressive,* 24 (November, 1960): 35.
20. Richard Wright, "Chicago Slums Are Recreated In Buenos Aires for Film Scenes," *Ebony,* 6 (January, 1951): 84; "Native Son," *Newsweek,* 38 (July 9, 1951): 94.
21. Ellison, p. 279.

8. A Pale Black Imitation

1. "Jam Session In Movieland," *Ebony,* 1 (November, 1945): 38.
2. *Variety,* July 20, 1938, p. 10.
3. *Age,* May 28, 1932, p. 7.
4. Pressbooks for *Harlem on the Prairie, The Bronze Buckaroo,* and *Harlem Rides the Range,* NYPL-TC; "California Dude Ranch," *Ebony,* 2 (February, 1947): 5.
5. *Courier,* March 2, 1939, p. 21; *Defender,* January 13, 1940, p. 18.
6. *News,* January 16, 1937, p. 8.
7. *Variety,* March 17, 1937, p. 9; *Age,* March 20, 1937, p. 9; *News,* March 27, 1937, p. 10.
8. "Negro Movie Boom." *Ebony,* 1 (September, 1946): 44.
9. *Age,* July 16, 1932, p. 6.
10. "Spirit of Youth," *Time,* 31 (January 31, 1938): 36.
11. "Negro Movie Boom," p. 42; *Variety,* January 27, 1954, p. 69.
12. *Afro-American,* November 14, 1936, p. 12; Frazier, pp. 69–73; *Variety,* October 2, 1935, p. 3; MPH, April 12, 1947, p. 18.
13. *Variety,* August 12, 1933, p. 7.
14. Ibid., February 9, 1938, p. 20.
15. "Negro Movie Boom," p. 44.

16. Horne and Schickel, p. 89; *Age*, January 23, 1937, p. 1; "Making a Movie On a Dime," *One World*, 2 (May, 1948): 18; *News*, September 30, 1939, p. 10.
17. Noble, p. 181.
18. Andrew Sarris, *The American Cinema* (New York: E.P. Dutton, 1968), p. 143; "Mr. Washington Goes to Town," *Time*, 35 (April 29, 1940): 84; New York *World-Telegram*, June 16, 1939, p. 2.
19. New York *Post*, April 16, 1942, p. 12.
20. MPH, July 15, 1939, p. 41; January 24, 1942, p. 34.
21. New York *World-Telegram*, August 17, 1946, p. 25.
22. *Courier*, November 30, 1929, Sec. 2, p. 2, April 26, 1930, p. 6.
23. *Age*, January 10, 1931, p. 6.
24. Cripps, *Negro Digest*, p. 27; *Courier*, March 14, 1931, p. 8; *Age*, May 23, 1931, p. 6.
25. *News*, September 30, 1939, p. 10; *Afro-American*, May 20, 1933, p. 10; *Age*, May 25, 1935, p. 4.
26. *Age*, May 10, 1938, p. 4.
27. William Harrison, "The Negro and the Cinema," *Sight and Sound*, 8 (Spring, 1939): 17.

9. Toward a New Image

1. *Perspectives on Twentieth Century America*, ed. Otis L. Graham, Jr. (New York: Dodd, Mead & Co., 1973), p. 361.
2. Vroman and Belafonte quoted in Arnold Shaw, *Belafonte* (New York: Chilton, 1960), p. 101; "See How They Run," *Ebony*, 7 (April, 1953): 45, 48.
3. Quoted in Era Bell Thompson, "Why Negroes Don't Like Porgy and Bess," *Ebony*, 14 (October, 1959): 54.
4. James Baldwin, *Notes of a Native Son* (London: Michael Joseph, 1964), pp. 48, 51.
5. Dorothy Dandridge and Earl Conrad, *Everything and Nothing* (New York: Abelard-Schuman, 1970), p. 183; Earl Mills, *Dorothy Dandridge* (Los Angeles: Holloway House, 1970), p. 213.
6. Carolyn Ewers, *Sidney Poitier: The Long Journey* (New York: New American Library, 1969), 87.
7. NYT, December 11, 1957, quoted in Ewers, p. 88.
8. Young quoted in Thompson, p. 54.
9. Dandridge and Conrad, p. 183.
10. *Courier*, September 19, 1953, p. 19; Darryl F. Zanuck, "Controversy Is Box Office," *International Film Annual*, ed. Campbell Dixon (London: John Calder, 1957), p. 80.
11. Albert Johnson, "Beige, Brown, or Black," *Film Quarterly*, 13 (Fall, 1959): 40; Shaw, p. 243.
12. NYT, December 15, 1957, II, p. 7.
13. *Sirk on Sirk: Interviews with Jon Halliday* (London: Secker and Warburg, 1971), p. 129.
14. Pressbook of *I Passed For White*, NYPL-TC.
15. Dai Vaughan, "Sapphire," *Films and Filming*, 5 (June, 1959): 25.
16. Albert Johnson, "Shadows," *Film Quarterly*, 13 (Spring, 1960): 32; Johnson, "The Negro in American Films: Some Recent Examples," ibid., 18 (Summer, 1965): 22.

17. *Variety*, July 10, 1957, p. 1.
18. Colin Young, "Nobody Dies/Patriotism in Hollywood," *Film: Book 2*, ed. Robert Hughes (New York: Grove Press, 1962), p. 96.
19. "Movie Maker Belafonte," *Ebony*, 14 (June, 1959): 95.
20. Robert Kotlowitz, "The Making of *The Angel Levine*," *Film 69/70*, ed. Joseph Morgenstern and Stefan Kanfer (New York: Simon and Schuster, 1970), p. 176; "Belafonte Plays Angel On and Off Screen," *Ebony*, 24 (October, 1969): 80.
21. *Time* quoted in *Film Facts*, February 11, 1959, p. 6.
22. Edward Mapp, *Blacks in American Films: Today and Yesterday* (Metuchen, N.J.: Scarecrow Press, 1972), pp. 130–31.
23. Lerone Bennett, Jr., "Hollywood's First Negro Star," *Ebony*, 14 (May, 1959): 100; Alexander Walker, *Stardom* (London. Michael Joseph, 1970), p. 348.
24. Poitier quoted in Ewers, p. 77.
25. Gavin Lambert, "The Defiant Ones," *Film Quarterly*, 12 (Fall, 1958): 42; Richard Maynard, *The Celluloid Curriculum* (New York: Hayden Book Company, 1971), p. 156.
26. Dworkin, p. 34.
27. Walker, p. 348.
28. *The Village Voice*, August 17, 1967, p. 15.
29. Quoted in Ewers, p. 116; Maxine Hall Elliston, "Two Sidney Poitier Films," *Film Comment*, 5 (Winter, 1969): 27; Andrew Greeley, "Guess Who's Coming to Dinner," *The Reporter*, 38 (March 21, 1968): 40.
30. *Courier*, April 25, 1964, p. 19; quoted in Ewers, p. 122.
31. Poitier quoted in Charles L. Sanders, "Sidney Poitier," *Ebony*, 23 (May, 1968): 178; NYT, September 10, 1967, II, p. 5, July 19, 1970, II, p. 5; Louie Robinson, "The Expanding World of Sidney Poitier," *Ebony*, 27 (November, 1971): 112.
31. NYT, July 2, 1972, II, p. 7; James Baldwin, "Sidney Poitier," *Look*, 31 (July 23, 1968): 56.

10. BLACK IS BOXOFFICE

1. *Variety*, May 9, 1956, p. 5, May 8, 1957, p. 3; Junius Griffin quoted in *Variety*, August 16, 1972, p. 5; Charles Michener "Black Movies," *Newsweek*, 80 (October 23, 1972): 74.
2. *Variety*, August 26, 1970, p. 5.
3. Philip T. Hartung, "Dark of the Sun," *Film 68/69*, ed. Hollis Alpert and Andrew Sarris (New York: Simon and Schuster, 1969), p. 88.
4. Pauline Kael, *Going Steady* (New York: Little, Brown, 1970), p. 185; Brown quoted in Charles L. Sanders, "Film Star Jim Brown," *Ebony*, 24 (December, 1968): 202.
5. *Playboy's Sex In Cinema 1970* (Chicago: Playboy Press, 1970), p. 10.
6. St. Jacques quoted in Charles L. Sanders, "Raymond The Magnificent," *Ebony*, 24 (October, 1969): 177; *Monthly Film Bulletin*, August, 1970, p. 164.
7. Louise Sweeney, *Christian Science Monitor*, July 8, 1972, p. 8.
8. Davis quoted in "Cotton Comes to Harlem," *Jet*, 39 (August 27, 1970): 62.

9. Quoted in Chester Higgins, "Black Films: Boom or Bust," *Jet*, 42 (June 8, 1972): 59.
10. Quoted in Verina Glaessner, "The Negro in the Contemporary Cinema," *Film*, Spring, 1971, p. 16, and in "The Story of a Three Day Pass," *Ebony*, 24 (November, 1968): 54.
11. Melvin Van Peebles, *Sweet Sweetback's Baadasssss Song* (New York: Lancer Books, 1971), p. 92.
12. Ibid., pp. iii, 36, 43.
13. Joseph Gelmis, *The Film Director as Superstar* (Garden City, N.Y.: Doubleday, 1970), p. 38; WNET transcript, p. 4; Lerone Bennett, Jr., "The Emancipation Orgasm: Sweetback In Wonderland," *Ebony*, 27 (September, 1971): 16.
14. *The New York Herald*, September 5, 1971, II, p. 6; Bennett, "Emancipation," pp. 112–18, *passim*.
15. Quoted in Theophilus Green, "The Black Man as Movie Hero," *Ebony*, 27 (August, 1972): 145; Joseph Gelmis quoted in Gary Houston, "Audiences and Black Movies," *Showcase*, Chicago *Sun-Times*, May 30, 1971; Van Peebles, p. 107.
16. Quoted in Variety, July 28, 1971, p. 5; *Shaft* pressbook, NYPL-TC.
17. Nigel Andrews, *Monthly Film Bulletin*, January, 1972, p. 15; John C. Mahoney, Los Angeles *Times*, quoted in James P. Murray, "Do We Really Have Time for a Shaft?" *Black Creation*, 3 (Winter, 1972): 14; NYT, July 25, 1971, II, p. 13; Parks quoted in *Monthly Film Bulletin*, op. cit.
18. Roger Greenspun, NYT, August 7, 1969, p. 30.
19. *Variety*, September 8, 1971, p. 25, February 23, 1972, p. 2.
20. *New Yorker*, 48 (December 2, 1972): 161.
21. *Variety*, October 3, 1973, p. 14.
22. Vincent Canby, NYT, November 2, 1972, p. 46.
23. Hamilton quoted in Arthur Knight, "Sex Stars," *Playboy's Sex In Cinema 4* (Chicago: Playboy Press, 1974), p. 142.
24. Variety, April 17, 1974, p. 16.
25. NYT, December 17, 1972, II, pp. 3, 19; March 13, 1973, p. 10, May 2, 1973, p. 41; *Variety*, November 22, 1972, p. 77, Alvin F. Poussaint, "Cheap Thrills That Degrade Blacks," *Psychology Today*, 7 (February, 1974): 98.
26. *Wall Street Journal*, July 22, 1974, p. 9.
27. WNET transcript, p. 7; Brad Darrach, "Hollywood's Second Coming," *Playboy* (June, 1972), 227.
28. *Variety*, October 20, 1971, p. 62.
29. Ibid., July 17, 1974, p. 22, May 8, 1974, p. 1.
30. Ellen Holly, "Where Are the Films about Real Black Men and Women?" NYT, June 2, 1974, II, p. 11.

Bibliography

BIBLIOGRAPHY

ANYONE WRITING about films must look at them. During the past few years I have viewed hundreds of films for this book. Film researchers in this country are blessed because of the multiplicity of TV stations, all of which spend much of their air time showing movies. And television was one of my main resources for film, for the United States has no single repository for films. The revival of many old movies at campus showings, repertory theaters, and the like further allowed me to run down films that otherwise could not have been seen. A number of private collectors were kind enough to make certain titles available to me. I was also fortunate in having access to films at Eastman House, the Museum of Modern Art Film Study Center, and the Library of Congress (where the American Film Institute collection is deposited). It simply is not possible to list the sources for all the films mentioned in the text. The bibliography that follows deals with nonfilm material.

COLLECTIONS OF MATERIALS

D. W. Griffith scrapbooks, Museum of Modern Art Library, New York City.

George Johnson Negro Film Collection, Bancroft Library, University of California, Los Angeles.

George Johnson Oral History, Bancroft Library, University of California, Los Angeles.

Schomburg Collection, New York Public Library, New York City.

Theatre Collection, Research Library for the Performing Arts, New York Public Library, New York City.

BOOKS

Abramson, Doris. *Negro Playwrights in the American Theatre.* New York: Columbia University Press, 1969.

Agee, James. *Agee on Film: Reviews and Comments.* Boston: Beacon Press, 1958.

Baker, Ray S. *Woodrow Wilson: Life and Letters.* Garden City, N.Y.: Doubleday, Doran, & Co., 1931. Volume 4.

Baldwin, James. *Notes on a Native Son.* London: Michael Joseph, 1964.

Barkas, Natalie. *Behind the Camera.* London: Geoffrey Blas, 1934.

———. *30,000 Miles for the Films.* London: Blackie & Son, 1937.

Bergstern, Bebe, ed. *Biograph Bulletins 1896–1908.* Compiled by Kemp Niver. Los Angeles: Locare Research Group, 1971.

Blumer, Herbert. *Movies and Conduct.* New York: Macmillan, 1933.

Bogle, Donald. *Toms, Coons, Mulattoes, Mammies & Bucks.* New York: Viking Press, 1973.

Butcher, Margaret Just. *The Negro in American Culture.* Revised and updated. New York: New American Library, 1971.

Capra, Frank. *The Name Above the Title.* New York: Macmillan, 1971.

Dandridge, Dorothy, and Earl Conrad. *Everything and Nothing.* New York: Abelard-Schuman, 1970.

Daniels, Roger. *The Politics of Prejudice.* New York: Atheneum, 1968.

Dickenson, Thomas, ed. *Chief Contemporary Dramatists.* Boston: Houghton Mifflin, 1921.

Dunning, William. *Reconstruction: Political and Economic: 1865–1877.* New York: Harper and Brothers, 1907.

Elkins, Stanley. *Slavery.* 2nd Ed. Chicago: University of Chicago Press, 1968.

Ellison, Ralph. *Shadow and Act.* New York: Random House, 1924.

Ewers, Carolyn. *Sidney Poitier: The Long Journey.* New York: New American Library, 1969.

Farber, Manny. *Negative Space: Manny Farber on the Movies.* New York: Praeger, 1971.

Focus on The Birth of a Nation, edited by Fred Sieva. Englewood Cliffs, N.J.: Prentice-Hall, 1971.

Freedman, Lawrence. *The White Savage.* Englewood Cliffs, N.J.: Prentice-Hall, 1970.

Gelmis, Joseph. *The Film Director as Superstar.* Garden City, N.Y.: Doubleday, 1970.

Gish, Lillian, with Anne Pinchot. *The Movies, Mr. Griffith, and Me.* Englewood Cliffs, N.J.: Prentice-Hall, 1969.

Gorelik, Mordecai. *New Theatres for Old.* New York: Samuel French, 1940.

Graham, Otis L., Jr., ed. *Perspectives on Twentieth Century America.* New York: Dodd, Mead, 1973.

Green, Abel and Joe Laurie, Jr. *Show Biz.* New York: Holt, Rinehart and Winston, 1951.

Gussow, Mel. *Don't Say Yes Until I Finish Talking.* Garden City, N.Y.: Doubleday, 1972.

Halliday, Jon, ed. *Sirk on Sirk: Interview with Jon Halliday.* London: Secker & Warburg, 1971.

Hampton, Benjamin. *History of the American Film Industry.* New York: Dover, 1970.

Hardy, Forsyth, ed. *Grierson on Documentary*. Los Angeles: University of California Press, 1966.

Hart, James, ed. *The Man Who Invented Hollywood: The Autobiography of D. W. Griffith*. Louisville, Ky.: Touchstone Publishing Co., 1972.

Henderson, Robert. *D. W. Griffith: His Life and Times*. New York: Oxford, 1972.

————. *D. W. Griffith: The Years at Biograph*. New York: Farrar, Straus & Giroux, 1970.

Higham, Charles, and Joel Greenberg. *The Celluloid Muse*. London: Angus & Robertson, 1969.

Horne, Lena, and Richard Schickel. *Lena*. Garden City, N.Y.: Doubleday, 1965.

Hughes, Langston. *I Wonder as I Wander*. New York: Rinehart, 1956.

Hughes, Langston, and Milton Meltzer. *Black Magic*. Englewood Cliffs, N.J.: Prentice-Hall, 1967.

Hunnings, Neville. *Film Censors and the Law*. London: George Allen and Unwin, 1967.

Inglis, Ruth A. *Freedom of the Movies*. Chicago: University of Chicago Press, 1947.

Jablonski, Edward, and Lawrence Stewart. *The Gershwin Years*. Garden City, N.Y.: Doubleday, 1958.

Jacobs, Lewis. *The Rise of American Film*. New York: Harcourt Brace, 1939.

Jarvie, I. C. *Towards a Sociology of the Cinema*. London: Routledge & Kegan Paul, 1970.

Kael, Pauline. *Going Steady*. New York: Little, Brown, 1970.

Lindenmayer, Otto. *Black History: Lost, Stolen, or Strayed*. New York: Discus Books, 1970.

Lindgren, Ernest. *The Art of the Film*. London: George Allen and Unwin, 1963.

Lindsay, Vachel. *The Art of the Moving Picture*. New York: Liveright, 1970.

Lingeman, Richard. *Don't You Know There's a War On?* New York: Putnam, 1970.

Link, Arthur S. *The New Freedom*. Princeton: Princeton University Press, 1956.

Logan, Rayford. *The Betrayal of the Negro*. New York: Collier Books, 1965.

Mapp, Edward. *Blacks in American Films: Today and Yesterday*. Metuchen, N.J.: Scarecrow Press, 1972.

Maynard, Richard A. *The Celluloid Curriculum*. New York: Hayden Book Company, 1971.

Micheaux, Oscar. *The Case of Mrs. Wingate*. New York: Book Supply Co., 1945.

————. *The Forged Note*. Lincoln, Neb.: Western Book Supply Co., 1916.

Mills, Earl. *Dorothy Dandridge*. Los Angeles: Holloway House, 1970.

Mitchell, Loften. *Black Drama*. New York: Hawthorn, 1967.

Munden, Kenneth, ed. *The American Film Institute Catalog of Motion Pictures Produced in the United States: 1921–1930*. New York: Bowker, 1971.

Murphy, George, with Victor Lasky. "*Say . . . Didn't You Used To Be George Murphy?*" No place: Bartholomew House, 1970.

Myrdal, Gunnar. *An American Dilemma*. New York: Harper, 1944.

Noble, Peter. *The Negro in Films.* London: Skelton Robinson, c. 1947.

Osofsky, Gilbert. *Harlem: The Making of a Ghetto.* New York: Harper & Row, 1965.

Peterson, Ruth, and L. L. Thurstone. *Motion Pictures and the Social Attitude of Children.* New York: Macmillan, 1933.

Playboy Press Editors. *Playboy's Sex in Cinema 1970.* Chicago: Playboy Press, 1970.

Quigley, Jr., Martin, and Richard Gertner. *Films in America 1929–1969.* New York: Golden Press, 1970.

Ramsaye, Terry. *A Million and One Nights.* New York: Simon and Schuster, 1964.

Randell, Richard S. *Censorship of the Movies.* Madison, Wis.: University of Wisconsin Press, 1968.

Rhodes, James F. *History of the United States from the Compromise of 1850.* Vol. 6. New York: Scribner's, 1906.

Robeson, Eslanda Goode. *Paul Robeson: Negro.* London: Victor Gollancz, 1930.

Robinson, Jackie, and Alfred Duckett. *I Never Had It Made.* New York: Putnams, 1972.

Rotha on Film. Fairlawn, N.J.: Essential Books, 1958.

Rowland, Mabel, ed. *Bert Williams: Son of Laughter.* New York: English Crafters, 1923.

Sarris, Andrew. *The American Cinema.* New York: E. P. Dutton, 1968.

Seton, Marie. *Paul Robeson.* London: Dennis Dobson, 1958.

Shaw, Arnold. *Belafonte.* New York: Chilton, 1960.

Silva, Fred, ed. *Focus on The Birth of a Nation.* Englewood Cliffs, N.J.: Prentice-Hall, 1971.

Short, Bobby. *Black and White Baby.* New York: Dodd, Mead, 1971.

Sullivan, Mark. *Our Times.* Vol. I. New York: Scribner's, 1926.

Tindall, George B. *The Emergence of the New South: 1913–1945.* Baton Rouge: Louisiana State University Press, 1969.

Van Peebles, Melvin. *Sweet Sweetback's Baadasssss Song.* New York: Lancer Books, 1971.

Vidor, King. *A Tree Is a Tree.* New York: Harcourt Brace, 1953.

Walker, Alexander. *Stardom.* London: Michael Joseph, 1970.

White, Walter. *A Man Called White.* New York: Viking Press, 1948.

White, W. L. *Lost Boundaries.* New York: Harcourt Brace, 1948.

Woodward, C. Vann. *Origins of the New South.* Baton Rouge: Louisiana State University Press, 1951.

——. *The Strange Career of Jim Crow.* New York: Oxford University Press, 1966.

ARTICLES

Alabrook, James. "Historic Color Bias in Print." *Journalism Quarterly,* Spring, 1971.

Anderson, Lindsay. "Lost Boundaries, Pinky, Home of the Brave." *Sequence,* January, 1950.

Baldwin, James. "Sidney Poitier." *Look,* July 23, 1968.

"Belafonte Plays Angel On and Off Screen." *Ebony,* October, 1969.

Bennett, Jr., Lerone. "The Emancipation Orgasm: Sweetback in Wonderland." *Ebony,* September, 1971.

————. "Hollywood's First Negro Movie Star." *Ebony,* May, 1959.

Boskin, Joseph. "Sambo: The National Jester in the Popular Culture." *The Great Fear,* edited by Gary Nash and Richard Weiss. New York: Holt, Rinehart and Winston, 1970.

"California Dude Ranch." *Ebony,* February, 1947.

Cook, Raymond. "The Man Behind The Birth of a Nation." *North Carolina Historical Review,* October, 1962.

"Cotton Comes To Harlem." *Jet,* August 27, 1970.

Cripps, Thomas. "Paul Robeson and Black Identity in American Movies." *Massachusetts Review,* Summer, 1970.

————. "Movies in the Ghetto, B.P. (Before Poitier)." *Negro Digest,* February, 1969.

————. "The Myth of the Southern Box Office." *The Black Experience in America,* edited by James Custer and Lewis Gould. Austin: University of Texas Press, 1970.

————. "The Reaction of the Negro to the Motion Picture *The Birth of a Nation." The Making of Black America,* edited by August Meier and Elliott Rudwick. New York: Antheneum, 1969. Volume 2.

Curtwright, Wesley. "Motion Pictures of Negroes." Typescript, c.1939. Schomburg Collection, NYPL, New York City.

Darrach, Brad. "Hollywood's Second Coming." *Playboy,* June, 1972.

Diamond, Geraldyn. "The Negro Actor and the American Movies." *Close Up,* August, 1929.

DuBois, W. E. B. "Dramatis Personae — *Hallelujah." The Crisis,* October, 1929.

————. "The Talented Tenth." *The Negro Problem,* ed. Booker T. Washington, *et al.* New York: James Pott & Co., 1903.

Dworkin, Martin. "The New Negro on Screen." *The Progressive,* October–December, 1960.

Ellston, Maxine Hall. "Two Sidney Poitier Films." *Film Comment,* Winter, 1969.

Frazier, E. Franklin. "Recreation and Amusement among American Negroes." Typescript, 1940. Schomburg Collection, New York Public Library.

Glaessner, Verina. "The Negro in the Contemporary Cinema." *Film,* Spring, 1971.

Gordon, Henry S. "The Story of David Wark Griffith." *Photoplay,* October, 1916.

Greeley, Andrew. "Guess Who's Coming To Dinner." *The Reporter,* March 21, 1968.

Green, Theophilus. "The Black Man as Movie Hero." *Ebony,* August, 1972.

Hackett, Francis. "Brotherly Love." *New Republic,* Vol. 7. March 20, 1915.

Harrison, William. "The Negro and the Cinema." *Sight and Sound,* Spring, 1939.

Hendrick, Burton. "The Great Jewish Invasion." *McClure's Magazine,* January, 1907.

Higgins, Chester. "Black Films: Boom Or Bust." *Jet,* June 8, 1972.

Holly, Ellen. "Where Are The Films About Real Black Men and Women." New York *Times,* June 2, 1974, II.

"Home of the Brave." *Ebony,* June, 1949.

"Home of the Brave." *Newsweek,* May, 16, 1949.

Hughes, Langston. "The Negro and American Entertainment." *The American Negro Reference Book,* edited by John P. Davis. Englewood Cliffs, N.J.: Prentice-Hall, 1966.

"Jam Session In Movieland." *Ebony,* November, 1945.

Johnson, Albert. "Beige, Brown, or Black." *Film Quarterly,* Fall, 1959.

———. "The Films of Minelli." *Film Quarterly,* Winter, 1958.

———. "The Negro in American Films: Some Recent Works." *Film Quarterly,* Summer, 1965.

Kagan, Norman. "Black American Cinema." *Cinema,* Volume 6, No. 2.

Killans, John O. "Hollywood in Black and White." *White Racism,* ed. Barry Schwartz and Robert Disch. New York: Dell, 1970.

Knight, Arthur. "Sex Stars." *Playboy's Sex In Cinema."* Chicago: Playboy Press, 1974.

Kotlowitz, Robert. "The Making of *The Angel Levine.*" *Film 69/70,* edited by Joseph Morgenstern and Stefan Kanfer. New York: Simon and Schuster, 1970.

Kupferman, Theodore, and Philip J. O'Brien. "Motion Picture Censorship — The Memphis Blues." *Cornell Law Quarterly,* Spring, 1951.

"Making A Movie On A Dime." *One World,* May, 1948.

Metzger, Charles. "Pressure Groups and The Motion Picture Industry." *Annals of the American Academy of Political Science,* November, 1947.

"Mister Washington Goes To Town." *Time,* April 29, 1940. Michener Charles. "Black Movies." *Newsweek,* October 23, 1972.

Moss, Carlton. "The Negro in American Films." *Harlem, U.S.A.,* ed. John Clarke. New York: Collier Books, 1971. Revised Edition.

"Movie Maker Belafonte." *Ebony,* June, 1959.

Murray, James P. "Do We Really Have Time for a Shaft?" *Black Creation,* Winter, 1972.

"Native Son." *Newsweek,* July 9, 1951.

"Needed: A Negro Legion of Decency." *Ebony,* February, 1947.

"Negro Movie Boom." *Ebony,* September, 1946.

Pouissant, Alvin. "Cheap Thrills That Degrade Blacks." *Psychology Today,* February, 1974.

Ramsaye, Terry. "The Rise and Place of the Motion Picture." *Annals of the American Academy of Political and Social Science,* November 1947.

Reddick, L. D. "Educational Programs for the Improvement of Race Relations." *Journal of Negro Education,* Summer, 1944.

Robinson, Louie. "The Expanding World of Sidney Poitier." *Ebony,* November, 1971.

Sanders, Charles. "Film Star Jim Brown." *Ebony,* December, 1968.

———. "Raymond The Magnificent." *Ebony,* October, 1969.

———. "Sidney Poitier." *Ebony,* May, 1968.

———. "Skirts Ahoy." *Ebony,* April, 1952.

"Spirit of Youth." *Time,* January 31, 1938.

"Stepin Fetchit Comes Back." *Ebony,* February, 1952.

Stern, Seymour. "Griffith's The Birth of a Nation." *Film Culture,* Spring–Summer, 1965.

Still, William G. "The Negro and His Music in Films." *Proceedings of the Writers Congress.* Berkeley: University of California Press, 1944.

"The Story of a Three Day Pass." *Ebony,* November, 1968.

Thompson, Era Bell. "Why Negroes Don't Like Porgy and Bess." *Ebony,*
    October, 1959.
Trumbo, Dalton. "Minorities and the Screen." *Proceedings of the Writers
    Congress.* Berkeley: University of California Press, 1944.
Vaugham, "Sapphire." *Films and Filming,* June, 1959.
Velie, Lester. "You Can't See That Movie." *Collier's,* May 6, 1950.
Warner, Virginia. "The Negro Soldier: A Challenge to Hollywood." *The
    Documentary Tradition,* ed. Lewis Jacobs. New York: Hopkinson and
    Blake, 1971.
"Whatever Happened to Stepin Fetchit?" *Ebony,* November, 1971.
Winnington, Richard. "Critics Forum." *Sight and Sound,* January, 1950.
Wolfenstein, Martha, and Nathan Leites. "Two Social Scientists View *No
    Way Out.*" *Commentary,* October, 1950.
Wright, Richard. "Chicago Slums Are Recreated In Buenos Aires For Film
    Scenes." *Ebony,* January, 1951.
Young, Colin. "Nobody Dies/Patriotism in Hollywood." *Film: Book 2,* ed.
    Robert Hughes. New York: Grove Press, 1962.
Zanuck, Darryl. "Controversy Is Box-Office." *International Film Annual,* ed.
    Campbell, Dixon. London: John Calder, 1957.
Zito, Stephen. "The Black Film Experience." *The American Film Heritage,*
    ed. Tom Shales, *et al.* Washington: Acropolis Books, 1972.

NEWSPAPERS AND PERIODICALS

Baltimore Afro-American
Close Up
Chicago Defender
The Crisis
Ebony
film facts
Films and Filming
Life

Lubin Bulletin
Monthly Film Bulletin
Motion Picture Herald
Moving Picture World
New Theatre
New York Age
New York Amsterdam News
The New York Times

Opportunity
Pittsburgh Courier
Sequence
Show World
Sight and Sound
Variety
Vitagraph Bulletin

PH.D. THESES AND MASTER'S ESSAYS

Belcher, Farrin. "The Place of the Negro in the Evolution of the American
    Theatre." Ph.D. thesis, Yale University, 1945.
Bloom, Samuel. "A Social Psychological Study of Motion Picture Audience
    Behavior: A Case Study of the Negro Image in Mass Communication."
    Ph.D. thesis, University of Wisconsin, 1956.
Buchanan, Singer A. "A Study of the Attitude of the Writers of the Negro
    Press Toward the Depiction of the Negro in Plays and Films 1930–
    1965." Ph.D. thesis, University of Michigan, 1970.
Burke, William L. "The Presentation of the American Negro in Hollywood
    Films, 1946–1961." Ph.D. thesis, Northwestern University, 1965.
Hutchins, Charles. "A Critical Evaluation of the Controversies Engendered
    by D. W. Griffith's *The Birth of a Nation.*" Master's Essay, University
    of Iowa, 1961.
Merritt, Russell. "The Impact of D. W. Griffith's Motion Pictures from 1908
    to 1914 on Contemporary American Culture." Ph.D. thesis, Harvard
    University, 1970.
Schlosser, Antol. "Paul Robeson." Ph.D. thesis, New York University, 1970.

Index

INDEX

Numbers in italics refer to photographs